VISIONS
OF
ONE WORLD

Alexander & the Talking Tree, on the cover and title page, was drawn by Aminta Marks from a reproduction of a late 15th-century manuscript of the Shah Namah. Bodleian Library. Ousely Add. 176 (Ethé 501), fol. 311 b.

"In the course of his wanderings, Alexander comes to a talking tree, which rebukes him for his lust of conquest and prophesies his death in a country far from his native land."

B. W. Robinson, in the introduction to
Thomas W. Arnold, *Painting in Islam,*
A Study of the Place of Pictorial Art in Muslim Culture,
Dover Publications, New York, 1965, pl. xxxviii.

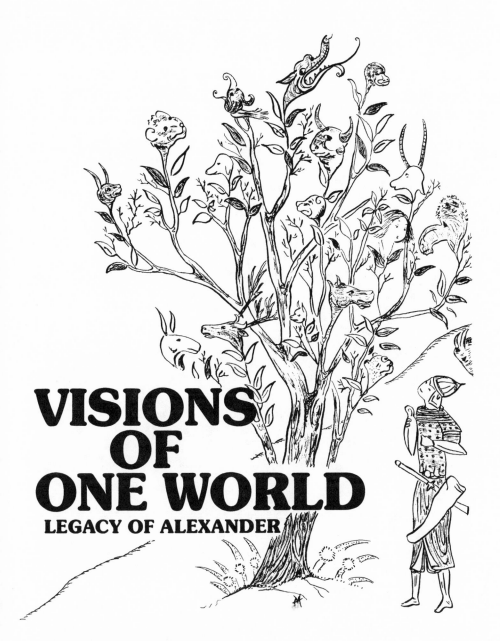

VISIONS
OF
ONE WORLD
LEGACY OF ALEXANDER

JOHN H. MARKS

Copyright ©1985 John H. Marks

Four Quarters Publishing Company
1200 Boston Post Road
Guilford, Connecticut 06437

Library of Congress Cataloging in Publication Data

Marks, John H. (John Henry)
  Visions of one world.

  Bibliography: p.
  Includes index.
  1. Alexander, the Great, 356–323 B.C.—Influence.
2. Hellenism. 3. Near East—Civilization.
4. Mediterranean Region—Civilization. I. Title.
DF234.2.M37 1985   930'.4   85-4441
ISBN 0-931500-10-9
ISBN 0-931500-09-5 (pbk.)

Composition by The Publishing Nexus Incorporated
Post Office Box 195, Guilford, Connecticut 06437

Printed in the United States of America

CONTENTS

LIST OF MAPS AND CHARTS

INTRODUCTION

THE ABIDING RIFT
BETWEEN WEST AND EAST

The civilizations that today confront each other west and east of the Mediterranean derive from opposing western and eastern conceptions of man and his place in the world. That opposition first began to appear clearly when Greeks and Near Eastern peoples mingled as rulers and subjects after Alexander's conquest. The story of that mingling is the subject of this account.

The Hellenistic age, inaugurated by Alexander, and its successor, the Roman empire, brought together into a unified world widely separated traditions of life and thought that would exist uneasily together for a millennium of mutual appraisal and conflict. Within a single decade the conquering Macedonians spread Greek language and culture eastward from the Aegean to the ancient centers of civilization in the river valleys of the Nile and Euphrates, and further east to the Oxus, Jaxartes and Indus; and their returning troops diffused eastern ideas and practices westward to Macedonia and Greece. Over the succeeding centuries, these new perceptions and practices spread to Rome and finally to all Europe.

This enforced and extended encounter between western and eastern perceptions of man and society inevitably produced modifications in both, but in general the centuries following Rome's decline saw the return of peoples east and west of the Mediterranean to their own distinctive and traditional ways of ordering human affairs. Despite the many unifying cultural features of western and eastern Mediterranean approaches to life that still prevail, and with due regard to the diversity of viewpoints and ideals in both western Europe and the Near East that prevent either from being perceived as a cultural monolith, one may still discern a cleft

1

separating their basic conceptions about man and the state.[1] The essential differences can be crudely but simply stated.

Western Europe has an aggressive view of man, whom it describes as a reasoning being, driven to discover, organize and synthesize knowledge of what is. This man abstracts philosophical, scientific and political generalizations from his total experience and seeks to know "the laws by which all things cohere." On the basis of this knowledge he wills to create a more perfect society. This European view derives essentially from the Greeks, with whom "scientific" study of matter as matter began, and for whom faith represented imperfect knowledge that would finally have to bow before demonstrable facts.

The Greeks knew, of course, that mere acquisition of facts does not constitute wisdom or education (*paideia*). They believed education consisted of a man's being molded by the cultural achievements he inherited from the past, which he appropriated in company and conference with his contemporaries. Such learning, they were convinced, enabled one to make trustworthy judgments about the nature of things, judgments that were necessary to achieve a good society. That educational goal, adopted and cherished in the western world, has meant and still means that western Europe values "humanistic education of the spirit" far above "rote learning."

This humanistic education is believed to take place in open discussion with one's peers and to depend on democratic interchange of ideas as the best means of advancing both knowledge and human government. The West therefore makes formal education compulsory, as the essential means to good government, and freely democratic, as the necessary road to investigation, the essential means for discovering truth, and the best hope for developing man's potential for good. The West understands freedom to be mutual interdependence and responsibility for creating and maintaining social and private order, making possible intellectual, moral and political discovery through peaceful, communal search for truth. One who participates responsibly in this search within the state is called a citizen; and this view of citizenship, basic to western European and American social and political thought, is Greek and Roman in origin.

The Near East, on the other hand (defined as the landmass extending,

---

1. This observation has long prevailed. Cf., e.g., George Rawlinson, *The Seventh Great Oriental Monarchy*, 2 vols., New York, n.d., vol. 1, part 3. "There is an essential antagonism between European and Asiatic ideas and modes of thought. . . . "

from Tunis along the eastern shores of the Mediterranean and Aegean seas as far as the Hellespont and the Bosporus, eastward into modern Afghanistan), has known but not adopted this essentially Greek view of man. No conception of city-state (*polis*), no accepted body of literature and tradition to provide the mold for a man's education (the Jews are a notable exception), no Platonic system of ideas, no notion of the eternity of the cosmos apart from divine creation has taken root in Near Eastern thought.[2] Facts in the Near East do not have the same force of necessity or eternity they have in the West, and one can therefore appeal to God against them. Facts are rather thought to have a beginning and consequently an end; they are thus, despite their self-evidence, dependent on and subordinate to divine will, which to be known must be revealed. One does not investigate; one apprehends. In the Near East, therefore, law comes basically by revelation rather than through reason, and trust in reason is subordinated to faith in God, as men seek salvation (*soteria*) rather than education (*paideia*).

This divergent emphasis is readily evident in political practice. Even late in the twentieth century, freedom in the Near East is primarily a personal rather than a social concern, and democratic process is often a veneer over patriarchal authoritarianism. Citizenship in a state tends to be a formality whose meaning has not yet been carefully explored or appropriated, and freedom therefore usually means escape from oppression rather than opportunity to create the orderly governmental process that guarantees to all citizens the possibility of doing what they believe they must.

This Near Eastern view of man and the world is alien to the European historical, critical attitude toward events, and to the western ideal of society as a community of autonomous, free, yet politically related and mutually dependent citizens. The western state is a political and social organism rather than a patriarchal family or tribal organization. Thus the often stated conviction that "we must accept an abiding difference between East and West" is still basically correct, though it has been wildly exaggerated in suggestions that Asia has never been permanently influenced by Europe.

Surprisingly, the intellectual and political differences between Europe

---

2. This thesis is cogently presented by Jörg Kraemer in *Das Problem der Islamischen Kulturgeschichte*, pp. 35–36. For a different view see F. E. Peters, *The Harvest of Hellenism*, who thinks of Hellenism as an ideal, formulated and normalized by the Greeks of Alexandria. In this book Hellenism represents the humanistic Greek view of man in the universe as contrasted with Near Eastern theism which makes man primarily a servant of the gods.

and the Near East exist today in spite of a millennium of Greek and Roman domination in the Mediterranean world. The formative influences that shaped western civilization were at work in Athens of the fifth pre-Christian century and throughout the Mediterranean and Near Eastern worlds until the days of the emperor Heraclius in Constantinople in the seventh century of our era. These western forces washed over the Near East, especially after Alexander, but in the backwash of the Muslim conquest, the essential Greek view of life was for the most part rejected by the resurgent, native, ancient Near Eastern spirit. Greek philosophy and science after their partial eclipse in Europe were revived briefly in Islamic thought from whence they passed to Europe in the Renaissance. Subsequent history, however, reveals how differently those Greek ideas fared in Western and Near Eastern cultural and institutional life. The Western "hither-worldly ideal," which reckons with the permanence of the world and man's obligation and will to achieve the good life for all, assisted the development of Europe; while the "prophetic ideal of the Orient," which subordinates the world and man to God's inscrutable will, helped to separate the Near East from European industrial and scientific achievement.

On the other hand, the introduction into the West of eastern ideas of rule, etiquette and protocol at royal courts, and, through Oriental religions (primarily Judaism, Christianity and Islam), of teleological ideas about salvation, an unseen world of spiritual beings, conversion, and judgment after death, has informed and modified the original Greek view of man. The West, since Augustine (died 430), sees man no longer simply as an analytic, reasoning being, but also as a will, a power shaping history; and it values man's ability both to perceive truth and even more to relate to it. This mixture of modified Greek and Near Eastern perceptions is alike the ground and goal of modern, western human activity. Our idea of human destiny is not Greek, but Near Eastern. Loyalty to the divine command is the Near Eastern counterpart to the Greek insistence on quality of thought and life. In the latter, quality is a matter of intellect; in the former, loyalty is a question of will. This significant modification of Greek thought in our modern world is traceable to the Near East.

Modern Near Eastern states are, to be sure, vastly different from their pre-Islamic predecessors. The will of the people is expressed in parliamentary discussion and decision, while the western ideal and practice of education is being increasingly adopted. Adherents of the religions of Mecca and Jerusalem are learning to speak with conviction and cogency in the halls of Athens, appropriating and exploring the values of western intellectual and political systems for their own societies. But this current development underscores the divergent paths followed by men of faith and reason after what we may call the Alexandrian millennium.

The attempt historically to understand this east-west divergence properly begins with Alexander. The Greeks had been active as mercenaries and traders in the Near East from the seventh century B.C., as both Herodotus (II 159) and Strabo (xiii.2.3 [C 617]) reveal. The Hebrew prophet, Ezekiel, who lived in the sixth century B.C., graphically described the trade of Tyre, mentioning Greece and Rhodes (ch. 27), and Joel (3:6-8) complained that Greeks were buying Hebrews offered for sale as slaves by Tyrian slave merchants. But not until the Macedonian conquest did it occur to Greeks systematically to subdue Palestine, Egypt, Syria, Mesopotamia, Iran and even the Indus valley. The decisive confrontation between basic eastern and western views of life did not occur before that western offensive.[3] Alexander's expeditions, however, brought into sharp focus the outlines of the contrast, and his life kindled differing, enduring spiritual and political dreams in men both east and west until recent times. As one of mankind's spectacularly successful figures, he became a paragon for immediate and distant successors who adapted to their own times and dreams the ideas his life had unleashed. So they kept them alive.

The story of the clash between the ancient Classical and Near Eastern worlds is long and complex, and its telling is anchored inevitably, because of the sources at our disposal, to western leaders whose careers mark off eras in Mediterranean history. Four western rulers epitomize the eras of east-west relationships during the millennium: 1. Alexander (365–323 B.C.), who launched the successful western offensive but died before he could consolidate his gains or give adequate political direction for the future; 2. Octavian Augustus (63B.C.–A.D. 14), who presided over the successful organization of the Roman empire; 3. Constantine (ca. A.D. 280–337), who during his thirty-year reign (306–337) allied the Roman state with Christianity and in his new Roman capital on the Bosporus established an impregnable center for the empire; and 4. Justinian in whose lifetime (483–565) Christian controversies, which revealed the basic religious cleavage between eastern and western Mediterranean thought, divided the empire, and during whose

---

3. Cf. the lectures of A. Momigliano on Greek influences on the Near East in his *Alien Wisdom: The Limits of Hellenization*, Cambridge, 1975.

rule (527–565) the increasingly consolidated Near Eastern reaction to western domination prepared the opportunity for Arab conquest.

No eastern rulers comparable with these four from the western Mediterranean, with the possible exception of the Iranian, Chosroes I Anoshirvan (ruled 531–578), are remembered for decisive roles in Mediterranean history. Ptolemaic and Seleucid rulers, oriented toward the Mediterranean and dominated by the Macedonian view of life as they were, were unable and unwilling to integrate their Near Eastern subjects into the political ruling structure of their states; Jewish politics were determinedly parochial; and Parthian records have not been found. The Near East, in fact, during the millennium before Muhammad produced few political or literary figures of note, but an impressive number of religious leaders: Zoroaster, prophets and priests of the Jews, Jesus and Mani, to name a few. Near Eastern political history during this period is thus an appendage to western Mediterranean history, and the Near Eastern, Islamic states arose as much on the ruins of earlier Assyrian and Achaemenid empires as on the thin, imported soil of Greek and Roman political philosophy and institution.

The post-Alexandrian millennium reveals those forces that would impel future Islamic and Christian development. One might expect that eastern and western Mediterranean cultures would affect each other equally. But however much Greek philosophic and Roman legal thought modified eastern perceptions of the world, they did not displace the ancient Near Eastern conception of man as an unruly servant of the gods. That conception, moreover, left its indelible stamp on western religious thought and permanently modified the Greek perception of politics and the state.

This book is for students who desire an overview of an extraordinarily fruitful millennium from whose cultural and political achievements flow in varying degrees the modern cultures of the Near East and western Europe. The story is told in the conviction of its central usefulness for understanding both western and Near Eastern civilizations. Two traditional views of life converged briefly after Alexander and separated after Muhammad, having accepted from each other what could enrich but not destroy the essential life-view of either.

SUGGESTIONS FOR FURTHER STUDY:

The history of Greece is conveniently told in J. B. Bury's classic account, *A History of Greece*, 3rd ed., revised by Russell Meiggs (London, 1951); and N. G. L. Hammond, *A History of Greece to 322 B.C.*, 2nd ed. (Oxford, 1967). Further studies, maps and extensive bibliography are provided in the *Cambridge Ancient History*. An excellent bibliographic introduction is Hermann Bengtson's *Introduction to Ancient History* (California, 1970).

An introduction to Hellenism in the East appears in the stimulating essay of Carl H. Kraeling, "The Greek and Roman Orient" in C. H. Kraeling and R. M. Adams, *City Invincible* (Chicago, 1960); and in F. E. Peters, *The Harvest of Hellenism* (New York, 1970). W. W. Tarn's *Hellenistic Civilization*, 3rd ed., revised by the author and G. T. Griffith (London, 1952), is encyclopedic. Edwyn Bevan's essay, "The East and the West" in his collection, *Hellenism and Christianity* (London, 1921), gives older but timely perspective. The works of A. D. Momigliano are mind-expanding; see especially his collected *Studies in Historiography* (New York, 1966).

The complex problem of the cultural relationship between Islam and its eastern and western forbears and contemporaries has been succinctly stated by Jörg Kraemer, *Das Problem der Islamischen Kulturgeshichte* (Tübingen, 1959). Fuller treatment is provided by Carl H. Becker, *Das Erbe der Antike im Orient und Okzident* (Leipzig, 1931), an expansion of theses stated in his *Islamstudien* I (Leipzig, 1924). Becker could write that without Alexander there would have been no Islamic civilization (*Der Islam* I [1910], p. 15; cf. Ulrich Wilcken, *Alexander the Great*, p. 323f.). Islamic cultural history was treated by the late G. E. von Grunebaum, *Medieval Islam*, 2nd ed. (Chicago, 1954), and *Modern Islam* (New York, 1964). Useful are Norman Daniel's *Islam and the West* (1960); *Islam, Europe and Empire* (1966), *The Arabs and Mediaeval Europe* (New York, 1975); and C. E. Dubler's article, "Survivances de l'ancien Orient dans l'Islam," in *Studia Islamica* VII (Paris, 1957). A stimulating philosophical view is given by Lev Shestov, *Athens and Jerusalem* (New York, 1968).

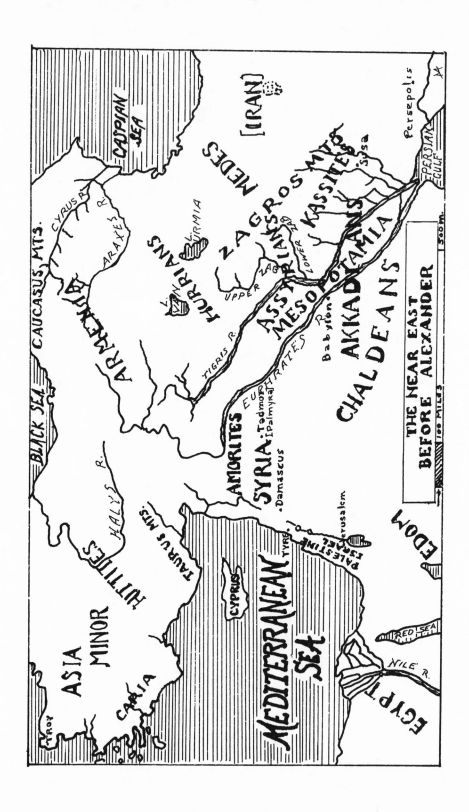

THE NEAR EAST
BEFORE ALEXANDER

I

ALEXANDER'S
POLITICAL HERITAGE

The military campaigns of Alexander and his generals exposed them to three forms of government, with which the generals would have to come to terms when they tried to govern their own territories after Alexander's death. The assumptions undergirding those political forms rested on conceptions of man's place in the cosmos, which would converge and clash in the post-Alexandrian millennium of Near Eastern and Mediterranean history.

The forms were the following. A. The states east of the Mediterranean were territorial empires, in which an elite ruling group controlled large numbers of people whose traditions, languages and cultures were often distinct from those of their political overlords. Those peoples were expected to be loyal to their masters by refraining from rebellion and by paying the costs of a government that gave them stability and order. B. The Greek city-states, best known and represented in history by Athens and Sparta, were elite democracies, in which citizen participation was a postulate of acceptable government. Loyalty to the state called all citizens to active participation in its deliberations rather than to unwavering obedience to its chief. C. The monarchy of Macedonia was a patriarchal, nascent feudalism, which differed from eastern empires mainly in its smaller territorial extent and thus more limited control of natural resources, and in its non-theocratic basis. These three systems require elaboration.

A. The Persian empire, which fell before the Macedonian advance, was the culmination in theory and practice of a long tradition of Near Eastern rule. The major contributors to that tradition were the Semitic-speaking peoples, most recently represented in the Assyrian and Chaldaean empires, and the Indo-Persians, whom Alexander would dethrone from their centers of power at Sardes, Susa and Persepolis. The long tradition of subjecting independent peoples or states to the political domination of a conquering elite arose in the Near East. It was not achieved by Alexander for the first time in history, however much western ideas of empire may owe him. Neither was empire achieved by Greeks. The so-called Athenian empire began as an alliance of Greek cities against Persia in the fifth century B.C. and lasted but a few decades, from ca. 480 to 400, primarily because traditions of citizenship within the Greek city-states made the Athenian "empire" non-viable from the beginning. The tradition of empire arose when Semitic-speaking rulers first took control of Mesopotamia, and it was transferred to the west by the Persians.

Two extraordinary rulers from Akkad (near modern Baghdad), Sargon (ca. 2300 B.C.) and his grandson, Naram-Sin (ca. 2230 B.C.) created the first territorial empire in history. Their drive to conquest can be seen as part of a perennial vicious cycle of acquiring more and more raw materials to maintain and increase a voracious military superiority. For them the raw materials were primarily copper and tin, necessary to win superiority over their less aggressive Sumerian neighbors and their unruly Semitic kinsmen to the northwest. By demonstrating the advantages accruing to a strong city that could exercise military and economic control over vast subject territories, these Akkadian masters launched Near Eastern history on its monotonous, millennial career of conquest. No matter how much subsequent rulers like Ur-Nammu (ca. 2100 B.C.), Lipit-Ishtar (ca. 1930 B.C.) and Hammurapi (ca. 1790 B.C.) might legislate "justice for the widow and orphan," they were unable to halt the drive to conquest successfully inaugurated by Sargon and Naram-Sin and thereafter idealized in Mesopotamia. Amorites and Elamites conquered the Akkadians and were in turn subjected by Kassites and Hurrians, Hittites and even Egyptians.

By the eighth century B.C. the Near East had fallen into the grip of Assyrian empire-builders. Their bloodthirsty records of conquest, made available to the world only after the decipherment of cuneiform in the mid-nineteenth century, have confirmed western, biblically derived ideas, still unfortunately widely prevalent, about the essentially predatory and despotic nature of Near Eastern peoples. The Assyrian empire fell to Medes and Chaldaeans in the seventh century, and the new empire of the Indo-European Persians arose during the sixth century on the ashes of the former Semitic structures. Alexander's successors thus had to erect their Near Eastern governments on the vestiges of Assyrian and Persian rule.

That rule had claimed dominion over the universe, described as "four quarters of the world." That description, first used by Naram-Sin to designate the vast resources both necessary and at his disposal to provide fuel for his war machine, showed that management of the world's wealth by conquest was an overriding Akkadian goal. That same purpose was later to be adopted by successive imperial powers. The burdens, however, of administering the subjected territories soon proved to be costly, and the conquerors sought to ease them wherever possible. Common practice was for the ruling peoples to create politically independent enclaves that would pay tribute, permit trade to be monopolized by the conqueror, and above all eschew treacherous intrigues and wars for liberation. To be of greatest benefit to the conquering states, subject territories had to be supervised by minimal armies of occupation. The problem, of course, was to prevent rebellion, and the simplest, handy solution was to threaten the annihilation of uncooperative peoples. So long as a threat of extinction could be fulfilled it served to check rebellions of the conquered. The empires were thus collections of intimidated vassal states.

The victorious Near Eastern ruler represented his own people who alone enjoyed the privileges of national identity and gave name to the entire subjected and loosely defined territorial state. Identity for the conquered was either territorially or ethnically derived from their rulers. The kings of Akkad, Babylon and Assur established kingdoms named for their royal cities. Hurrian, Hittite and Israelite states, on the other hand, are remembered more as ethnic groups than as extended city-states. Whatever their claim to rule, however, the ruling people, represented by their kings, alone enjoyed political and religious identity. Their sovereign presence dominated every subject community by means of the army, the religious cult, the language of law and the collection of tribute. They considered all men to be servants of the ruling gods, but only the ruling people entitled to enjoy the full rewards of pious obedience.

A common human right to justice was everywhere accepted, though its definition was more assumed than attempted. An ancient text stated what must have been axiomatic, "If a king does not heed justice his people will be thrown into chaos and his land will be devastated."[1] Though this

---

1. "Advice to a Prince," in W. G. Lambert, *Babylonian Wisdom Literature*, Oxford, 1960, p. 113.

claim to justice might indeed be popularly urged, its content was rather mechanically defined, and what was accepted as just could be achieved at all only when enforced by the king. The rights of subject peoples appear to have extended primarily to exemption from further oppression in exchange for grateful submission to the benign, conquering gods. The ruler was thought to be the servant of his divine lord, whose law was intended first for his own people and only by benevolent extension for conquered subjects. Within this general, philosophical framework, the states of Assyria and Persia developed special features.

The Assyrians tried to unify their conquered subjects and discourage rebellion by creating a homogeneous people in Mesopotamia and Syria. Over several hundred years they perfected the practice of deporting selected groups of conquered peoples from their homelands to new settlements elsewhere within the empire. By this stratagem they effectively broke the resistance to Assyrian rule of independent peoples, especially in Syria and Palestine, and inadvertently guaranteed that the language of the deportees, Aramaic, would become dominant throughout the Near East. The language of diplomacy became perforce Aramaic for half a millennium, as the evidence of Persian royal correspondence reveals.

The homogeneous, Aramaic-speaking people, however, did not form an organic, self-sustaining state of their own, nor were they given an integral role in Assyrian or Neo-Babylonian governmental structure. They were subjected to Assyrian rule, in a state appropriately described as an organization of homogeneous slaves, which left for posterity a ruined field of once independent life. The Hebrew prophet, Isaiah, described the Assyrians of his time in words that have become proverbial for despotism: "He (Assyria) has said . . . I have removed the boundaries of peoples, and have plundered their treasures; like a bull I have brought down those who sat on thrones. My hand has found like a nest the wealth of peoples; and as men gather eggs that have been forsaken, so I have gathered all the earth; and there was none that moved a wing, or opened the mouth, or chirped" (Isa. 10:13-14 *RSV*).

That despotism was a national act of obedience to god; the world had to be won for Assur, who commanded his people to conquer on his behalf.[2]

---

2. The systematic, religiously motivated Assyrian conquests can be likened in some respects to the "conquests" of Christian missionaries in the nineteenth century.

The commercial by-products of the conquest were no doubt considered to be the just deserts of Assyrian obedience to divine command. Egyptians and Babylonians made claims to world domination similar to those of the Assyrians, but they never attempted to create a homogeneous people or to force them to worship Egyptian or Babylonian gods. The Assyrian rationale for conquest was, however, explicitly religious. The biblical report about Ahaz's submission to the Assyrian Tiglath-Pileser III relates that Ahaz had an altar constructed in Jerusalem like the Assyrian altar he had seen in Damascus (2 Kings 16:7-18). One may infer that Ahaz, in exchange for Assyrian protection, was forced to adopt Assyrian forms of worship.

The Assyrian kings zealously asserted superiority over other peoples, in obedience to the commands of Assur to whom they wrote dedicatory prayers at the conclusion of their accounts of conquest. Their state was thus not so much a commonwealth of citizens whose welfare was essential to that of the state as it was a god's personal possession, presented to him by his loyal, obedient, Assyrian servants. Conquered peoples were not entitled, even had they so desired, to refer to themselves as Assyrians. The Assyrian kingdom was thus not a political power capable from within of sustained organic growth or development. It was rather a grateful king's offering to his god, Assur.

What was new in the Assyrian conception of the state was not the fact of domination but the principle supporting it. Assur was believed to be an exclusive, conquering god, and he retained restricted, regional character and superiority. The god was example and inspiration for the merciless Assyrian ruler, determined to break all resistance to his own power. All conquered gods were thought to be dependent on Assur's mercy, as conquered peoples were subservient to his king. The monotheistic religious insight sanctioned the imperialist political ideal, from which it perhaps arose.

One insurmountable obstacle for Assyrian religion was the widespread worship in Assyria of the Babylonian God, Marduk. Marduk seems at all times to have enjoyed popular devotion in Assyria, while Assur remained primarily the royal Assyrian divine patron. This religious dualism adversely influenced Assyrian politics, for popular Assyrian homage to Marduk, which prevented the creation of a consistent, official Assyrian policy toward Babylon, contributed to the swift Assyrian fall in the late seventh century.[3]

---

3. Cf. J. A. Brinkman, "Sennacherib's Babylonian Problem," *JCS* 25, 1973, pp. 89–95.

The Persian conception of the state differed from the Assyrian. Though Persian territorial claims were also worldwide, as the world was known in the fifth century B.C., and though the sovereignty of the Persian god, Ahuramazda, was thought to be universal, Persian claims to absolute dominion were somewhat tempered by distinctive Iranian insights. The kings at Persepolis recognized and respected ethnic and cultural differences among their subjects. Instead of seeking cultural conformity with Persian ideals they permitted regional diversity in the conviction that state welfare derives in large part from popular contentment. Further, the religion of Ahuramazda, the wise Lord, was Iranian rather than locally Persian (from Fars). Its appeal to a religiously diversified people redeemed it from the exclusive chauvinism that marked Assur-worship, for the universality latent in Mazda-worship allowed conquered peoples to share in truth without the military and political compulsions of Assyrian demands for conformity. All men could participate in the propagation of truth, and through the deed of Ahuramazda's pious worshipers the world could gain in purity. The appeal of Mazdaism was thus broad, granting all adherents of the faith dignity and worth, and the Persian state consequently based its theoretical concern for the welfare of Persian subjects on ethical considerations.

The inscriptions on the grave of Darius I (522–486) at Naqsh-i-Rustam, a few miles north of Persepolis, reveal the new religious spirit. "A great god is Ahuramazda, who created this earth, who created yonder sky, who created man, who created happiness for man, who made Darius king, one king of many, one lord of many." "A great god is Ahuramazda, who created this excellent work which is seen, who created happiness for man, who bestowed wisdom and activity upon Darius the king. Saith Darius the king: By the favor of Ahuramazda I am of such a sort that I am a friend to right. I am not a friend to wrong. It is not my desire that the weak man should have wrong done to him by the mighty; nor is that my desire, that the mighty man should have wrong done to him by the weak. What is right, that is my desire. I am not a friend to the man who is a Lie-follower. I am not hot-tempered. What things develop in my anger, I hold firmly under control by my thinking power. I am firmly under control by my thinking power. I am firmly ruling over my own (impulses)."

Clearly, Ahuramazda's law, revealed to the Persians, was not considered to be dependent on Persian rule, though Persian responsibility was to rule the world according to its precepts. The universalism of this legal conception helped to knit the far-flung empire together, while the humanistic intent of the religion, restricted no doubt in the practical legal formulations of the state, was nevertheless that all should participate in and enjoy the worship of Ahuramazda. Thus, being a Persian national did not, in theory at least, mean having religious privilege. Emphasis in Mazdaism rested on one's personal relationship to god rather than on the relationship of an ethnic group to its god. Iranian religion was therefore less chauvinistic, nationalistic, and territorially limited than were the Semitic cults, and its appeal transcended the limits of contemporary Near Eastern religious faiths. The Babylonian inspiration for Darius' laws is likely, but the universalism and humanism of the latter were new to the Near East.

The universalism of Iranian religion did not, however, include political equality for all men. Though Ahuramazda's lordship was meant for all, the center of his sovereignty on earth was Fars, and the agents of his rule were Persian. Positions of authority were controlled by Persians, and this parochialism prevented the establishment of a state that could win the loyalty of its non-Persian subjects. Effective rule, as opposed to domination, rests on the consent of the governed; and Persian rulers, like their Mesopotamian predecessors, had repeatedly to quell the rebellions of non-consenting subjects. The Iranian satraps controlled commerce and administered public life in their districts, but their satrapies were essentially tax areas, receiving the benefits of political order in exchange for regular tax offerings.

The Persians, like the Assyrians before them, thought of themselves as a chosen people. That exalted self-view deprived them of a worthy view of others. They dominated subject peoples whom they would not amalgamate into the ruling political structure. Thus they never erased the age-old distinction between "the rulers" and the "ruled." Only those chosen by birth could think of themselves as Persians, and "the government" was therefore for all others an institution to be feared, distrusted, or even ignored whenever possible. Identification of subjects with their government was never strong and usually lacking altogether, while the king was identified with a *chosen* people and their *chosen*land. Wherever Darius went, e.g., he was recognized as *the* Persian, from Persepolis, the overlord to whom service and obedience were due. He was the one elected by Ahuramazda to instruct his subjects in the truth. Allegiance to him, where it was not personally or ethnically motivated, arose from expedience, prudence, or religious feeling. Loyalty to the state, where it existed, meant subservience to the authority and consanguinity of the dominating class.

Near Eastern empires were thus conceived and administered in the service of gods. Those gods, known to chosen peoples, were thought to have commanded them to subdue other peoples to that truth; and the rewards of conquest belonged to the chosen few, while the god's mercy was his gift to the willingly subservient masses. Large territorial states were consequently the logical outgrowth of the idea of an elect people. The view of man as servant to the gods carried with it the imposition of divine service on all men. The great rulers of Near Eastern history attributed their motivation and successes to their national and city gods, even when they composed flagrantly egotistic annals of their own personal achievements. That ancient Near Eastern religious perception of man and the state as being agents of a jealous god, has troubled the world from the beginning. It still dominates the thoughts of people who believe God to be on their side or themselves to be particularly, even exclusively his beloved.

The weakness of the Persian empire was apparent long before its collapse. Darius' successors were unable to hold it together as the local satraps gradually achieved more and more power and independence. The famous expedition from Asia Minor into Mesopotamia by Cyrus the younger, supported by a Greek mercenary army, to wrest the Persian throne for himself from his brother Artaxerxes II revealed to most Greeks the meager limits of Persian military power. When Cyrus was killed in 401 B.C. at Cunaxa and his ten thousand Greek mercenary troops, led by Xenophon, safely returned home fifteen hundred miles through Persian territory along the Black Sea, the truth was clear for the world to see. The Persian military colossus was helpless. Thereafter the desperate Persian kings so eagerly and successfully sought Greek troops that Greek mercenaries came gradually to dominate the Persian levy and become the strongest force in the Persian army. Only the divisions among the warring Greeks and their irresistible greed for Persian gold preserved Persian rule in Asia Minor.

SUGGESTIONS FOR FURTHER STUDY:

Concise surveys of Mesopotamian history have been written by S. Moscati, *The Face of the Ancient Orient* (Chicago, 1960); H. W. F. Saggs, *The Greatness that was Babylon* (New York, 1962); S. N. Kramer, *The Sumerians* (Chicago, 1963); Georges Roux, *Ancient Iraq* (Harmondsworth, 1964; 2nd ed., 1980); W. W. Hallo and W. K. Simpson, *The Ancient Near East* (New York, 1971). Fuller treatments and extensive bibliography are contained in the *Cambridge Ancient History*, especially the third edition, of which Vol. I, parts 1 and 2 and Vol. II, parts 1 and 2, have appeared (1971ff.).

An outstanding introduction to the study of Aramaic is the article, "Aramaic" by A. Jeffrey in the *Interpreter's Dictionary of the Bible* (New York, 1962).

For Achaemenid history consult the convenient works of G. G. Cameron, *The History of Early Iran* (Chicago, 1936), and A. T. Olmstead, *History of the Persian Empire* (Chicago,

1948). The *Cambridge History of Iran*, now in preparation, will treat the Achaemenid period in Vol. II. The inscriptions on the grave of Darius have been translated and published by Roland G. Kent, *Old Persian: Grammar, Texts, Lexicon*, 2nd ed. (New Haven, 1953). The passages quoted above appear on pages 138 and 140. For a comparison of Darius' laws with those of Hammurapi, see Olmstead, *History of the Persian Empire*, pp. 119–134.

B. The conception of the state at work in Athens on the eve of the Macedonian conquest differed basically from that common to the Near East. It rested on the Greek sense of individual human worth, which did not relegate man to the status of slave of the gods, but rather set him in judgment over against his experience. From that sense of human value arose the Greek perception, most comprehensively explored by Aristotle (384–322 B.C.), that political organization both fulfills and restricts private life, and that those restricting and liberating qualities of the state demand careful scrutiny, regulation and balance. The political activity involved in achieving this desired regulation and balance took place for the Athenian Greeks in the city-state (*polis*), which thus became the stage for that interaction which was the source of all Greek achievement.

The city-states were fellowships of like-minded people, held together by social ideals and goals commonly debated and agreed upon rather than enforced by obedience to ruling gods and their royal, human representatives. The city-states did not encompass extensive territory, nor were their inhabitants thought to be primarily or essentially servants of the patron deities. The cities were territorially compact, and their citizens considered themselves to be both independent of the gods and subject with them to unknown and ineluctable fate. Affairs of state were in principle the affairs of all, everybody's business, and not simply the domain of the god and his chosen representatives. Thus instead of the Near Eastern theocracy with its chosen people, where the goals of the state were declared to have been established by and received on earth from gods, there arose in Greece a democracy, where the goals of the state were derived from critically examined tradition, agreed upon in public discussion, and where public opinion was consequently a powerful force in the common political experience. The critical difference between Greek and Near Eastern politics was ultimately a difference in court of final appeal: the Near East appealed in the search for truth to God's revelation, mediated in the cult; Greece appealed to men's reason, refined in public discussion.

Commonly accepted goals of state, settled upon after extensive, free discussion among reasonable men, can obviously be only as good as the men who make them. The Athenians, therefore, in their active pursuit of a perfect state, postulated man's perfectability. They recognized that public and private welfare are correlatives: as the state helps the individual to be perfect, to that extent the individual also contributes to the welfare of the state. For them the state thus became a moral association, and political science largely a matter of ethics, related both to an underlying theory of law and to the practical necessities of statecraft. The institutions of the state were intended to administer the popular will and to insure that it was directed toward the ideal state. Thus the Greek thinkers expected the state to act in pursuit of goals and according to procedures sketched out by its citizens. Greek democracy was intentionally "a system of collective control of a common life."

The Greeks appear to have been the first people to distinguish clearly between the affairs of public and private interest and to struggle with the conflict between uniform compulsion by the state for the public good and voluntary cooperation within the state for private ends. Some accommodation of the two, they recognized, is essential if a political form is to be viable. The city-states were attempts to unite and integrate both. Claims of the state upon its citizens as well as private claims against the state were subjects of continued inquiry and discussion in Athens especially, as they had never been in the Near East, where justice was not defined with respect to both social (public) and personal (private) goals and norms, as the two impinge on each other. The great playwrights of Greece agonized over the politics of justice in a way unknown in the Near East. Does justice for the community, they asked, differ from justice for individuals, and is reconciliation of the two possible?

The Greek city-states may thus be said to have fostered three lines of Greek thought—humanism, which is individual worth asserted against divine power; politics, which is individual responsibility and freedom balanced against public welfare and compulsion; and justice, which is the reconciliation achieved by common consent between personal and public order. All three lines occupied fourth century Greek thinkers, whose dramatic and philosophic works are eloquent witness to their probing search for man's proper place in the world.

Greek political thought did not, of course, spring like Athena full-blown from the head of Zeus. City government had known a long cycle of change, from monarchy through aristocracy and tyranny to democracy, and that history provided data for contemplating both the nature and necessity of change as well as for proposing ideal forms of government to achieve just, humane, social goals. The differing political experiences from city to city at any given time naturally suggested comparisons and judgments about the best forms of government. Consequently, discussion of the facts and fundamentals of political society was basic to Greek life, and it must be simply and truly said that political thought began with the Greeks. Glimmers had, to be sure, appeared in the Near East, especially among the Hittites and Hebrews, but political light first dawned in Athens and Sparta, and by the fourth century it shone brightly.

That light, as we have seen, illuminated the purposes of statehood as much as the means of statecraft. Aristotle, writing in the fourth century, accurately reflected Greek traditional experience when he wrote that a constitution was not simply "an arrangement of offices," but "a manner of life." He began with the premise that the backbone of all worthy political structure is morality, which for him consisted in living according to reason. Since he identified law ultimately with reason, he believed justice to be equivalent to action in accordance with reason. Justice thus became the fulfillment of all moral (and thus legal) obligations between members of the community, and also the realization of good, which the state expressed in its laws. A constitution conceived as "a manner of life" derives the purposes and power of government from the active minds and wills of its subjects.

The Greeks saw that the minds of citizens had therefore to be developed to reflect on and participate in honorable government, and that education (*paideia*) was essential if worthy statehood and citizenship were to be achieved. They understood education to mean that process by which the human personality is formed, and the goal of Greek education was therefore what today we may call culture, i.e., the ability to make informed and intelligent judgments on all matters relating to the common life. The cultivated, educated citizen in Athens, whether or not he took an active part in political life, would be able to decide intelligently about political matters and thus make his necessary and valuable contribution to the life of the state. Athens, declared the orator Isocrates in 380, has made the name, Greek, count not as a stock but as a type of mind; Greeks are those who share in "our culture" rather than in "a common physical type."[4]

Enduring as the Greek political insight was to be, however, the city-

---

4. *Panegyricus* 50. Quoted by E. Barker, *The Politics of Aristotle*, Oxford, 1958, p. xii, n. 2.

states were too parochial to endure in the world upheavals of the fourth century. They were too exclusive to govern large territories, in which the traditions of citizenship associated with local communities would require modification and adaptation to the larger, new political unity. Local sovereignty and national unity have always been somewhat antithetical, and that antithesis was to be a major source of conflict in the Hellenistic world. Furthermore, citizenship was reserved in the city-states for the worthy few, at the expense of the untutored mass. Nevertheless, the ideals of citizenship, inspired and fostered by the Greek city-states, dominated Hellenistic, Roman and Byzantine societies, as they have the political ideals of their successors; and the cherished Greek tradition of citizenship in a polis effectively prevented the simple transfer of oriental patterns and practices of empire to the Mediterranean after Alexander's conquests. The ideal of citizenship is an enduring Greek gift to mankind.

SUGGESTIONS FOR FURTHER STUDY:

Useful discussions of the polis appear especially in Ernest Barker, *Greek Political Theory* (London, 1918); Alfred Zimmern, *The Greek Commonwealth*, 5th ed., rev. (Oxford, 1931); H.D.F. Kitto, *The Greeks* (Harmondsworth, 1951); W. G. Forrest, *The Emergence of Greek Democracy, 800–400 B.C.* (New York, 1966).

On Greek education the comprehensive work of Werner Jaeger, *Paideia: The Ideals of Greek Culture*, translated by Gilbert Highet, 3 vols. (Oxford, 1943–45), is indispensable. H. I. Marrou, *A History of Education in Antiquity*, translated by G. Lamb (London, 1956), is equally valuable. A brilliant assessment of Greek civilization from the time of Homer to the fall of Athens in 404 B.C. is given by C. M. Bowra, *The Greek Experience* (New York, 1957).

C. The catalytic agent in the interaction of Greek and Near Eastern political ideas and practices that ultimately produced the Roman empire was the Macedonian monarchy. The Macedonian conquest of Greece and the Near East brought to light opposing ideas about man and government and produced a crisis in ideas about the ruler's relation to law. Both Macedonians and Greeks knew the ruler to be fallible, subject to the frailties of human reason. His will, therefore, had for them the force of law only by common consent. The Near Eastern king, on the other hand, was the god's representative and at times the incarnation of truth. Since law in the East was thought to be revealed by gods rather than reasoned among men, loyalty to the king meant obedience to his will rather than discussion and search for truth. One of the great struggles of the Alexandrian millennium in Mediterranean and Near Eastern history thus became the reconciliation of these two views and the definition of legitimacy for a ruler and his government. The role of the Macedonians in the struggle was critical.

The Macedonian kingdom arose in the seventh century B.C. in the Balkan Peninsula north of Greece and the Thermaic gulf of the Aegean Sea, bounded on the west by Epirus (modern Albania) and on the east by Thrace (modern Bulgaria). This land power, possessing practically no protected harbor besides those in the Chalcidic Peninsula between the Thermaic gulf and the Dardanelles, and generally ignored as being inconsequential in world affairs by the Greeks of the fifth century, was within three centuries to spread Greek thought and culture throughout the world. The Macedonians were probably Greeks, as Herodotus seems to confirm when he omits them from his list of barbarians who look down upon trades and craftsmen: Persians, Lydians, Scythians and Thracians (II, 167). The Athenians, however, regarded the Macedonians as barbarians and never accorded them cultural equality. This widely adopted Greek attitude of superiority toward the Macedonians persisted, even though Greek was spoken at the Macedonian court and Euripides wrote his *Bacchae* there, and it troubled political dealings between the two states until after the Roman conquest.

Macedonia, however, is geographically the connecting link between Greece on the one hand and the Adriatic, Europe, Thrace and the lands bordering the Danube River on the other. It offered the Persians the only land approach to Greece, and perhaps not surprisingly in the fourth century its people had to shoulder the burden of controlling the eastern Mediterranean world, a task which neither Persians nor Greeks had undertaken with success. The subsequent Macedonian supremacy in the eastern Mediterranean eventually was to open the entire Mediterranean to Roman control.

The Macedonians under Philip II (359–336 B.C.) demonstrated to a waiting world the advantages of a strong monarchy and in the process became intermediaries between Hellenic (Greek) and Near Eastern cultures, producing the amalgam known as Hellenistic. Enlightened monarchy, as seen in the reigns of Philip and his son, Alexander, became the goal not only of fourth century philosophers but also of the masses of war-weary, deprived peoples. To the ambitious it offered a structured and carefully stratified society, to the poor and needy a shepherd, and for mankind in general a benefactor. To us it seems almost obvious that some form of monarchy should have become a middle road between oriental despotism and Greek democratic leveling of the populace in the fourth century; but to most Greeks monarchy of any kind represented political retrogression.

The Macedonian monarchy was a patriarchal, military kingdom, comprising the army of free Macedonians. In Greek contemporary literature "the Macedonians" is a composite designation for the people, its army and its state, leading one to conclude that the Macedonian state was represented by the Macedonian army. Never, even at the height of their world power, did the Macedonians develop a great city in Macedonia and thus they did not share in the Greek political experience of the city-state. Political power in Macedonia derived from territorial wealth and military prowess, both of which were held in the grasp of a few noble families. There is no evidence that independent Macedonian cities ever arose to challenge or limit the royal authority, and it thus seems probable that the seeds of European feudalism were first sown in Macedonia. Because of their long and successful military tradition, Macedonian armies retained extraordinary status and power in the post-Alexandrian era, but problems of statecraft were to be attacked and solved not by them but by the Romans.

The Macedonian army exercised two primary privileges: 1. that of naming its leader and king, usually by recognizing the son or relative of the deceased king or by acclaiming as king another man of distinguished ability or family;[5] and 2. that of acting as the supreme court in cases of capital punishment.[6] The king, as head of state, army and people, exercised the powers of general and priest and also of judge, except for matters that came for decision before the army. Among the Macedonian nobility the king was chief among equals, undistinguished from the rest in dress, accessible to them by right, and in solemn covenant with them to govern according to law, as they in turn were to preserve the government established by law.[7] He was not traditionally a tyrant, as Callisthenes in Iran would remind Alexander. When the latter demanded that his troops show their respect by prostrating themselves before him, Callisthenes emphasized that the Macedonians ruled in Macedonia "not as tyrants but as constitutional monarchs."[8]

The Macedonian state was thus a military kingship, and to be king of the Macedonians was different from being king of Macedonia, as subsequent Hellenistic history makes evident. The king was primarily the leader of his people, not the ruler of a definite territory. Lands conquered in war were the

---

5. Appian, *Syria* 54; Plutarch, "Demetrius" 18.
6. Arrian III.26; Curtius VI.8.25.
7. Plutarch, "Pyrrhus" 5.
8. Arrian IV.11.6.

king's personal possession, over which he alone could dispose. For those wars of personal conquest, as distinguished from wars of national or royal self-defense, his troops volunteered their services for hire.

Among the most important of the king's hired troops were the cavalry Companions (*Hetairoi*), a small class of royal servants, drawn primarily from Macedonia and Greece but also from Asia, who were given the use of extensive royal lands for their service. The Hetairoi numbered during Philip's lifetime only eight hundred, but they controlled more land than ten thousand wealthy Greeks.[9] They were personally bound to serve the king in all his wars, and to prepare their adolescent sons for royal service they sent them to court to serve as pages and royal guards.[10] The Companions thus formed a special elite, dependent on the king in accordance with definite legal arrangements. Among their number were some of Philip's and Alexander's most trusted friends and advisers, and perhaps because of their dependence on the king the Companions did not survive the break-up of the Macedonian empire.

Philip II brought Macedonia to the pinnacle of its power. He emerged from a long succession of able rulers to lead his people to military, political and economic superiority by subduing and dominating their neighbors, opening their land to the sea, importing Greek culture and preparing the way for the spectacular career of his son, Alexander. Philip is often judged from the standpoint of his chief opponent, Demosthenes (385?–322 B.C.), as having been a barbarian intent on the destruction both of Athens and of Greek freedom. Whatever may be the merit of that Greek view, from the Macedonian viewpoint Philip was the creator of a Balkan empire, stretching from the Adriatic to the Black Seas, and including Greece and Athens. The operating principles and practices of the Macedonian monarchy Philip forged launched Alexander on his dramatic career and were strongly to influence the thought and practice of his successors around the Mediterranean for generations.

When Alexander died without an heir in June, 323 B.C., he left a legacy of Macedonian world conquest, a new sense of world unity and the gigantic problem of governing Macedonia, Greece and the Near Eastern spear-won territories. That problem had to be solved in the light of the

---

9. Theopompus, fr. 225, in F. Jacoby, *Die Fragmenta der griechischen Historiker*, Berlin (later, Leiden).

10. Arrian IV.13.1.

prevailing Greek and Near Eastern philosophical and theological conceptions of man and the state as they were embodied in the practices of statecraft in the Near East, Greece and Macedonia. The conquered nations required new political structure, a structure that had to be derived from existing models of territorial empire, city-state, and patriarchal monarchy. The structure would require centuries to accomplish and the efforts to achieve it would launch Europe and the Near East on their respective routes to modern statehood.

SUGGESTIONS FOR FURTHER STUDY:

An excellent geographic and archaeological history of Macedonia, containing maps and bibliograhy, is provided by Stanley Casson, *Macedonia, Thrace and Illyria* (Oxford, 1926). A useful supplement to the study of Greek and Roman history is M. Cary's *The Geographic Background of Greek and Roman History* (Oxford, 1949).

The king's role in the Macedonian state was described by Franz Hampl in his doctoral dissertation, *Der König der Makedonen* (Leipzig, 1934). The favorable review by Karstedt (*Gnomon*, 1934, pp. 401–03) and the critical estimate of Momigliano (*Athenaeum* 13, 1935, p. 3ff.) provide perspective.

A new study of Macedonia is being written by N. G. L. Hammond and G. T. Griffith, *A History of Macedonia*, to be completed in three volumes. The first volume, *Historical Geography and Prehistory*, was published by the Oxford University Press in 1972.

Note: Estimates of Alexander among the Greeks and Romans

Alexander left to his successors the political problems of legitimacy and government that he himself had faced temporarily but never settled satisfactorily. Their solutions to those problems inevitably involved estimates of Alexander himself, the studies of whose life are in many respects an index to political change in the west. Divergent estimates of Alexander's career arose during the centuries after his death, and a review of the earliest estimates will introduce the political events with which the Hellenistic era began.

A perversion, when parochial European literature called him the first "world conqueror," has made Alexander the originator of empire-building in world history. More accurately, as we have seen, he is the founder of empire-building in the west; but his title "the great," was bestowed on him only several decades after his death, by the Roman playwright, Plautus.[11]

---

11. *Mostellaria* 775.

Alexander's reputation as world conqueror arose slowly over centuries in which the consequences of his extraordinary military and cultural feat were gradually recognized. Emerging philosophies of rule and life, based on the new knowledge of the world he left to posterity, stimulated the development of an Alexander ideology which interpreted and used Alexander's conquest to buttress new political goals and ideals. He became the symbol of unlimited authority and power, and his career became a legend to legitimize subsequent imperial dreams.

Alexander's contemporaries, however much they admired his military genius, do not seem to have been impressed with the worldwide significance of his career. They dubbed him simply "the unconquered." Even his teacher Aristotle died in 322 never suspecting that the lifework of his one-time student, who had himself succumbed to fever in Babylon the previous year, marked the end of the autonomous Greek city-state and the dawning conception of a world-state. Greek thinkers generally found fault with aspirations to world dominion, and their admiration for Alexander rested, therefore, on his stunning success against their traditional foe, the Persians, rather than on any hope they entertained of world rule. Indeed, many Greeks hated Alexander for destroying Greek political independence and were encouraged by Demosthenes to ascribe Alexander's success simply to "good fortune."[12]

Though general praise for the "fearless and blameless knight," Alexander, prevailed during the century after his death, the darker side of his character was not forgotten. Nearchus, his admiral, chided him for the "fantastic and romantic march" of his troops across the Gedrosian desert. Chares, his one-time master of court ceremonies, reported Alexander's drinking bouts, an apple fight staged by the conquering general in Babylon and the unseemly marriages of Macedonian men and Persian women at Susa. The Athenian, Menander, dubbed him in effect a wine-bibber par excellence by making his drinking excesses proverbial.[13] These scattered allusions, however, did not greatly diminish the general admiration for Alexander's military genius. Though muckraking reports of Alexander's

12. Ep. 1, "On Political Harmony," par. 146, in the Loeb Edition, vol. 7. The same view, that Alexander owed his success to chance, was espoused by the Lyceum of Aristotle, no doubt because of Alexander's murder of Aristotle's nephew, Callisthenes, in 328.

13. *Kolax*, fr. 293.

intemperance may have circulated widely, his contemporaries on the whole marveled at the fact of his success rather than at reports of his excess.

For two centuries (ca. 250–50 B.C.), as Greek attention converged on the rising power of Rome, literary interest in Alexander decreased, to be revived by the Parthian-Roman struggle for control of the Near East. Mithridates of Pontus, in fact, in his effort to unite Asiatics and Greeks against Rome, claimed descent from Darius and Cyrus on his father's side and from Seleucus and Alexander on his mother's, thus revealing that Alexander counted for something among the Greeks at that time.[14] Both Pompey and Antony sought to assume features of Alexander's physical appearance;[15] Lucullus and Crassus aped him in Asia; and Julius Caesar compared himself unfavorably with Alexander, weeping because at Alexander's age he himself had accomplished so much less.

Polybius probably deserves the credit for making Alexander the Greek national hero who spread Greek culture to Asia.[16] His praise of Alexander, who made Asia subject to Greece, strengthened the Greeks' self-esteem in the face of their own subjections to Rome after Pydna (168 B.C.) and the Roman destruction of Corinth (146 B.C.). At the same time, however, it elicited compensatory, detracting estimates of Alexander from the Romans. Thus was joined the fruitless debate, whether Alexander could or would have defeated Rome had he lived to try. Livy berated those Greek panegyrists as foolish (*levissimi*) who sought to diminish Rome by exalting Alexander, and he epitomized his argument with the memorable epigram, "Alexander was fortunate in his death" (*iuvenem fortuna morbo extinxit*).[17]

Among the Romans, defenders of the Augustan principate discovered favorable parallels between Augustus and Alexander, while the defenders of republicanism sought to diminish Alexander. He was the subject of noteworthy accounts by Pompeius Trogus (excerpted in Justin XI–XIII), Diodorus of Sicily (XVII–XVIII.6) and Quintus Curtius Rufus; and he was an object of praise or blame to Livy, Strabo and Seneca. The interest of these three men lay in questions about Alexander's good fortune (did he owe his success to his fortune or to his fortitude?) as well as about the Greek character of his work (was he a great Greek nationalist or simply an Asiatic

14. Justin 38.7.1; Appian, *Mithridates* 20.
15. Plutarch, "Pompey" 2.2; Sallust, *Historiae* 3.88 M.
16. IX 34.
17. VIII.3.7.

despot?). For the matter-of-fact Strabo, Alexander was the great world-discoverer, but for the philosophical Seneca he was a man "swollen beyond the limits of human arrogance," uneducated, intemperate and wild.[18] In an age of Roman power and expansion both Greeks and Romans tended to admire Alexander's conquest but impugn his motives and character.

Alexander's image as world conqueror achieved particular significance during the reign of Trajan (98–117) who sought to surpass him. The admiration of Plutarch who wrote about A.D. 100 knew few bounds and even Arrian, who died in A.D. 180 and is conceded to have given the world its most objective appraisal, concentrated his work on Alexander the conquering general. By the third century, however, Alexander was becoming a legendary hero, a great man of an age now past, revered as a god of fortune whose image would bring fortune to its bearer. Alexander had become co-regent with Tyche, the goddess of fortune.

More recent historians have properly associated Alexander with a major turning in classical history (Droysen) as well as with the ideal of one world and the brotherhood of man (Tarn).[19] One is, in fact, tempted to trace western conceptions and drives for empire back to him. The temptation, however, leads as we have seen to over-simplification.

SUGGESTIONS FOR FURTHER STUDY:[20]

An annotated list of works on Alexander is provided by Nancy J. Burich, *Alexander the Great: A Bibliography* (Kent State, 1970). The second-century author, Arrian, has given us our best account of Alexander; it is available in a translation by Anthony de Sélincourt, revised by J. R. Hamilton, in Penguin paperback. On the problem of an "Alexander ideology" the following are basic: Franz Weber, *Alexander der Gosse im Urteil der Griechen und Römer bis in die konstantinische Zeit*, Diss. (Leipzig, 1909); Alfred Heuss, "Alexander der Grosse und die politische Ideologie des Altertums," (*Antike und Abendland* 4, 1954, pp. 65–104); Gerold Walser, "Zur neueren Forschung über Alexander den Grossen," (*Schweizer Beiträge zur allgemeinen Geschichte* 14, 1956, pp. 156–189; reprinted in G. T. Griffith, ed., *Alexander the Great, The Main Problems* [New York, 1966]); F. Pfister, "Alexander der Grosse. Die Geschichte seines Ruhms" (*Historia* 13, 1964, pp. 37–79). The Alexander Romance is treated by Reinhold Merkelbach, "Die Quellen des Griechischen Alexander-romans" (*Zetemata*, Heft 5 [Munich, 1954]); George Cary, *The Medieval Alexander*

---

18. *Quaest. Nat.* VI 23; Cf. *Ep.* 91.17.
19. Cf. the review of E. Badian in *The New York Review of Books*, September, 1974.
20. Cf. Chapter II, n. 9.

(Cambridge, 1956); Israel Kazis, *The Book of the Gests of Alexander of Macedon* (Cambridge, Massachusetts, 1962).

The influence of Aristotle on Alexander is discussed by V. Ehrenberg, *Alexander and the Greeks* (Oxford, 1938), especially chapter 3, "Aristotle and Alexander's Empire." See also P. Merlan, "Isocrates, Aristotle, and Alexander the Great," *Historia* III, 1954, pp. 60–81. An extremely useful introduction to the problem is given by S. M. Stern, *Aristotle on the World State*, (Cassirer) (Oxford, 1968), who discusses an Arabic translation of a letter allegedly sent by Aristotle to Alexander. A. Momigliano tends to discount the letter's authenticity, *Alien Wisdom: The Limits of Hellenization* (Cambridge, 1975), p. 136f.

Ulrich Wilcken's *Alexander the Great*, translated by G. C. Richards and edited by Eugene N. Borza (New York, 1967), is the most comprehensive and illuminating work on all aspects of Alexander's life and career readily available.

II

THE MACEDONIAN CONQUEST

Alexander was thrust into his career by the ambition and successes of his father, Philip, who brought Macedonia to the pinnacle of its power and influence. Philip's admiration for Athens as well as his dreams for his son may be glimpsed both in his engagement of Aristotle to instruct Alexander in Greek learning and statecraft,[1] and in his appointment of the youth to positions of military command where he could learn the arts and uses of war which he himself had mastered.

Philip had spent three of his adolescent years as a hostage in Thebes, where he had learned to admire the military leadership of Epaminondas and to respect the discipline of his troops. In that experience Philip discovered new tactical possibilities for an army and how to develop them. He subsequently "made history" by forming a standing force of professional soldiers and instituting the practice of constant drill and exercise with the result that his troops fought at any time of day or year.

His royal army consisted of the select cavalry (*hetairoi*), and foot guards (*agema*), augmented by the lightly armed and easily maneuverable infantry (*hypaspists*). The famed phalanx, armed with small round shield and sarissa (a spear or pike about 13 feet long), made up what has been called Philip's territorial army. All forces were organized into tactical units that combined in each all classes of fighters. Philip adopted Epaminondas' oblique order of attack for the phalanx, according to which the strong assault of the attacking wing was supported by the circling movement of the other wing

---

1. Aristotle was Alexander's tutor in Pella from 342–336, while the royal heir matured from a boy of 13 to a young man of 19 years.

THE BALKANS

0   200
         miles

DANUBE RIVER

ILLYRIA
[YUGOSLAVIA]

ADRIATIC SEA

[BULGARIA]

MACEDONIA

STRUMON R.

THRACE

BLACK SEA

Bosphorus

Byzantion

SEA OF MARMORA

Pydna

Crenides
Amphipolis

CHALCIDIC PENINSULA

Olynthus

SAMOTHRACE

EPIRUS

THESSALY

HELLESPONT
[DARDANELLES]

Actium

AETOLIA

Thermopylae

GREECE

PHOCIS

EUBOEA

AEGEAN SEA

Corinth

BOEOTIA
Thebes

Athens

CHIOS

CYCLADES

COS

CRETE

RHODES

MEDITERRANEAN SEA

to squeeze the opposing army into a clinch from which escape was impossible.

In addition, Philip introduced into warfare the strategy of annihilation or what today is quaintly called "mopping up," and perfected assault engines with protective devices for their operators in order to overcome fortified cities. He thus created an awesome fighting force, in which the terror-inspiring phalanx was supported by mobile units for greater variety and maneuverability in the assault. The adaptability of his troops to changing battle conditions gave him the same advantage over Greek and Persian battle tactics that later Roman legions and maniples would, in their turn, achieve over the Macedonian. This total war machine and effective operating procedure became part of Alexander's heritage and training.[2]

The confederation of Macedonians and Greeks in a war against Persia was also achieved by Philip after a twenty-year period in which he steadily subjected Athens to his own will. His first clash with Athens (over Amphipolis, the Athenian outpost at the mouth of the Strymon [modern Struma] River in Thrace in 357) gave him an important port city as well as control of the timbered hinterlands, where material for ship-building and the gold-mining operations on the Pangaean mountain east of the river greatly enriched his treasury. The mines were said to produce one thousand talents per year, which at the Greek standard of about 81 pounds represented a fortune. Philip's minting thereafter of the Macedonian gold stater helped to unify his kingdom while at the same time it created a competitor in Mediterranean markets for the Persian gold daric. Moreover, from Amphipolis Philip could interfere in Athenian trade with the Black Sea and threaten to reduce or even curtail the grain supply for Athens.

The Greeks at the time were locked in the third Sacred War (a war declared by the Delphic amphictyony against one or more of its members on the ground of sacrilege against Apollo), and Athens had been unable to defend Amphipolis. To make matters worse, the Thessalians invited Philip to assist them in that same war against the south, and Philip's ready acceptance of the Thessalian request in the summer of 353 gave him both strategic advantage in northern Greece and opportunity in the south to engage in Greek inter-city political intrigues. The Thessalian invitation to

---

2. Consult Diodorus 16.3.1f.; J. W. C. Fuller, *The Generalship of Alexander the Great*, New Brunswick, N.J., 1960, pp. 39–54, (reprint, 1968); W. W. Tarn, *Hellenistic Military and Naval Developments*, Cambridge, 1930.

Philip thus not only shifted the course of the Sacred War but also became a turning point in the direction of Greek history as well. The Macedonian entry into Thessaly gave Philip virtual control of the territory from the Hellespont to Thermopylae, increasing his command of the sea; and it inaugurated the long and fruitless Greek struggles for independence from the Macedonian state.

Prevented by Athens for the time being from continuing south into Greece, Philip concentrated his efforts against Thrace, subjecting its entire Aegean coastline and entering into alliance with Byzantium. This connection with a former member of the Athenian League brought Philip the support of two other former members, Chios and Rhodes, and the Athenians now found their influence in the northern Aegean Sea severely reduced and their position in the Chalcidicean Peninsula dangerously isolated. While Philip continued to strengthen his own dominant position both westward in Illyria and eastward in Paeonia, some of his Greek allies began in alarm to repent of their new-found Macedonian allegiance. The people of Olynthus, a city in the Thracian Chacidice, renounced their treaty with Philip, for reasons not entirely clear to us, and signed a pact of mutual defense with Athens. This precipitated war between Philip and Athens in the winter of 349/8, and it brought the political furor in Athens about Greek relations with Persians and Macedonians to its highest level.

Demosthenes, the Athenian spokesman for Greek independence of Philip, feared, correctly as it turned out, that Philip's aggressive policy would mean the end of Athenian political freedom; and he concluded that a weak and distant Persia was less to be feared than a strong ^nd neighboring Macedonia. Demosthenes' oratory against Philip was eloquent,[3] but he failed to understand that all Greece would have to unite to resist Macedonia successfully, and that Macedonian policy might indeed benefit Greece by uniting Greece and Macedonia against their common, ancient foe, Persia. Demosthenes was an Athenian, ambitious for Athenian glory, fearful of Athenian defeat, and unwilling to see that the fate not only of Athens but of all Greece demanded Greek unity of purpose and policy. His opponent, the orator Isocrates (436–338 B.C.), pursuing one of his favorite themes, which his teacher, Gorgias, had proposed half a century earlier, urged the Greek

---

3. First Philippic 351; Olynthiacs 349/8; Second Philippic 344; Third Philippic 341.

cities to unite in a Panhellenic war against Persia; and when they failed to unite politically, he agitated for a military confederation by urging on Philip leadership of the Greeks in a war against Darius.[4] The heat from this political discussion in Greece became intense after the peace treaty of 346 between Philip and Athens, which confirmed the legitimacy of Philip's presence in Greece.

The negotiations for that treaty, which began after Philip took and destroyed Olynthus[5] in 348, were undertaken by ten Athenian envoys, including Demosthenes. The latter gained adherence in Athens to his anti-Macedonian position by pointing to the Macedonian enslavement of the Olynthians and Philip's continued destruction of towns in the peninsula. But in Greece the third Sacred War dragged on, and in the midst of the peace negotiations regarding Olynthus the Thebans appealed to Philip for help against the Phocians. Philip sent a token force and thereby became a party to that war, too. Then, in the negotiations with Athens to conclude the Sacred War, Philip won alliance with Athens, and the Athenians sacrificed Thessaly and Phocis, excluding them from specific mention in the treaty for the sake of peace in Greece with Philip. The treaty (346) is known by the name of its chief architect, Philocrates.

Philip subsequently defeated the Phocians, and their votes in the amphictyonic council were transferred to him. Philip thus not only gained votes in the Greek council but also received by treaty the Chalcidic Peninsula, Amphipolis, and part of the Thracian Chersonese. That Philocratean agreement, legalizing the territorial *status quo*, together with Philip's dramatic gains in bringing to a conclusion the Greek Sacred War, represented a stunning victory for Macedonia.

Philip's military success, however, his political acumen and unexpected forbearance in victory over Athens undermined Demosthenes' anti-Macedonian arguments and added cogency to Isocrates' arguments for Greek unity under Philip "Euergetes" (the beneficent, bountiful, doer of good) in a national war for liberation from the Persians. Philip, urged Isocrates, by such a war could bring Greek dissension to an end and inaugurate for all Greece an age of peace and prosperity. Isocrates thus

---

4. In his pamphlet, the *Philippus*, 346.
5. The site was uncovered by D. M. Robinson, *Excavations at Olynthus, 1929–1938*, 14 vols., Baltimore, 1929–1938.

became in effect the herald of Athenian culture, while Demosthenes narrowly espoused and stressed an Athenian political mission. Both men, loyal Athenians as they were, failed to appraise the total situation accurately.[6]

The correct political appraisal was Philip's who seized every advantage to achieve Macedonian hegemony in the Balkans. The Peace of 346 had made him a member of the Greek amphictyonic council, which permitted him to serve as an arbiter in amphictyonic disputes, and he exploited that opportunity fully. He had hoped and tried to achieve friendship with Athens, but the Athenian insistence that Philip give up all his gains in Greece and the Thracian coast forced him to abandon that hope. He thus found himself being drawn gradually and steadily into war against Athens. Through the political agility of Demosthenes, Thebes was brought into alliance with Athens, and the mounting animosities between Philip and the Athenian-Theban alliance culminated in the decisive battle on the plain of Chaeronea in Boeotia, on August 2, 338. There the professional Macedonian cavalry under the command of Alexander, then a young man of eighteen, breached the Greek battle line and brought swift defeat to the allied Greek citizen-recruits. One thousand Athenian citizens died, and two thousand more were taken captive. Isocrates lived to hear the news from Chaeronea but not to know Philip's terms of peace.

Guided perhaps by grievances from his years as a hostage as well as being stung by the Theban alliance with Athens, Philip showed no mercy to Thebes. He executed or banished its anti-Macedonian partisans. He sold his Theban prisoners into slavery and placed a Macedonian garrison on the citadel. Athens, on the other hand, he treated with unexpected magnanimity. Alexander went to the city, returning all Athenian prisoners and the bones of those who had been cremated after their deaths at Chaeronea, to assure Athens both freedom from Macedonian invasion and continued possession of her primary Aegean outposts. Philip refrained from marching into Attica in exchange for the Athenian promise to join his proposed, new Hellenic union; and the grateful city erected a statue to him, granting him and Alexander citizenship. It seems probable that Philip, in spite of his treaty of peace and friendship with the Persian Great King after the latter's reconquest of Phoenicia and Egypt, by now had begun to perceive the way

---

6. For a useful collection of texts and a concise introduction to the end of an age in Greece (346–322) consult W. R. Connor, *Greek Orations*, Ann Arbor, 1966.

to Macedonian supremacy over Persia offered by a united Greek and Macedonian offensive against The Great King. It would be seized ostensibly to liberate the Greek cities of the Ionian coast that had been held by the Persians since "the King's Peace" of 386 B.C.

Whether Philip perceived that or not, his victory at Chaeronea, coincident as it turned out with the death by poison of the able Persian king, Artaxerxes III Ochus, was decisive for Mediterranean history. Leadership among the Greek states now passed to Macedonia, and the independent city-states had to submit not only to monarchy but to a people they considered to be inferior outsiders. In Persia the rule passed after two years to the forty-five-year-old Darius III Codomannus, who seems to have been an irresolute incompetent, called by Arrian "weak and incapable in warfare."[7] In the Mediterranean as a whole, throughout the next ten centuries, generals, statesmen and thinkers would struggle to establish the meaning, legitimacy and prerogatives of kingship. They would do so under the dominating influences of fourth-century Greek political theory, ancient oriental ideas of divine rule, and the stunning military successes of Philip and Alexander.

The immediate political consequence of Chaeronea, however, was the congress Philip convened at Corinth in the winter of 338/7, to which all the Greek states except Sparta sent representatives. The congress attempted to promote general peace in Greece and Macedonia by establishing a Hellenic federation known to historians as the Corinthian League. Its members, represented by an agreed number of delegates to a council of the League, agreed to an alliance of peace among themselves and of mutual defense against outside attack forever. They agreed specifically to recognize Philip as leader of the League, to refrain from attacking him or his descendants, to give up all feuds and aggression among themselves, and to guarantee freedom of the sea to all.[8] The treaty stipulated the preservation of local autonomies, Macedonian garrisons being stationed only in Thebes, Corinth and Chalcis. The Council was empowered to make decisions about war and peace, to determine requisite levies of men and means for League projects, and to assess penalties for violations of League decisions. Superficially the

---

7. III.22.2.
8. Diodorus XVI.89. Justin 9.5.1–2.

League was the achievement of Panhellenism; in fact, as the Macedonian garrisons made clear, it was the triumph of Macedonian imperialism.

At its meeting in 337 the Council voted war with Persia under the military command of Philip. That vote no doubt followed the urging of Philip, for whose ambition the common military effort against Persia now seemed opportune. His proposed war of vengeance doubtless appealed to the pride and crusading instincts of the Greeks and obscured for posterity the precise reasons for war. His announced goal was the liberation of the Greek territories in Asia Minor, and in the spring of 336 he sent a contingent of ten thousand men under the command of his most trusted general, Parmenio, across the Hellespont. Opposed by inadequate and irresolute Persian forces, Parmenio secured a foothold in the Troad (the region around ancient Troy). That Macedonian success may have disheartened the Persians, but Philip's death shortly thereafter, in June 336, and the energetic defenses of Memnon, admiral of the Persian fleet, doubtless lulled the Persians into a false sense of well-being.

Philip was forty-seven years old at his death. The reasons for his murder by a certain Pausanias can only be conjectured, but among them the dissatisfaction of Philip's nobles with his arbitrary methods may be surmised. It is difficult to assess his work. He did unite Greece, providing for the Aegean coastal states a fresh opportunity for increased commerce as well as economic and political development. His most enduring work, however, was to demonstrate the power of an efficient, monarchical system in a national state, supported by a loyal and professional army. The demonstrated power and effectiveness of Macedonian monarchy, joined as it would be with Greek ideals of community and the oriental tradition of the territorial state, provided foundation for the Hellenistic state systems that arose after Alexander's death.

Alexander inherited his father's ambition and will, his role as king of Macedonia and leader of the Corinthian League and his command of the impending war against Persia. What his own part in Philip's death may have been is not known, since the immediate murder of Pausanias, Philip's assassin, prevented effective investigation of the plot. Quickly thereafter, however, he saw to the execution of all possible contenders for the Macedonian throne, on the ground that they were parties to the assassination plot, and received the army's allegiance as king. Subsequently, within the brief span of thirteen years, he would give men the vision of a united world by means of his extraordinary conquering expedition into the centers of ancient civilization; and his name would become a symbol for world domination.

Almost every aspect of Alexander's career has been subjected to careful scrutiny, and many have attempted to tell his story. There is thus no need to recount in detail the stages of his march through Asia. Several aspects of his work, however, which became reference points in the military and cultural struggles of succeeding generations require notice here.[9]

Alexander's accession to the Macedonian throne after Philip's death was not a simple matter of course. Alexander owed his crown to the loyalty of Philip's generals, especially to Antipater and the three slayers of Pausanias: Leonnatus, Perdiccas, and his brother-in-law, Attalus, all of whom appear to have supported Alexander throughout his career. Among the other generals, however, an opposing faction seems gradually to have clustered around Parmenio, forming a clique which required time and patience for the young king to crush. Its influence and power may be inferred from the fact that Parmenio's sons held high posts in the army. Philotas, his oldest, commanded the Hetairoi (see above, pp. 23, 29), and Nicanor, his other, the hypaspists. Parmenio's son-in-law, Coenus, commanded one of the regiments and is credited with having made the decisive speech before Alexander, that brought the Indian expedition to a halt.[10] Among these men Alexander had to move circumspectly.

To begin with, therefore, he summoned Parmenio from Asia Minor in the fall of 335 to help with the preparations for war, but he did not assign him command of a division, making him instead second-in-command of the army. Then, in the course of the long campaign, Alexander removed Parmenio's relatives one by one from active combat until finally, in the summer of 330, he ordered the execution of Philotas and Parmenio himself. Five years later Coenus too was dead, and by the end of Alexander's life, Parmenio's family seems to have been extinguished. This sketch of family

---

9. For a bibliography see above pp. 27–28. Among the Greek and Roman authors, Diodorus Siculus, whose history of Alexander forms books XVI.66–XVII of his Universal History, wrote ca. 54 B.C.; Quintus Curtius Rufus wrote his history of Alexander ca. A.D. 50; Plutarch lived ca. A.D. 46 to 120; the work of Trogus, the Augustan historian is preserved in Justin's abridgment (third century A.D.); and Arrian died in A.D. 180. The works of Ulrich Wilcken, C. A. Robinson, Jr., and W. W. Tarn on Alexander the Great are available in English. The Alexander Romance is translated by E. H. Haight, *The Life of Alexander of Macedon by Pseudo-Callisthenes*, New York, 1955, and by A. M. Wolshojian, *The Romance of Alexander the Great by Pseudo-Callisthenes*, translated from the Armenian, New York, 1969.

10. Arrian V.27; Curtius X.3.10.

history together with the many familiar stories of Parmenio's unacceptable advice to Alexander on the one hand and the high esteem known to exist for him among Philip's troops on the other cast light on the rivalries and ambitions that existed from the beginning among the Macedonian generals. [11]

In less than two years, however, before the second anniversary of Philip's death, Alexander established his own authority in the Balkans. He fixed the northeastern border of Macedonia at the Danube River, subdued the Illyrians on the west, nipped a Greek uprising in the bud by destroying Thebes, confirmed his position as leader of the Corinthian League, crossed the Hellespont into Asia Minor with an army of some 35,000 troops, leaving Antipater in Pella to govern Macedonia, and was facing the Persian forces massed across the Granicus River (modern Kocabas), a small stream emptying into the Sea of Marmora. His speed, military skill and resourcefulness, together with his ferocity against the rebellious Thebes and leniency toward the temporizing Athens, guaranteed tranquility in the Balkans under Antipater's watchful eye while the young king marched off against the Persians. Thus by the time Alexander set foot in Asia his kingship over the Macedonians was accepted, the homeland was secure, his army seasoned, and the Greeks united with him in a treaty of allegiance and mutual support. His political power depended on his skill in preserving both the army's allegiance and Greek popular support. His military successes would preserve that power and support, and the Macedonian pattern he inaugurated would dominate the politics of the ensuing era.

Alexander's expedition was, as we have said, nominally a Panhellenic crusade for punishment of Persia and liberation of the Greeks in Asia Minor. [12] At the time, that rationale seemed sufficient for the Greek support of the war, but for us Alexander's subsequent career clouds his motives. Whether his thought moved entirely within the sphere of the Corinthian alliance or whether from the outset he had dreams of a more extensive or complete conquest of Persia cannot be known for certain. His youthful ambitions were certainly fed by successes which in turn inevitably determined his policies.

For the first few years of the campaign Alexander emphasized vengeance against the Persians, even after Darius' death in July 330, treating as

---

11. This material was first presented by E. Badian, "The Death of Parmenio," *Transactions of The American Philological Association* 91, 1960, pp. 324–38.

12. Diodorus XVI.89.2–3; XVII.72.6.

traitors the Greek mercenaries captured in Persian employ, except for those who had joined the Persians before the signing of the Corinthian treaty. In that way he signified to the Greeks his continuing role as leader of the Corinthian League. But Alexander was also conquering lands for himself, spear-won territory, as his successors would call the lands they claimed as their own by right of conquest. Those Greek cities he freed from Persian domination he appears to have subjected to his own. For the rest he assumed for himself the rights of the Great Persian King wherever he went. His personal ambition seems always to have triumphed over any obligation he may have felt to the Greek alliance.

The Macedonian conquest of Persia was accomplished with three major battles. The first attack at the Granicus in May or June of 334 crumbled the Persian defenses in Anatolia and allowed Alexander to take Asia Minor, including the main centers of trade and communication: Sardes, Ephesus, Miletus, Halicarnassus and Ancyra. The second pitched battle, this time against the Persian forces commanded by Darius himslf, was fought at Issus on the narrow maritime plain of Cilicia in October or November of 333. The defeat of the Persian king there on his own soil opened to Alexander the way into the heart of the Persian empire. Two years were required, however, for Alexander first to secure the Syro-Palestinian coast and Egypt before his final, decisive battle with Darius, which occurred about October 1, 331, not far from Nineveh, between the towns of Gaugamela and Arbela (modern Erbil, near the confluence of the Upper Zab and Tigris rivers).[13] When the battle turned against the Persians, Darius fled, leaving to Alexander the treasures of his camp at Arbela and the prize cities of Babylon and Susa, containing the millennial riches of oriental civilization. Shortly thereafter the Macedonians took Persepolis, the residence city of the Persian kings some 1200 miles east of the Granicus River, and they could rightly have boasted that Greek vengeance against Persia had been achieved, Persian suzerainty abolished, and the way opened for the founding of a new kingdom. That boast, however, seems not to have been made; and the far-reaching implications of the Macedonian presence in Babylon, Susa and Persepolis seem to have occurred to no one.[14] The

---

13. For a description of those battles cf. J. F. C. Fuller, *The Generalship of Alexander the Great* (N2).

14. Cf. Arrian III.18.11–12, who regrets Alexander's burning of Persepolis.

political and cultural consequences of Alexander's campaign would require half a millennium to become evident.

Indeed, the symbolic value of the conquest was to last long after the expedition itself was but memory, and the components of the symbol have fascinated historians from the beginning. A brilliant, conquering general, descendant of a family of generals and commanding the loyalty of a superb fighting force gave basic shape to the symbol. The elaborating features, however, refined the essential image that persists into the present, the image of a king whose brilliant exploits reveal his divine nature and qualify him for world rule. Those features, part of the literary heritage about Alexander, are themselves enigmatic and deserve mention.[15]

First Alexander stopped at Troy to pay homage to Achilles, thereby suggesting his own place in a tradition of semi-divine, invincible heroes. Later he allowed the queen of Caria, Ada, to adopt him as her son and in that way legitimize his sovereignty over the Carian satrapy, the civil government of which he left to her direction. He became by adoption the son of an Oriental and demanded the tribute formerly due the Great King. Then he went to Gordium, near Ancyra, where he cut the knot that fastened the carriage of Gordius to its yoke, thus claiming the prize of world rule said to be given the one who untied it. The tradition most widely accepted, that Alexander cut the knot rather than attempting to untie it, suggests historians' belief that he abandoned established rules and precedents, as his consuming ambition for world dominion drove him eastward. That ambition would justify any means.

In Egypt during the winter of 332 Alexander called on the oracle of Ammon at the oasis of Siwah in the Libyan desert, an excursion requiring about six weeks and resulting in his being addressed by the priest as Ammon's son who would conquer whomever he wished. At Persepolis the following winter he burned the royal palace, a wanton act, whose significance was to symbolize for Greece her complete revenge on the Persians: the end of Achaemenid rule. In the spring of 330, in pursuit of Darius, he released the Thessalian cavalry together with the other Greek contingents, sending them home laden with the spoils of plunder. This dismissal turned the future campaign to Alexander's personal purposes; it announced that the

---

15. For the following cf. C. A. Robinson, Jr., "The Extraordinary Ideas of Alexander the Great," *American Historical Review* 62, 1957, p. 326ff.

Panhellenic war of revenge was finished, and that the emerging empire did not depend on Greece for its existence. He enrolled those Greeks who continued with him as mercenaries in his army rather than allies, and he retired Parmenio from combat by leaving him in command of treasure and communication at Ecbatana. When, in Media, Alexander came upon the body of Darius, whom his eastern satraps had killed rather than let him be captured by the Macedonians, Alexander returned the body to Persepolis for royal burial. Thereafter he began to act as Darius' legitimate successor by right of conquest, adopting Persian dress and court ceremonial and embarking on that arduous campaign that would compel allegiance to him from the rebellious eastern satrapies.

It seems clear that the Macedonian general intended not only to become successor to the Persian king, but also to turn the allegiance of his Macedonian army away from homeland or state to himself as commander and king. Certainly the existence of an independent military body, freed of compelling home ties or superior loyalty outside itself and its leader, became a characteristic feature of Hellenistic politics. Alexander now represented absolute monarchy. As the son of Ammon, he was a divinized king, whose territorial and political limits were defined solely by his own power and initiative and expressed in the exploits of his loyal army.

The three years of conflict in the heartland of Iran were the most difficult of Alexander's life. Here he faced Iranian resistance where it was strongest and most fanatical. Kingship was here regarded as the gift of Ahuramazda, and the king as Ahura's chosen, leading the fight against the spirits and forces of darkness, of whom Alexander must have seemed the chief.[16] No doubt the physical and psychological strains of fierce combat, exhaustion and depression contributed to Alexander's loss of temper and murder of Philotas and Parmenio (330), Cleitus (328) and Callisthenes (327) during these years. Near their end he married Roxane, the daughter of Oxyartes the Bactrian.[17] This union of the Macedonian king with the Iranian people may have symbolized the reconciliation Alexander sought with Iran, but it may as well have been his first accommodation to the Iranian religious scruple that their king should be subject to Ahuramazda.

Accounts of Alexander's campaign in India (summer 327 to summer

---

16. Cf. F. Dvornik, *Early Christian and Byzantine Political Philosophy: Origins and Background*, 2 vols., Washington, 1966, Ch. III "Iranian Kingship."

17. Arrian IV.19.5.

325) set in relief his image as world conqueror. His biographer, Arrian, thought the subjection of India was an essential step in Alexander's conquest of Asia,[18] and others have maintained that it was the continuation and completion of his Persian conquest, since Darius had reckoned India in his empire. Whatever Alexander's motives may have been, however, his campaign in India lay outside the limits of his mandate as leader of the Corinthian League and his legitimate claim as king of Persia. The Indian campaign was, as Arrian correctly surmised, part of a plan to actualize the Persian title, "world ruler," and it revealed Alexander driving his army forward for his own purposes until the loyalty of his men would endure no more.[19]

Halted at last by the stubborn refusal of his troops to proceed further east, Alexander turned back, and after exploring the Indus River valley, he set out for Susa. Early in 324, after one of the most difficult marches of his life from the Indus across the Gedrosian desert (in Baluchistan), where the army suffered greatly from the heat, lack of water and supplies, Alexander again reached Susa.

Now the Macedonian king, leader of the Corinthian League, Great King of the Persians and ruler of the world, had to knit his conquests together with government. That meant, for a start, closing the rift between conquering Macedonians and conquered Persians, a goal sometimes regarded as the fusion of the two peoples. What Alexander may have intended cannot be known, but in a great marriage feast at Susa he and eighty of his nobles, including Hephaestion, Craterus, Perdiccas, Ptolemy, Nearchus, Seleucus and Eumenes, married Persian and Iranian noblewomen; and Alexander gave wedding gifts to ten thousand of his Macedonian troops who had then or earlier taken Iranian brides. The nuptial rites were performed according to Persian custom, and therewith a lasting symbol for the union of Macedonians and Iranians was left to posterity.[20] The symbolism was doubtless reinforced and preserved by the contemporary Stoic belief in the unity and brotherhood of mankind. At the time, however, the marriage feast, accompanied as it was by the enrollment of Persians in the select Macedonian Cavalry Guard (*agema*), summed up

---

18. IV.15.5–6.
19. Arrian V.27–28.
20. Arrian VII.4.4–8; Diodorus XVII.107.6; Plutarch, "Alexander" 70.2.

for many Macedonians the estrangement of their commander-in-chief from his own people.

From Susa Alexander requested that the Greek allies pay him divine honors. This order is not mentioned by any Alexander historian, and historians disagree whether the initiative for the divinization came from Alexander himself or the Greeks. Aelian attributed the idea to Alexander. Demosthenes scoffed at it. Apotheosis certainly was a Greek rather than an oriental custom, and since there is no doubt that divine honors were conferred, not by Orientals but by skeptical Greek envoys whose appearance at Susa would have been gratuitous had Alexander not summoned them, the probability is that Alexander initiated the proceeding.[21] The Greek attitude may have been summarized by Demosthenes, who is said to have quipped, "Let Alexander be son of Zeus and of Poseidon too if he wishes."[22] But for all that, Arrian's later report is that in 323 Greek ambassadors arrived in Babylon to honor Alexander as a god.[23] Alexander's rule was thus consecrated, and that tie with the divine fixed the rationale for rule that was, with varying political and theological supports, to dominate statecraft in the Mediterranean until the Middle Ages.[24]

Also from Susa went Alexander's decree to the Corinthian League that all Greek exiles from League territory, except murderers and temple-robbers, should be repatriated and their properties restored.[25] This edict, issued without prior consultation with the federal council of the League, was in violation of the Corinthian treaty and reveals the extent to which Alexander had expanded the original limits of his own authority and prerogatives. His decree empowered Antipater in Macedonia to enforce

---

21. Aelian, *Varia historia* II, 19, ed. R. Hercher, 1887; J. P. V. D. Balsdon, "The 'Divinity' of Alexander," *Historia* I, 1950, pp. 363–88, argues for the initiative having come from the Greeks.

22. Hyperides, *In Demosthenem*, Fragment VII (VIII).31.14 in J. P. Burtt, *Minor Attic Orators* 2, p. 522 (Loeb, 1954).

23. VII.23.2.

24. Alfred Heuss, "Alexander der Grosse und die politische Ideologie des Altertums," *Antike und Abendland* 4, 1954, p. 71: "Truly Alexander the Great became as it were the incarnate symbol (Begriff) of absolute monarchy for posterity, and to study his career is to pursue a constantly renewed political orientation."

25. Marcus N. Tod, *Greek Historical Inscriptions* II, No. 202; Diodorus XVII 109.1–2; XVIII 8.1–7.

compliance and was doubtless intended to create a strong corps of Alexander-supporters in Greece. The suggestion is attractive that Aristotle's oft-cited advice to Alexander to treat the Greeks as a leader (*hegemon*) and the barbarians as a master (*despotes*) was a reproof, given in 324 in the wake of this edict. Certainly the enlistment of all Greeks, especially the discontented, in support of the divinized ruler became a constant concern of Hellenistic dynasts, and the proclamation of promise of freedom to Greeks a continual inducement to their cooperation.

In the summer of 324 Alexander left Susa for Ecbatana and thence for Babylon; and at Opis, on the Tigris River, where the main road west joined his road to Babylon, he made a final test of his army's commitment to himself and his plans: he released some ten thousand of his veteran troops, encouraging their desire for home and rewarding them with gifts for their long service.[26] As commanders of the returning contingent he appointed Craterus and Polyperchon, with instructions that in Pella Craterus should relieve Antipater of his command, and Antipater in turn should lead a fresh levy of recruits to Alexander. The troops, perhaps as Alexander expected they would, understood their discharge to reveal Alexander's preference for Persians over themselves, and their consequent mutiny revealed their widespread feeling that Alexander was no longer their comrade, the Macedonian king, but rather, increasingly, an oriental despot. Alexander quickly pacified the veterans by exploiting their feelings of camaraderie and loyalty to himself. The discharged troops did set out for home, but after a year they had reached only Cilicia. The uses a personal army might serve were not lost from the view of his future successors.

On the evening of June 10, 323, in Babylon, in his 33rd year, Alexander died, probably of malaria.[27] At his death he had, superficially at least, brought the civilized world under Macedonian military and Greek cultural domination, and he himself had become the guiding force of an empire. That empire was his, existing primarily because of his vision, initiative, leadership and prowess in war. The empire did not represent a ruling people, though a Macedonian and Greek army had brought it into being, so much as it did the ambition and military genius of a single man. Alexander represented no land or people so much as he did himself. His

---

26. Diodorus XVII 108.1–3; 109.2–3.
27. Cf. Alan Samuel, "Alexander's Royal Journals," *Historia* 14, 1965, p. 8 for the date.

conquest was his personal possession, and his power resided both in his personal ability and the loyalty and capability of his fighting force. When he died there was no people except the army to name a successor, and the army was by then only loosely representative of any land or people.

The idea that a state is its ruler's personal possession, an idea already evident at Alexander's death, became a distinguishing feature of the Hellenistic era. The oriental territorial state, composed as it had been of many ethnic groups, organized by allegiance to a pantheon of deities and their royal, earthly representatives, had now become incorporated into the empire of a conquering general and become his state. He, rather than any people or land, defined the extent and purpose of the new state, a fact that emerges clearly in its name. Instead of Assyrian, Persian, Egyptian or Greek states there now appear dynasties of Seleucids, Ptolemies, Attalids and Antigonids, later to be replaced by Roman and Persian empires and still later by religious groupings of Christians and Muslims. The basis of statehood was subtly being transferred from land, people or political form to a man, his dynasty, a culture or a religion. Not until the rise of European states was government itself again to become basic, as it had once been in Greece, to the definition of "state."[28]

This transfer inevitably altered the prevailing conception of kingship. In the Near East the ruler had represented a definite people and territory in the service of their gods, which restrained him within well-known ethical limits. Alexander's authority and power, however, were not simply extensions of his Macedonian origin and privilege, nor were they rights conferred upon him by deities jealous for their own prerogatives. Rather they were his own by virtue of his extraordinary achievement. His were prerogatives residing not in his kingly office so much as in his own worthiness and competence as victorious general. He, the man, created his kingdom. His kingship derived only indirectly from the existing Macedonian kingdom in the Balkan Peninsula. Rather his empire found its basis and unity in his person, and the "government" was thus embodied in him, to whom all subjects were asked to become loyal, whatever their traditional, ethical values and principles. The fact becomes apparent in his coins. The Persian daric bore the symbolic stamp of the king, lacking individual character, but the Greek coins of Alexander bore his own likeness, representing the

---

28. Cf. J. R. Strayer, *On the Medieval Origins of the Modern State*, Princeton, 1970.

imprint not of a state but of a person. Significantly, the practice of placing the ruling sovereigns' portraits on the coins was retained by the Hellenistic kings.

These coins also reveal the religious foundations of Hellenistic rule to be personal rather than ethnic or national. The Egyptian pharaoh had been the incarnation of Ammon-Re, and the Persian king had ruled as the chosen representative of Ahuramazda, but Alexander and his successors represented no established religion other than one derived from and based upon their own achievements and aspirations. They represented no gods but themselves. In Greece pictures on coins had usually been those of gods or heroes who had been intimately connected with the state issuing the coins, but after Alexander the ruler's imprint appears with or instead of the god's picture. The ruler thus represents, either in himself or in combination with some divine symbol, the power and extent of the state. He replaces the patron god of the city-state, and his unlimited authority proceeds from his divine right. Alexander's new state was thus rooted in his person, defined by the territorial limits of his power and authority, and rationalized by his divine right to rule.

Three consequences of this emerging conception of the state were to dominate political aspiration for the succeeding millennium. The first was the conviction that the prerogative of divine kingship was world rule. The new king, despot by divine right, a right justified by his conquests, would fully realize his rule only in world dominion. Near Eastern monotheistic tendencies in religion here received their political counterpart: just as one god demanded the obedience and loyalty of all men, so his representative on earth could properly claim their submission. The idea may have seized Alexander himself. During the last months of his life the idea of world conquest seems to have driven him to ever greater and bolder plans that may well have been related to his request for divine honors.[29] But whether he drew the connection between his own apotheosis and world rule or not, Alexander's conquest did change the picture of the world and give Greek scientific, empirical method that broad field for inquiry which later blossomed in the achievements of Hellenistic science. By then the world was recognized as one. Alexander thus came to represent both military and

---

29. Diodorus XVIII 4.1–6; cf. F. Hampl, "Alexanders des Grossen Hypomnemata und letzte Pläne" and F. Schachermeyr, "Die letzten Pläne Alexanders des Grossen," reprinted in G. T. Griffith, *Alexander the Great: The Main Problems*, Cambridge, 1966.

scientific world conquest, and the idea of one world under one leadership with one culture, which was later realized in part by the Romans, had its genesis with him.

Corresponding to the idea of world rule was the second conviction, later expressed in the Stoic doctrine of human brotherhood: the oneness of mankind. The extension of rule and the equality of subject peoples were correlative. The more extensive the king's rule, the more all men might be regarded as brothers, and the more the tendency toward human brotherhood, the more the tendency toward political and cultural uniformity. To be sure, Alexander joined his empire to the existing national or local powers. He became the Achaemenid successor, the new pharaoh, the Babylonian king. But this did not lessen the cosmopolitan character of his kingdom. His accommodation to the conceptions and practices of conquered peoples whose cultures had earlier played decisive roles in the world, was merely a means to the recognition in these provinces of his world authority. Nevertheless, characteristic of his expedition and symbolically decisive for the Stoics was his potential removal of two distinctions: 1. the political one between ruling and subjected people; and 2. the cultural one between Greeks and barbarians. After Alexander, to be a barbarian no longer meant being a speaker of an unknown language; it meant being an uncultured person, unfamiliar with the Hellenistic ways of life. The ethical consequences of this human brotherhood were to be worked out much later.

Thus the third consequence, deriving from the other two, was the conviction that world rule and the oneness of mankind should result in a single world culture. Indeed Near Eastern cultures were grecized and Greek culture orientalized, a fact which our modern adjective, Hellenistic, expresses. Certainly Alexander was not animated solely by his desire to spread Greek culture, but he was its bearer and he had a clear consciousness of the superiority of Hellenic civilization over any other. He died before the influences of oriental civilizations on his own cultural outlook could become fully known to his contemporaries.

The diffusion of these convictions accompanied the increased ease of communication in the post-Alexandrian world. Alexander's epic conquest reduced the world to more manageable proportions, opening to the Greeks new trade routes and markets, and making accessible to traders, travellers and soldiers places remote from their traditional spheres of contact. The numerous Greek settlements, founded at strategic points in the East, became focal centers for the exchange and integration of ideas and products, all made possible by the release and distribution of the Persian treasure hoard. Trade in the Near East ceased being a royal prerogative, and Near Eastern conceptions of man and the world travelled westward to be appraised and appropriated by western participants in the new economy. Alexander's coinage linked together symbolically the widely separated parts of his empire.

Greek curiosity about the universe, which had suddenly received for consideration a vast amount of new data, would not only adapt these new facts to political and commercial ends but also stimulate Greek inquiry into the nature of the world and matter to such an extent that there would emerge the first great scientific era in western history. Thinkers were assisted by compilers who delighted in assembling data and issued in profusion lists, manuals, travelogues and catalogues. From this era come such lists as "the seven wonders of the world," a compendium of sight-seeing requirements for the well-travelled tourist. The discovery that elsewhere customs and laws prevailed that differed markedly from Greek traditional practices raised afresh the ancient quest for wisdom in the new context of relativism.

The plain fact was that Greeks were no longer isolated and independent. They were now caught up in the political, economic, social and religious movements of the much larger world. Their city fathers were no longer the ultimate political authority but were subject to the demands of empire and the authority of its ruler. The self-contained world of the city-state had been exploded beyond repair. Hellenism paid the price of world conquest with the loss of its own freedom, but Greek ideas about freedom were thereby diffused throughout the world where they combined with Near Eastern notions of loyalty, obedience and love. Western ideas of citizenship grew from Greek, Near Eastern, Roman and Augustinian roots in soil that was turned and fertilized by the Alexandrian expedition to the East.

SUGGESTIONS FOR FURTHER STUDY:

In addition to works cited in the notes the following may be consulted with profit: H. Bengtson, *Griechische Geschichte*, 2nd ed. (Munich, 1960); C. Bradford Welles, *Alexander and the Hellenistic World* (Toronto, 1970); and J. B. Bury, S. A. Cook, F. C. Adcock, *The Cambridge Ancient History*, Vol. VI (Cambridge, 1927).

III

THE HELLENISTIC STATES

The ideas about rule and kingship that were introduced into the world by Alexander's conquest dominated the politics of his successors, often known by their Greek designation, *diadochi*. None of them, however, was able to command the loyalties of the army and other generals, as he had, or to equal his mastery of military command, strategy and tactics. Alexander's legendary hope of achieving world dominion thus became for his successors an impossible dream. That dream, which all of them shared in diverse ways, finally dissolved before the surviving realities of absolute oriental monarchy in conflict with Greek traditions of democracy and independence, the divided loyalties of the victorious Macedonian army, the costs of finding and hiring Greek mercenaries to reinforce the Hellenistic armies, and the necessity for dominating the sea. The complex problems of world dominion were far more intractable than those of initial world conquest had been, and each of the successors could only seize upon those resources available to him that would best support his own dream of dominion. The ensuing, forty-year scramble for power is witness to the world-shaking consequences of Alexander's life.

There could be only one king of Macedonia, but that fact did not prevent the successors from claiming kingship over the Macedonians at will. The Macedonian army alone could legitimately confer Macedonian kingship, but at the time of Alexander's death the army was widely separated as well as divided in its allegiance to Alexander's generals. Craterus and Polyperchon were in Cilicia with ten thousand veterans, and Perdiccas, who would soon be declared regent for both Alexander's half-brother, Philip Arrhidaeus, and the yet unborn child of Alexander's wife, Roxane, was in Babylon with the royal family and a greatly reduced

Macedonian army. The generals quickly therefore claimed for themselves strategically important provinces of the empire and established themselves in their chosen territories with as many soldiers as they could. The provinces they selected were westward oriented, and the generals hoped from their new centers of power to influence to their own advantage the course of events in Macedonia and Greece. Perdiccas had, as we have seen, the regency, the royal family, and the main Macedonian force; Antipater controlled the ancestral seat of Macedonian rule; Ptolemy, son of Lagus, claimed the rich and isolated Egypt, Lysimachus the entrance to the Black Sea, Antigonus a foothold on the Ionian coast, and Seleucus a foothold in Babylon. These claims to Alexander's legacy would, within two decades of his death, become the basis for permanent division of his empire into dynastic states.

The inevitable cheapening of Macedonian kingship made the support of Greece critical to the hopes of the Successors, for a leader who had the support of Athens had therein a sign of legitimacy and authentic power difficult to surpass. The prevailing principle seems to have been that whoever controlled Greece controlled the heart of the world—testimony to the enormous prestige of Athens and the desperate need for qualified, i.e., Greek and Macedonian, soldiers to police the world. The Successors, therefore, struggled to renew the Corinthian Alliance, which was dissolved when Alexander died without issue, and thus to stabilize their control over Greece; and their exaggerated cry of freedom for Greece would reverberate against Macedonian absolutism in the eastern Mediterranean until the Romans invested that call with new meaning.

The automatic dissolution of the Corinthian League at Alexander's death was quickly recognized by the Athenians at the urging of Demosthenes. They made haste to form a new, Hellenic league in an effort to regain their accustomed leadership in Greece; and this, in turn, produced an offensive response from Antipater, who marched south from Pella with a small force to quash the attempt. Outnumbered by the Greek armies, Antipater took refuge in Lamia in southern Thessaly (which gave its name to the war), where he was besieged. When Craterus and Polyperchon finally reached him with reinforcements in the summer of 322, they defeated the Greeks in a pitched battle at Crannon in central Thessaly in July. That same month the Macedonian fleet under Cleitus destroyed the Athenian fleet at Amorgos in the Cyclades islands. Those two defeats, which also imposed an army of occupation on Athens, permanently impoverished Athens on land and sea. Demosthenes, sought by Antipater, condemned by Athens, and seeing his life's work undone, committed suicide in October. The Lamian war thus sealed the fate of Athens while it emphasized the necessity for Hellenic cooperation in the future. Aristotle had died the same year at Chalcis,[1] and the deaths of Demosthenes and Aristotle within months of each other may be said to mark the end of the era of the Greek city-state.

The end of the Lamian war also marked the outbreak of armed conflict among Alexander's successors for the control of his empire. The complicated story is surprisingly well known and can be briefly summarized. In 321 Perdiccas died in a mutiny of his officers as a result of his abortive effort to take Egypt; two years later Antipater died of natural causes, leaving the regency in Macedonia to Polyperchon instead of his own son, Cassander. Chagrined, Cassander cultivated the friendship of Athens and made Demetrius of Phalerum (a coastal suburb of Athens) his representative there. Under Demetrius' leadership Athens experienced a decade of cultural revival (317–307)[2] that would be transferred to Egypt, when, after Cassander's death in 297, the exiled Demetrius would help found the famous library and museum at Alexandria. When in 317 Alexander's mother, Olympias, saw to the murder of Philip Arrhidaeus and his wife, Eurydice, a crime for which she herself was put to death by the Macedonians the following year, the Macedonian royal house was reduced to Roxane and her seven-year-old son, Alexander IV, whom Cassander kept under guard at Amphipolis. The death in 317 of Eumenes, the only Greek among the Macedonian successors, left Antigonus, "the one-eyed," master in Asia; and Seleucus, in Babylon, fled from him to Ptolemy in Egypt in the summer of 316.

At Tyre, in the spring of 315, Antigonus, refusing to accept the demands of the other successors that he give up the territories he had taken from Eumenes and Seleucus, proclaimed himself regent of the empire, justifying his act by recalling that Antipater had appointed him marshal of Asia after Perdiccas died in 321. Antigonus' design was evidently to win Greek support by proclaiming freedom for the Greek cities that Ptolemy, Lysimachus and Cassander had invested with garrisons of their own troops. From Tyre Antigonus therefore declared the cities to be free and called upon his troops to remove Demetrius and the Macedonian occupying force from Athens, a "deliverance" they were unable to accomplish for eight years.

In 312, attempting to ruin Ptolemy, Antigonus sent against him his

---

1. The Athenian hostility toward Aristotle and his friendship with Antipater are noteworthy. Aristotle named Antipater the executor of his will.

2. Cf. W. W. Tarn in *CAH* VI, ch. 15, p. 496f. and the bibliography on pp. 607–08.

son, Demetrius Poliorcetes, "taker of cities," but the campaign was premature. Ptolemy met Demetrius at Gaza and defeated him so decisively that Seleucus felt it safe to return from his asylum in Egypt to Babylon. His return in 312 B.C. marks the beginning of the Seleucid era (calendar). The general peace that was reached in the autumn of 311 left Antigonus supervisor of Asia, Ptolemy confirmed in Egypt, Lysimachus in Thrace and Cassander in Macedonia until the young Alexander should come of age. That effective death warrant for Roxane and her son was carried out by Cassander in the winter of 310/309, and the death of Polyperchon in battle in 309 left Cassander master in Macedonia.

Thus by 309 Alexander's "empire" had been broken into five territorial states: 1. the Asiatic kingdom of Antigonus, stretching from the Hellespont to the Euphrates and commanding the main trade routes from the East; 2. the kingdom of Ptolemy, consisting of Egypt and its outposts, Cyrenaica, Cyprus and parts of southern Syria, rich, self-contained and least vulnerable of the five to attack; 3. the Thracian kingdom of Lysimachus, stretching from the Aegean to the Danube and including the Greek cities on the western shore of the Black Sea, controlling the passage of goods between the Aegean and Black Seas, but also faced with warding off the northern barbarians; 4. the Macedonian homeland of Cassander, politically and militarily prestigious but lacking strong economic foundation; and 5. the eastern territory of Seleucus, who was declared king of Babylon in 309/8, oriented initially toward Iran and India until in 305 Seleucus gave India including Gedrosia to Chandragupta, the Indian, Mauryan king, in exchange for five hundred war elephants, and thereafter turned his attention primarily to Mediterranean politics. Greece, however, which was now claimed by both Macedonia and Egypt as a consequence of the Lamian war, remained a problem.

Antigonus' effort to dislodge Greece from Egyptian and Macedonian control began when his son, Demetrius, made a successful attack on the Piraeus in 307 and liberated Athens from Cassander and Demetrius of Phalerum. Antigonus and his son then defeated Ptolemy's navy at Salamis in Cyprus the following year. That victory gave them a command of the Aegean and eastern Mediterranean seas that was to endure for two decades; and it so exhilarated Antigonus that he declared himself king and his son co-regent, successors to Alexander. The other successors, not to be outdone, also assumed the royal title, thus further debasing its meaning. The next year, when Rhodes, which stood for freedom of the sea, refused Antigonus' order to boycott Egypt, Demetrius besieged the island city a full year without success, being forced finally to give up the siege in order to relieve

Athens of Cassander's renewed threat. That successful Rhodian resistance marked the beginning of Rhodian ascendancy in the Mediterranean, and within a few decades Rhodes became the leading commercial power of the world and her port a clearing house for commerce and trade.

In the Peloponnese, however, Demetrius had such success against Cassander that he re-established the old Corinthian alliance in 302, naming Cassander the common enemy at the initial League meeting to which all the Hellenic states except Sparta, Messenia and Thessaly sent representatives. Cassander responded with an alliance of the successors against Antigonus, and the inevitable war with Antigonus broke out in Asia Minor in 301. That summer at Ipsus in Phrygia (perhaps modern Sipsin) the eighty-year-old general was defeated and killed. In the treaty negotiations that followed, Seleucus and Lysimachus divided Asia between them, ordering an unwilling Ptolemy to give up "Hollow Syria" (Coele-Syria)[3] to Seleucus, but

---

3. Precise identification of Coele-Syria is difficult because of its varied usage in antiquity. In general it refers to northern Palestine, including the valley between the Lebanon and anti-Lebanon mountain ranges. But the evidence is not conclusive. G. A. Smith informs us that "In the Greek period the general name for all Eastern Palestine was Coele-Syria" (*The Historical Geography of the Holy Land* [London, 1903]: 538). Polybius remarks (V.80.3) that Raphia "is the first city of Coele-Syria on the Egyptian side after Rhinocolura," i.e., Coele-Syria is the whole of southern Syria, except Phoenicia. 2 Macc. 3:4-9 includes Jerusalem as a town in Coele-Syria. According to Josephus (*Antiquities* XIV.IV.5) the Romans restricted the term to Trans-Jordan: "Pompey committed Coele-Syria, as far as the river Euphrates and Egypt, to Scaurus, with two Roman legions . . . ." Edmund S. Bouchier describes the Leontes (Litani) River as breaking through the mountains to the sea near Tyre, "its basin being Coele-Syria, in the proper sense of that vaguely used term" (*Syria as a Roman Province* [Oxford, 1916]: 2). E. Schürer (II.i.97) believed that ca. 95–85 B.C. Damascus was "the capital of a kingdom called Coele-Syria separated from the kingdom of Syria . . . ." A. H. M. Jones (*Oxford Classical Dictionary*, 1949, p. 873) concluded that Syria was often called by the Greeks Coele-Syria, to distinguish it from 'Syria between the rivers' or Mesopotamia. No doubt the term was defined and delimited in antiquity according to the preference of its user for either the Seleucid or Ptolemaic regime. More recently Benjamin Mazar ("The Aramean Empire and Its Relations with Israel," *The Biblical Archaeologist Reader* 2 [ed. D. N. Freedman and E. F. Campbell: New York, 1964]: 150–51; rpt. from *The Biblical Archaeologist*, 24/4 [December 1962]: 97–120) has accepted the argument that *koile* "is a Grecized form of the Hebrew word" *kol*" and that *koile Syria* means "all Syria," i.e., "upper Syria" between Cilicia and the Orontes River, and "lower Syria" south of the Orontes. After the Ptolemaic conquest, *koile Syria*, he argues, was restricted to lower Syria, Ptolemy's territory, as opposed to "upper Syria," which belonged to Seleucus. The argument is not convincing. Cf. M. Avi Yonah, *The Holy Land*, rev. ed. (Grand Rapids, Mich., 1977): 44–45.

awarding Cassander nothing except perhaps a free hand in Greece. The immediate result of the treaty was thus to defer permanent settlement of Macedonia and to pit Seleucus and Lysimachus against one another, while its more lasting effect was to foster a prolonged dispute between Ptolemy and Seleucus over "Hollow Syria."

The Hellenistic state system was confirmed with the death of Antigonus at Ipsus. Four kings claimed most of Alexander's territory, basing their right to rule on their proven ability to take and hold their territories. Ptolemy held Egypt, Seleucus Asia east of the Taurus mountains, Lysimachus Thrace and Anatolia, and Cassander Macedonia and Greece. Demetrius controlled the sea from firmly held points in western Asia Minor, Cyprus and Phoenicia, and his alliance with Agathocles of Sicily suggested the possibility of a Mediterranean empire that Rome would later realize. The four kings, however, had to legitimate their own rights to rule and to establish self-sustaining political structures.

To establish his legitimacy, as we have noted, each king at one time or another had his troops acclaim him king of the Macedonians (a cogent witness to the continuing importance popularly attached to Macedonian military approval of the rule). Then, to build their states, the monarchs by co-regency established dynastic successions within their territories and founded capital cities named after themselves: Seleucia on the Tigris and Antioch on the Orontes, Lysimachia on the Chersonese, Cassandria on the Chalcidice, and Alexandria in Egypt, which became the leading city of the world. With the exception of Seleucia on the Tigris the cities faced the Mediterranean, the arena of political and economic rivalry, and relegated Iran, Iraq and central Asia Minor to the status of barbarian hinterland. Unable any longer to think of taking the world, the new dynasts were content to manage their own Mediterranean shares of it and resist any political, military or economic shift that might threaten the new balance of power.

That precarious balance was first imperiled after Ipsus by Demetrius, whose ambitions for rule had not died with his father and whose control of the port cities in western Asia Minor defied Lysimachus' claims to rule there. Ptolemy's claim to "Hollow Syria," against the agreement at Ipsus, brought him into open conflict with Seleucus, and, to counterbalance that, led him to give his daughters Arsinoe and Lysandra in alliances of marriage to Lysimachus and to Cassander's son, Alexander. Seleucus in return sought confederation with Demetrius by marrying the latter's young daughter, Stratonike (298). That union, however, was short-lived. The war in Syria, nevertheless, seemed to offer Demetrius the chance he had been seeking for non-interference by the Near Eastern dynasts in his designs on Asia Minor. Cassander's death in 297 after a long illness, the deaths of his sons shortly thereafter and the end of Antipater's house gave Demetrius the kingship by acclamation of the Macedonian army in 294. He now had a base from which to launch a reconquest of Asia and undo what Ipsus had achieved. But Lysimachus had found a new ally in Pyrrhus of Epirus, and the two were able to thwart Demetrius' plan to take Ionia from Lysimachus. They invaded Macedonia and divided it between them, forcing Demetrius to flee to Asia Minor, while leaving behind his son, Antigonus, to look after what remained of his Macedonian kingdom.

In Asia Demetrius' forces were unequal to those of Lysimachus; and on sea he was effectively isolated by Ptolemy, whose fleet had seized control of the Aegean islands. Forced to retire eastward he sought refuge finally in 286 with Seleucus, who held him prisoner in Syria, where he died in 283 in his fifty-fourth year. Ptolemy's death that same year, together with the scheming of Arsinoe, the new Ptolemy's sister and also Lysimachus' wife, to favor her own children over those of Lysimachus' earlier wives who had taken refuge in Syria, brought Lysimachus and Seleucus into open conflict. Their decisive struggle took place at Corupedium northeast of Smyrna (modern Izmir), probably in February 281, where Lysimachus was defeated and killed. Later that summer, Seleucus, who, considering himself to be Lysimachus' successor and king of Macedonia, was making his way from Asia to Lysimachia in Europe to take up his claim, was stabbed to death as he stepped off the boat that had carried him across the Hellespont. His assassin was Ptolemy Ceraunus (Thunderbolt), the oldest son of Eurydice, Antipater's daughter. Ptolemy I had passed over Ceraunus' claim to the Ptolemaic throne in favor of his own son by Berenice, Ptolemy (later Philadelphus). Ceraunus, having taken refuge in Thrace, seems to have expected to succeed Lysimachus; and his murder of Seleucus gave him the support of the army who declared him king of Macedonia. Seleucus' son, Antiochus, who had been co-regent with his father, became ruler of Asia.

Seleucus' death ended the era of Alexander's generals. Alexander's empire had become irrevocably divided, with political interest focused on the Mediterranean, and Near Eastern peoples became pawns in the Macedonian and Greek struggles for supremacy among themselves. The Persian territorial state had been broken up and the Macedonian kingdom of Philip attenuated. The Greek cities had lost their independence and now formed confederations to pursue Greek interests and oppose Macedonian domination. The two most prominent leagues were the Achaean in the Peloponnesus, reorganized in 280 B.C. and the Aetolian in central Greece. These

Greek experiments in federalism, offering illusory hope to the Greeks, would soon fail, together with Macedonia, before the sweep of Roman might.[4] Meanwhile, however, the new Hellenistic rulers would have to establish an acceptable, official legitimation for their sovereignty that would take account of the heterogeneous ethnic populations they aspired to rule. They would also have to stabilize their precarious economies, which depended on favorable control of trade and trade routes as well as on a continuing supply of silver and gold for their monetary systems. The economic stability they sought could be achieved by a careful strategy of military conquest, when desirable or possible, and by political and economic domination at home and abroad. The administrative organizations they inherited, however, which were unwieldy and often unacceptable to them, had to be modified to make room for the new Macedonian ruling class whose ambitions often exceeded their abilities to rule. The new kings had, in short, to achieve stability in their society, government and economy, in an age of discovery and enlightenment and a world ringed with envious and often hostile peoples.

The first of those outside peoples to profit from the confusion attending the deaths of Lysimachus and Seleucus were the Gauls (Galatians). They had been migrating slowly into the Balkan Peninsula from southern Germany ever since the eighth century B.C. Alexander had stopped them at the Danube, and after his death Lysimachus had restrained them from entering Thrace. The weakening of the northern defenses following Lysimachus' death now allowed the Gauls to continue their southward movement and unwittingly determine the course of Hellenistic history in Macedonia and Asia Minor.[5]

In the early spring of 279 Ptolemy Thunderbolt marched against them to his own defeat and death in the battle. That disaster left the floundering government of Macedonia leaderless for nearly two years and the Gauls free to continue their movement south and eastward unimpeded. A coalition of Greeks headed by the Aetolians halted them at Thermopylae in a victory that marked the beginning of Aetolian pre-eminence in Greece, but the

---

4. Cf. J. A. O. Larsen, *Representative Government in Greek and Roman History*, Los Angeles, Cal., 1955; W. W. Tarn, *CAH* VII, ch. xxiii.

5. See the full account in Justin XXIV.4–5; also A. Momigliano, "The Celts and the Greeks," in his book, *Alien Wisdom: The Limits of Hellenization*, Cambridge, 1975, pp. 50–73.

following year, 278, with the aid of the Northern League of Bithynia and Pontus, some Gauls crossed the Hellespont into Asia Minor to help in the native struggle against the Seleucid, Antiochus I. Against them Antiochus prevailed with the stunning use of his elephant corps,[6] forcing them to settle in central Anatolia in what later became known as Galatia, where they remained until Roman times, a constant terror to their neighbors. Thirty-six years later, in 241, Attalus, king of Pergamum, would rise to world power in the wake of his victory over the recalcitrant Gauls. Before that, however, in 277 in Thrace, near Lysimachia, Demetrius' son, Antigonus, nicknamed Gonatas (the meaning is unknown), gained a decisive victory over them and therewith won his kingship over Macedonia by acclamation of the Macedonian army. Eventually the Gauls established their kingdom of Tylis in Thrace, and with the Northern League of Asia Minor troubled the Greek and Macedonian coastal cities of Thrace and the Black Sea for more than a century.

The settlement of the Gauls confirmed the Antigonid dynasty in Macedonia and the Aetolian ascendancy in Greece; it also established the reputation and power of the Attalids in Pergamum, and created the Galatian district in Asia Minor, whose population was more often to be found on the side of the native Anatolians than on that of the Seleucids or Greeks. In this way, within four years of Lysimachus' death at Corupedium, the political stage was set for the cultural achievements of the third century. Two Greek leagues, the Aetolian and the Achaean, would dominate Greek politics; Rhodes would continue its fight for freedom of the sea; Pergamum would enjoy a brilliant cultural and political flowering, while Antigonids, Seleucids and Ptolemies would seek to control the rest of the world according to the principle, "Your neighbor is your enemy and your neighbor's neighbor is your ally,"[7]

The cultural achievements of the century were evident in the goals and accomplishments of the dynasts, the most representative among whom was Antigonus Gonatas, who ruled Macedonia almost half a century from 283–239. He was one of the best educated monarchs of the age, having studied at Athens under Zeno of Citium (in Cyprus), the founder of the

---

6. E. R. Bevan, *House of Seleucus*, 2 vols., London, 1902: 1.143; W. W. Tarn, *CAH* VII, p. 702.

7. C. B. Welles, *Alexander and the Hellenistic World*, p. 75. For a clear account cf. Pierre Grimal, *Hellenism and the Rise of Rome*, New York, 1968.

Stoic school, so-called because of Zeno's fondness for the porch (stoa) where he taught. Zeno would die in his 98th year in 264, having inspired his royal pupil with his ideal of the king as first servant of the state. A simple, unostentatious man, Gonatas spoke of kingship as a "glorious service"[8] rendered to those whose welfare was his primary concern.[9] His influence in the Mediterranean was wide-ranging because Macedonia with its incomparable army was still regarded as the heart of the world. That army had vanquished the Persians and most recently the Gauls. Now it was stationed in Thessaly and parts of all Greece, and Gonatas dreamed of wresting control of the Aegean Sea to himself, thereby siphoning off into Macedonia some of the wealth flowing into Alexandria and Egypt.

Gonatas' contemporaries in Egypt were the second and third Ptolemies: Philadelphus, who reigned from 285–246, and his son, Euergetes I, who succeeded him from 246–222. These men created a totalitarian state on the foundations laid by Ptolemy I Soter (323–283) following existing Egyptian models which they turned to their own economic advantage. Paradoxically in the process they made Alexandria rival Athens as the leading cultural center of the world. The Alexandrian library was unexcelled, and royal subventions to scholars and literati attracted to the Museum, the ancient equivalent of a modern Institute for Advanced Study, some of the best thinkers of the day. Athens preserved its preeminence as a center for philosophy, but Alexandria became the home of science, literature and literary studies. Egypt thus participated in Greek intellectual life and gave it direction, while clever economic and political policies made the first three Ptolemies masters of the world.

Serious problems troubled the Ptolemies, however, from the beginning. They had first of all to incorporate millennia of native Egyptian administrative, religious and economic tradition into their new Macedonian state, and they desired to do this without at the same time losing their own political and social superiority. Even more important, the Ptolemaic state could rely on an army composed only of Macedonian and Greek soldiers; and since the bulk of Alexander's army remained in Asia and Asia Minor or Macedonia, Ptolemy was forced from the start to find and pay for

---

8. Aelian, *Varia Historia*, II.20.

9. Cf. M. Hadas, *Aristeas to Philocrates*, New York, 1951; sections 187–292 of the letter of pseudo-Aristeas probably reproduce a Hellenistic treatise on kingship. Cf. S. Tracy, *III Maccabees and Pseudo-Aristeas*, Yale Classical Studies I, New Haven, 1928.

Greek mercenaries. For this he needed capital, which could be raised only with the aid of experienced Greeks. He therefore had to make immigration into Egypt as attractive as possible for Greeks, which he did by treating Egypt as a money-making machine, to use W. W. Tarn's apt phrase,[10] and in the process Alexandria became a center not only of Greek culture and society but also for Jewish, Syrian and Anatolian immigrants. At the same time, the native Egyptian work force had to be dominated and directed, and for this purpose the Ptolemies established military colonies at strategic points along the Nile, which they populated with Greek and Macedonian soldiers and officials, as well as with Greek and Near Eastern traders, artisans, and farmers. Still, however, the natives far outnumbered the immigrants, and their traditional life persisted throughout Ptolemaic times. An index to the Ptolemaic respect for the natives is the royal prohibition for nearly a century, from 312 to 217, that natives bear arms. The new rulers thus tried to respect both primary sources of their power, i.e., the technical and economic gifts of the new Greek and Macedonian immigrants, and the industry and stubborn disposition of the native Egyptian labor force, upon whose loyalty the new managers had to depend.

Ptolemaic control of Egypt rested on "the rights of conquest," which was interpreted to mean "the rights of ownership," but the new rulers had to secure at least the passive support of their subjects. The allegiance of the army depended on its privileged political and economic position in the country, and the loyalty of the immigrants to their social and economic advantages as masters of the native fellahin. But the Ptolemies, like their Macedonian contemporaries, were necessarily interested in finding a philosophy of kingship that could unite all the people behind them; and the titles they adopted, 'benefactor,' 'savior,' reveal their efforts to propagate a doctrine of the ruler as promoter of his subjects' welfare. For the Egyptian populace the Ptolemies posed as a new dynasty of Pharaohs and adopted Egyptian religious practices associated with worship of the Pharaoh as god. But the Egyptians were not deceived and continued to regard the intruders as foreign overlords.

The difficulties of creating an enduring Ptolemaic state were never resolved, as a glance at Ptolemaic history makes clear. That history falls into

---

10. W. W. Tarn and G. T. Griffith, *Hellenistic Civilization*, 3rd ed., London, 1952, p. 179.

three periods: 1. the initial imperial era of 120 years (from 323 until the accession of Ptolemy V in 203);[11] 2. a succeeding native era of 120 years (from 200 until the Roman interference under Sulla in the Ptolemaic succession in 80 B.C.; and 3. the final period when Egypt was at the mercy of the Roman generals (80–30 B.C.). The great period, the period contemporary with Gonatas' rule in Macedonia, about which we know the most because of our recovery of vast numbers of Ptolemaic papyri, is the first. The second was an era in which the native reaction to Ptolemaic weakness abroad and oppression at home returned the country to Egyptian control.[12] The final era can be described as the dying gasp of the once most formidable of Hellenistic states.

Center of gravity for the Ptolemaic state was 'the city,' Alexandria. It supplanted Memphis, the ancient capital of the country, and became the hub for Ptolemaic foreign policy. Round it were ranged the supporting outposts of Ptolemaic power: Cyrenaica, Cyprus, Southwest Asia Minor, and the islands of the Aegean. It early became clear to Ptolemy I that the road to independence of the other successors lay in controlling the sea, which separated Egypt from the Greco-Macedonian world, by a series of outposts, strategically located on the islands and shores of the Aegean. Through clever diplomacy and economic monopoly Ptolemy was able to insure the continued flow of goods across the sea from all directions into and out of Alexandria, and at the same time by means of his overseas outposts both to restrict Seleucid access to the Mediterranean, and to keep Greece and Macedonia so at war with each other that neither was able to threaten Egypt.

The drain on Ptolemaic financial resources involved in keeping this operation functioning was considerable, but when the Ptolemies gave up their expensive naval operations after 240, their empire crumbled at once, dragging with it to anarchy the other Hellenistic states. To keep the empire together meant financial ruin; to let it fall apart caused political chaos. There was no way to keep the oppressive Hellenistic state system viable. Ptolemaic foreign policy, which at the beginning had been "nationalistically" aggressive, in time became necessarily defensive, to

---

11. This era saw the steady eastward advance of Rome. The Romans signed a peace treaty with Philip and the Greek cities at Phoenice in Epirus in 205, thus ending the First Macedonian War; they defeated Carthage at Zama in 202.

12. Cf. W. S. Ferguson, *Greek Imperialism*, New York, 1913, p. 151.

preserve Hellenistic political balance. Only with Roman help did the Ptolemaic states continue throughout the first century B.C., until the Romans finally annexed Egypt and provided a new, imperial administrative system.

The Ptolemies embarked on imperialism because their domestic situation demanded it. Their stance in the world was "a plain consequence of holding Egypt as a foreign country,"[13] which made an adequate philosophy of home rule difficult. The Ptolemaic kings espoused three concurrent, conflicting constitutional theories. One, for the native Egyptians, made Ptolemy the divine Pharaoh; one, for the Greeks, carefully refrained from any assertion of apotheosis, since the only theological basis for it would have been acceptance of the Egyptian theory of a divine incarnation of the Pharaoh, a theory no Ptolemy could with self-respect parade before the Greeks; and one, for the Macedonians, made the Ptolemies descendants of Philip, Alexander's father. These three theories did not satisfy those they were intended to serve, nor could they be administratively or theologically combined to unify the realm. Internal political stability required a powerful boost from lucrative, foreign trade.

But, as we have seen, Ptolemaic world trade had to be protected by Macedonian and Greek mercenaries, since the Ptolemies could not recruit troops from the bitter fellahin of Egypt. Furthermore, the great Ptolemaic economic machine, which depended on the initiative and support of the Macedonians and Greeks who lived in the cities of Alexandria, Naucratis and Ptolemais, had, it seems, in return for their services, to exempt them from military service. Ptolemy was thus forced to maintain contact with the Greek world as the only recruiting ground for his entrepreneurs and troops in order to preserve a semblance of order in Egypt and so exploit successfully the Egyptian peasants. But by excluding Egyptians from any effective part in the government, the Ptolemies not only alienated them but also placed themselves at the mercy of their Hellenistic competitors elsewhere in the Mediterranean, for whom mercenary armies were less necessary.

Consequently, the Ptolemies never attempted great territorial conquests, since they were too expensive to undertake and impossible to maintain. The cost of Greek armies of occupation no doubt varied with the desirability of the occupied territory to the other dynasts and it would have been greater than its value to Ptolemy. Ptolemaic policy, therefore, was not

---

13. W. S. Ferguson, *Greek Imperialism* (N12).

to conquer territory in war but rather to prevent rival dynasts from affording the necessary troops of occupation for their conquered lands. For this purpose a few Ptolemaic outposts to sow dissension and suspicion served adequately. Ptolemaic foreign policy pursued the preservation of a balance of power, maintained by international threat and intrigue, which appears often to have been pursued for its own sake.

The internal administration of the state was accomplished by a vast bureaucracy, about which we are relatively well informed.[14] The strength of bureaucracy lies in its allocation of fixed responsibility and its ability to handle all kinds of business according to prescribed rules. With relatively few norms it can master the multiple variations of reality, and a society guided by bureaucratic rules can increase its output and accomplishment many fold. Bureaucracy has been aptly compared to the production line in manufacture, where each person has a limited task to perform, thus simplifying the process of production and radically increasing the output. But the limitation of bureaucracy is revealed by the appearance of exceptions before which it is helpless. The bureaucrat is unable to make decisions where the rules have to be abandoned. Smooth operation of the system becomes more important than people, and justice itself becomes bureaucratized. The Ptolemaic bureaucrat became a "foreign" state agent, who was not empowered to bargain or negotiate but only to execute orders from above. Such an agent easily becomes irresponsible, and those with whom he deals tend to become isolated. In their helpless, hopeless condition they seek some future in withdrawal or outright organized rebellion, losing their corporate will to embark upon any state ventures.[15]

The Ptolemaic state thus could not endure. But under the first four Ptolemies it prospered, being geographically invulnerable, taxably rich, and guided shrewdly by master politicians. Undisturbed by dreams of conquest like those afflicting the Seleucids, the Ptolemies soon became the strongest of the Hellenistic rulers and their state the keystone of the Hellenistic state system. When that state crumbled, the Hellenistic world crumbled with it. The other states might ape Egypt, but none had its geographic and economic advantage, and no other dynast was as shrewd as Ptolemy.

---

14. Cf. M. Rostovtzeff, *CAH* VII, p. 116ff.

15. The comparison was made by Franz Altheim, *Alexander und Asien*, Tübingen, 1953, p. 113ff.

Gonatas' long reign, coincident with the initial imperial Ptolemaic era, spanned also those of two Seleucid monarchs, Antiochus I Soter (280–261) and his son Antiochus II Theos (261–247), and it extended into that of Theos' son, Seleucus II Callinicus (246–226). Their Seleucid kingdom, as we have seen, was isolated from the Greek world by a ring of Ptolemaic possessions on the Asiatic coast of the Aegean, which seriously limited Seleucid access to the sea. The poor Seleucid harbors on the inhospitable Syrian coast were no substitute for great ports like Ephesus or Miletus. In addition, the Seleucid-Ptolemaic contest for possession of Coele-Syria, known as the Syrian wars, dominated Seleucid attention and energy during the third century. That struggle arose, as we saw, from Ptolemy's refusal to return the territory to Seleucus after the decision of Ipsus in 301, an agreement from which the Ptolemies felt they had been unfairly excluded. The wars dragged on because possession of Syrian timber and the seaports, Tyre and Sidon, were vital to Ptolemaic naval supremacy in the Aegean, which itself was necessary to check the rising power of Gonatas in Macedonia. The Syrian wars seemed for the moment to benefit the Ptolemies more than the Seleucids, but their final result was the exhaustion of both states and the collapse of the Hellenistic state system. The protracted Seleucid-Ptolemaic struggle made it possible for Iranian and Anatolian provinces to gain independence of the Seleucid state at mid-third century and for the native Egyptians before that century ended to wrest control of their country from their Ptolemaic masters. In the west, the Ptolemaic and Macedonian contest for control of the sea allowed the Romans, after their decisive victories over Carthage in the Punic wars, to subjugate the Hellenistic kingdoms as well.

The Seleucid state was the most vulnerable of the Hellenistic states, both to aggression from without and to dissension from within. Consisting of three geographical and cultural regions, the state was an aggregation of many peoples and civilizations: Iranians, Persians, Elamites, Babylonians, Assyrians, Aramaeans and Hittites. Its natural cultural and political center was in Babylonia and Assyria with their long traditions of rule and culture. To unite into one state the three parts of the empire—the eastern or Iranian, the central or Semitic, and the western or Greco-Oriental—was the Seleucid task.

Like the Ptolemies the Seleucids had to define that part of their empire on which they would rely for power. They perhaps could have orientalized the dynasty after Seleucus I, alone of the successors, kept his Iranian wife. But they chose instead to create a new Macedonia and Greece in those parts of their empire that seemed to offer the best hope of becoming unifying centers within the state. The Seleucids were never able to think of Iran as the center of their empire because they could not consider Asia Minor and north Syria as marginal areas of their state. Those areas, instead, loomed central to Seleucid thought, for they bordered on the Mediterranean, which was for them the focus of all the history and life that mattered.

No territorial state was ever confronted with greater difficulties than the Seleucid. It could not escape economic and political rivalry with Egypt, and it could not control Macedonia. It therefore dreamed of settling Greeks and Macedonians within the central regions of the empire, in Mesopotamia and Syria, where a strong state might be established that could eventually hold its own against both Egypt and Macedonia. The dream failed, however, for very few Greeks migrated into Seleucid Syria except from Seleucid-controlled cities in Asia Minor. Nevertheless the Seleucids did spread a network of cities, forts, and military colonies over the entire central area. The purpose of these settlements was to secure the frontiers, control the trade routes, and create islands of Hellenism that might gradually spread Greek culture throughout their districts. These city foundations, some of which dated from Alexander, extended from the Aegean coasts of Asia Minor all the way to Bactria and Sogdiana. Two of them played leading roles in Hellenistic history: Antioch on the Orontes became the political capital of the western part of the empire, while Seleucia on the Tigris became the political and economic capital of the eastern part and, in fact, the second capital of the state.

The major Seleucid problem was to make the kingdom more compact and thus to resist the pressures of an Iran in process of being reborn. But when the policy of Hellenization failed, Roman imperialism in the end prevented the Seleucids from dealing effectively with either Parthians or Jews. The Greek cities established by the Seleucids were little more than Greek islands in a sea of native population untouched by Hellenism, and indeed by the late Seleucid period the population of Syria was still not Greek but Aramaean.

The cultural interaction between Seleucids and Greeks cannot be satisfactorily assessed. Greek religion seems to have exercised no essential influence upon the native faiths. On the contrary, the Greek immigrants became the bearers of eastern religions to the west, so much so, that far from hellenizing the East they orientalized the Greek world itself. Aside from religious influences, however, lasting influences on Greece from the East are difficult to discern. Antioch was remarkably unimportant as a center of

Greek or Near Eastern artistic, literary or scientific learning, and Syrians like Zeno and Posidonius contributed little to Hellenistic learning that can be certainly traced to Near Eastern schools or modes of thought. Nevertheless, the Seleucids did maintain that contact between the Greek world and the East which had been established briefly and modestly by Alexander.

Encouraging Roman intervention in the disorderly contests among the Hellenistic kings were the princes of Rhodes and Pergamum. These leaders brought their so-called "middle kingdoms" to a brief lifetime of wealth and cultural flower in the short period between the decline of the Ptolemies in the Aegean and the Seleucids in Asia Minor and the rise of Roman empire. The more powerful of the two states was Pergamum, whose capital city was situated "on a crag" in the Caicus valley of western Anatolia. It had been from Persian times one of the major cities in Asia Minor, but its ascendancy began in 282 with its defection from Lysimachus to Seleucus. This defection seems to have amounted simply to an exchange of nominal masters, for the Pergamene coins of the period bear the portrait of Seleucus but the name of their own ruler without royal title, Philetaerus.[16] His policy consisted in winning the confidence of his Greek neighbors, building up his own army, and exploiting the natural resources of the immediate countryside, which he handed over to his nephew, Eumenes I, in 263.[17] Eumenes, however, broke with the Seleucids, defeated Antiochus I in 262 near Sardes and proclaimed his independence. He found a ready ally in Ptolemy who may indeed have incited his revolt. Eumenes' successor, Attalus I (241–197), for whom the dynasty is named, after defeating the Galatians and assuming therewith the title of king, continued the policy of weakening Seleucid and Macedonian power, which led him in the end to alliance with Rome. Attalid policy consequently has beeen characterized properly as "one poor in national aspirations and rich in short-sighted political ambitions," for after the Roman defeat of Antiochus III at Magnesia in 189 Pergamum received from Rome most of Asia Minor. But in 133 the kingdom ceased to exist, when the last Pergamene king deeded the territory to Rome.

---

16. E. T. Newell, "The Coinage of the Western Seleucid Mints from Seleucus I to Antiochus II," *Numismatic Studies* 4 (1941): Nos. 1528 and 1529, p. 316, plate LXVIII 9–10; The Pergamene Mint, p. 10ff. Cf. C. Seltman, *Greek Coins*, London, 1955, pp. 238–39.

17. R. B. McShane, *The Foreign Policy of the Attalids of Pergamum*, Illinois Studies in the Social Sciences 53, Urbana, 1964, pp. 30–31.

The other "middle state," Rhodes, had always been a commercial community. Limited in size and natural resources, the island was an intermediary in trading relations between Greece and the Near East, and its civilzation always retained a semi-oriental aspect. Its rise to power began in 305, the year the city successfully withstood the siege of Demetrius Poliorcetes and became the natural ally of Egypt, upon which it was dependent for wheat. But the Rhodians insisted that the sea remain free. As long as the Ptolemies appeared to respect this wish, the Rhodians remained loyal allies; but when Ptolemy II Philadelphus attempted to command the seas, Rhodes shifted her loyalty to Macedonia. Rhodes was responsible for the defeat of the Egyptian fleet in 259 off the coast of Ephesus, a victory that made Rhodes virtual master of the Aegean. Staunch in her insistence both on freedom for the Greek cities and peace and freedom in the Aegean, Rhodes kept communication open throughout the Aegean as long as she remained prosperous.

Like Pergamum, Rhodes curried Rome's favor, not simply for her own aggrandizement, however, but because she believed Rome to be the only force strong enough to keep peace in the East. Nevertheless, Rhodes was unwilling to sacrifice her long-standing insistence on freedom for Greeks and freedom of the sea to Roman imperial ambitions. When, therefore, in 168 Rhodes interceded with Rome on behalf of the Macedonians, in a matter which Rome considered to be no business of Rhodes, Rome determined to punish the city by making Delos in the central Cyclades islands a free port. The punishment ruined Rhodes. Rhodes remained thereafter a center of banking, but her customs revenue dropped within a few years from one million Rhodian drachmae to one hundred fifty thousand. This decline in prosperity made it impossible for her to police the sea, and piracy grew out of bounds until Pompey finally cleared the Mediterranean of pirates in the first century B.C..

It seems clear that the short period spanned by the reign of Antigonus Gonatas constituted a primary creative era for the Hellenistic states. During his lifetime the states were firmly established; their stability was not yet obviously undermined by disastrous rivalry, native uprising or Roman intervention; and the enlarged world of Alexander's conquests was being philosophically, religiously, politically, commercially and scientifically appropriated. Details of that appropriation, which would inform and enlighten all succeeding efforts to understand the world and order human affairs, reveal the "spirit of the age."

SUGGESTIONS FOR FURTHER STUDY:

P. Grimal, *Hellenism and the Rise of Rome* (New York, 1968), contains a basic bibliography. Also see P. Jouguet, *L'impérialisme macédonien et l'hellenisation de l'orient*, revised (Paris, 1961).

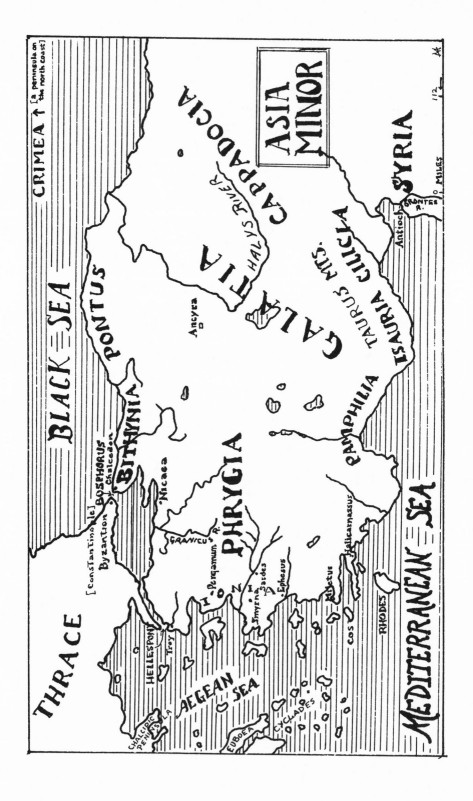

ASIA MINOR

CRIMEA ↑ [a peninsula on the north coast]

CAPPADOCIA

SYRIA

Antioch ·ORONTES R.

0 MILES

112

BLACK SEA

PONTUS

HALYS RIVER

Ancyra

GALATIA

CILICIA

TAURUS MTS.

ISAURIA

BITHYNIA

·Nicaea

[Constantinople]
Byzantium ·Chalcedon
BOSPHORUS

PAMPHILIA

PHRYGIA

GRANICUS R.

I O N I A

·Pergamum

·Sardes

·Smyrna

·Ephesus

·Miletus

·Halicarnassus

COS

RHODES

THRACE

HELLESPONT

·Troy

AEGEAN SEA

CHALCIDIC PENINSULA

EUBOEA

CYCLADES

MEDITERRANEAN SEA

IV

ASPECTS OF
HELLENISTIC CULTURE

Alexander's conquest opened to Greek thinkers the vision of a politically and culturally unified world, a possibility which previously appeared to them neither practical nor desirable. The Persian wars of the fifth century had left them scorning the Persians as despotic and all non-Greeks as culturally inferior. But Alexander, by defeating Darius and making Greeks and Macedonians masters of the world, forced them to accept, however tentatively and provisionally, the fact of world unity. Henceforth the ecumenical idea would inform Greek and Roman thought, and both Rome and the Christian church would claim universality.

Side by side with Alexander's ecumenical legacy appeared the conception of the divine ruler whose divinity was manifested in his abilities and successes. The idea of the monarch's divine right to rule, which the Near East had accepted with little discussion throughout its history, now became a legitimizing principle for kingship in the West. Greek cities gave Alexander divine honors, and the Hellenistic kings adopted epithets suggesting their god-like virtues in bringing beneficence and justice to their realms. As men of proven achievement they were expected to do so, and the peoples believed they deserved such leaders. A unified world would deserve a ruler of ability manifested in his conquest of territory, demonstrated ability that would qualify him as divine. Both ecumenism and ruler-cultism were characteristic of the Hellenistic appropriation of Alexander's world conquest.

Greek philosophy was particularly affected by the new political and cultural realities. The Greek philosophers who had considered the city-state to be the perfect form of organized community life now had to recognize that the city-state was an inadequate organ for world rule. Patterns of community life in the city-state could not embrace the complexities of size, organization and purpose involving community life in the world. Personal loyalty to the city-state would inevitably have to be modified if its citizens were to take advantage of the vast opportunities created elsewhere by Alexander's conquest. Furthermore, as the instability of all human affairs became manifest in the on-going struggle for control of the various Hellenistic states it called into question the Platonic world of enduring, ideal values on which the city-state had rested. There appeared now to be no actual, inner connection between world events; and a sense of community, therefore, would have to arise from a new view of the world that might make possible some kind of philosophical order amid the existing political and cultural chaos.

Such a view existed in the philosophies of atomism and cynicism. These doctrines, which made of atoms the ultimate unit and of the world a fortuitous agglomeration of units, attracted adherents because they could account for the individualism evident in the political and dynastic struggles that followed Alexander's death. By repudiating the traditional values that had hitherto governed ordinary men's lives and by insisting that true values cannot be known, these philosophies rationalized the nihilism and anarchy of the age. Their effect was to release men from responsibilities to their homelands and make them "citizens of the world." But this cos-mopolitanism that freed a man from communal responsibility in his own state could not and did not bind him responsibly to other people or institutions. Being a "citizen of the world" thus became a negative rather than a positive force in a world seeking community. When, e.g., someone asked Crates, the cynic from Thebes (365?–285), whether he wished to see the restoration of his country, he replied, "Why should it be? Perhaps another Alexander will destroy it again." Ignominy and Poverty he declared to be his country, which Fortune could never take captive!"[1]

Men sought new purpose, for their own cities could no longer exert

---

1. Diogenes Laertius VI 93, Loeb edition, trans. R. D. Hicks. On the early history of the Greeks in the Near East see the concise survey of T. J. Dunbabin, "The Greeks and their Eastern Neighbors. Studies in the Relations between Greece and the Countries of the Near East in the VIIIth and VIIth Centuries," *Journal of Hellenic Studies*, Supplement VIII, London, 1957.

exclusive claim on them. But as the comment of Crates makes clear, the world itself had no perceivable purpose. Philosophers addressed, therefore, not purpose or nature, but the satisfaction of practical needs, and Hellenistic philosophy became eudaemonistic, devoted to the pursuit of happiness. Philosophers devoted their efforts not to a study of the essence of things, not even to the problems of community, but essentially to what may be called the techniques of *autarchia*, i.e., self-sufficiency, "independence of the caprices of fortune." In the process of this shift in emphasis, natural science split off from philosophy to be pursued for its own sake, while philosophy became religious. The ideal man of philosophy, the man every man strove to become, was the "wise one," the one aloof and freed from everything that could disturb him, that could rob him of security of thought or feeling. Such an ideal, "wise" man, detached from concern with success or failure, could ignore fortune and discern the God (Nature, Reason) which alone gave satisfaction to life.

To be detached, however, one had to vanquish all false ideas of reality and value and to accept renunciation as a primary ethical goal. A man had to rid himself of the disturbing impressions and anxious thoughts made by passing events. He had to free himself from attachment to the world. Emphasis thus fell on passivity, freedom from worry, and the abolition of superstition which deprives men of tranquility. Epicurus (323–270) tried to put an end to deceptive ideas about the gods and human life and so to emancipate men from false ideas of the world. His concern was that they would take delight in the simplest pleasures of life, those unlikely to be removed by fortune. Skepticism sought to convince men of the relativity of all things and events and so to diminish their moral value that men would become indifferent to them. The wise man thus would not simply recognize and reject falsehood, he would also be indifferent toward the historical world, for the world of history existed by convention (*nomos*) alone; but it would be judged by the metaphysical, non-historical essence (*physis*) of things, which the wise man alone could know.

This independence of the world, achieved through the passive enjoyment of nature, was not a satisfactory way of life for most men, for whom the matters of daily life could not be matters of indifference. Epicurus could advocate a pleasant life, by which he meant the absence of pain and fear and a sober enjoyment of what nature provides, but he could not deny that the provisions of nature require human action and that all action is prey to Fortune. The well-known lines from Herculaneum sum up the Epicurean view of life:

> There is nothing to fear in God:
> There is nothing to fear in Death:
> What is good is easily procured;
> What is ill is easily endured.[2]

Epicurus would free a man from fate by having him turn away from interest in history and the state and find joy in friendship with another human being; but his remedy for pain, because it denied significance to history and statehood, could not satisfy the mass of mankind.

Zeno (335–263), founder of the Stoic school, advocated a different way to happiness: the exercise of virtue. Stoics shared with Epicureans the notion that the wise man can live above the differing false conceptions of life and morality, i.e., that he can so accommodate himself to them that they do not affect his happiness. But the Stoics differed from the Epicureans in their emphasis on right action, rather than withdrawal, as the means of avoiding pain. The exercise of virtue was the effort to live in harmony with reasonable Nature and divine Providence, to do one's assigned part in life's drama. Virtue consisted in playing the part, which was its own reason for being; such virtue was sufficient for human happiness, whatever the outcome of specific acts might be. Virtue, right action, freed a man from the vicissitudes and false values of the world, for it opened his mind and will to his god-decreed destiny. Stoics accepted destiny as wise and good, and their happiness derived from their calm assurance that they were living in harmony with the divine logos. For them self-consistency was the first mark of reason, and value in men's acts was to be found in their intentions. Citizens of the world as they were they held themselves aloof from parochial public service and tried to become free and sufficient to themselves, learning and teaching the art of self-control. The Stoic accent on duty instead of pleasure rendered their own withdrawal less opprobrious than that of the Epicureans.

Marcus Aurelius, emperor of Rome from 161–180 A.D., in his book in Greek, entitled, "Concerning Himself," known to us as "The Meditations of Marcus Aurelius," reveals the strong theological grip Stoic philosophy

---

2. Quoted by S. Angus in *CAH* VII, p. 234.

was finally to have on the ancient world. One of his best known passages is a moving statement of the Stoic view of life.[3]

> Man, you have lived as a citizen in this great city of the universe, and what does it matter whether you have lived there for five years or for five score? The portion allotted to each of us under its law is the same. What is the hardship, then, in your being dismissed from the city, not by a tyrant or unjust judge, but by Nature who brought you into it, even as the manager who has engaged him might dismiss a comic actor? "But" (he might say), "I have not finished the five acts; I have only had three." "True" (one may answer), "but in life three acts are all the play." He who was once the cause of thy being made, and is now the cause of thy being unmade, determines thy span. *Thou* hast not caused thy birth or thy death. Go, then, in peace. For He who dismisses thee is at peace with thee.

The image of an actor playing his part in the drama of life is characteristic of Stoicism and paradigmatic for the Hellenistic age. The actor has no other role than the one assigned him, which he is duty-bound to play well. What the play itself may signify or why it should be played or whether it succeeds or fails as a play is not the actor's concern. He has done his duty when he has played his part as it should be played, in accord with Destiny. Right action proceeds from right intention, for no act is good or evil in itself. Happiness is this simple awareness of being faithful to one's destiny.

Hellenistic philosophy, it can be seen, endorsed two incompatible ideas. On the one hand, the revolt against the structures of the city-state, implicit in the new cosmopolitanism, created the ideal of the "wise man" who would recognize the world rather than the city as his home. But on the other hand, that wise one, who recognized all men as fellow-countrymen, would also keep himself aloof from the world, and that detached aloofness would isolate him from the world of fools who did not know or care for virtue. What cosmopolitanism seemed to offer as brotherhood, the ideal of wisdom arose to exclude. To transcend in one's life the accidents of birth and position was wisdom, but to achieve that wisdom at the expense of a feeling of responsibility for one's fellows was to lose what had made Greece great.

---

3. XII.36. Translated by Ernest Barker, *From Alexander to Constantine*, Oxford, 1956, p. 323.

The individualism of the age led to the isolation of men from each other, as the "wise" withdrew more and more from the world.[4]

The rule of reason, which only the wise fully acknowledged, thus sharpened the division between their exclusive lives and those of the turbulent world. The separation was apparent in the secluded Epicurean garden but was no less real on the Stoic porch. The Stoic emphasis on virtue and duty seemed to offer a means of creating social community, but it led instead to a striving for individual, personal perfection. The wise man knew his destiny and was certain he knew it, and his virtue consisted in accepting it and living in harmony with reason, thus comprehending and restricting the proper objects of his action to what would make him perfect.

A sign of the increasing isolation of men from the ideal community once sought in the city-state (*polis*) was the gradual increase during the Hellenistic-Roman era in the number of exclusive social clubs throughout the Mediterranean world.[5] These were associations of the wise, cultivated, trained or committed individuals, generally for social enjoyment. In them the like-minded found fellowship, prominence and escape from the perils and demands of political fortune. Admission to membership was rigorously exclusive. Only those sharing the same knowledge, social background and purpose were welcome.

The ideal of a life in harmony with reason, emphasizing as it did personal acceptance of the destiny which one receives as one's portion in life, placed man finally in a world of necessity rather than freedom. History itself was seen to be cyclic and deterministic, and men were thought capable of

---

4. Stoic writings have been collected by A. C. Pearson, *The Fragments of Zeno and Cleanthes*, with Introduction and Explanatory Notes, London, 1891; J. Von Arnim, *Stoicorum Veterum Fragmenta*, 3 vols., Leipzig (Teubner), 1903–1905.

5. On the Greek clubs of M. N. Tod, *Sidelights on Greek History*, Oxford, 1932, p. 69ff., who gives in translation a complete copy of the statutes of one such club (pp. 87–91); F. Poland, *Geschichte des Griechischen Vereinswesens*, Leipzig, 1909, "the typical Greek union (*Vereinswesen*) is a Hellenistic phenomenon," p. 516. For comments about life in a Syrian club cf. Posidonius of Apamaea, in Athen., xii, 527, quoted by Bouchier, p. 202. "There were many clubs in which they amused themselves continuously, using the gymnasia as baths, anointing themselves with expensive oil and unguents, and using the schools, for so they called the dining-halls of the members, as if they were their own houses, stuffing themselves there for the greater part of the day with wines and food, and even carrying off much besides, amidst the sound of noisy lyres, which made whole cities ring with the uproar."

contributing little to it. The world was considered to be driven irresistibly by universal law, and to this grand theory the ideal of human freedom, one of the great achievements of Greek thought, was sacrificed. One further evil consequence of this determinism was the impetus it gave to efforts to discern the future, the most notorious of which was astrology.

Hellenistic religion, like Hellenistic philosophy, was in large part a result of the new configuration of political and cultural forces brought into being by Alexander's life. The destruction of the Persian empire in the East and the demise of the city-state as the chief center of political power in the West called to account the power of previously revered deities. Those gods had failed, and in the resulting religious turmoil and confusion faith in the gods yielded to trust in reason. Vastly increasing knowledge produced an enlightened age, in which feelings of dependence on higher powers were accommodated to the lordship of reason. Religion became, as a result, this-worldly.

The religious character of the age is best represented in its chief divinity, Tyche (luck, fate, destiny), who epitomized the course of world history. She was not blind chance but was independent of law and the general orders of life, bringing to all men changing fate and surprise.[6] In the first Christian century Pliny the Elder would complain that "Everywhere in the whole world at every hour by all men's voices Fortune alone is invoked and named, alone accused, alone impeached, alone pondered, alone applauded, alone rebuked and visited with reproaches; deemed volatile and indeed by most men blind as well, wayward, inconstant, uncertain, fickle in her favours and favouring the unworthy. To her is debited all that is spent and credited all that is received, she alone fills both pages in the whole of mortal's account; and we are so much at the mercy of chance that Chance herself... takes the place of God."[7] Men considered themselves to be helpless before the "great tempests of Fortune" who blindly tortured men with the worst perils.[8] To Fortune virtue availed nothing, and virtue was thus deprived of religious value.

The failure of the ancient gods and the incomprehensibility of the new goddess, Fortune, made Hellenistic religion inevitably humanistic. The

---

6. W. W. Tarn and G. T. Griffith, *Hellenistic Civilization*, 3rd ed., London, 1952, p. 340.

7. *Naturalis Historia* II.V.22 (Loeb).

8. A. D. Nock, *Conversion*, Oxford (paper), 1961, p. 140.

divinization of Hellenistic dynasts removed any aura of mystery from the gods and freed men from binding religious concepts. Religion consequently became free from rules, free of priestly class, free from hierarchy, and separated from the state. The Greek gods of the fifth century had been not only gods of the state, but also gods of the people, as opposed to the Near Eastern gods of the land. But as Hellenistic philosophy freed a man from superstition it enabled him to affiliate himself with the gods and gradually replace them. The Hellenistic cult of the king, seen religiously, was thus an outgrowth of Hellenic religion which had become progressively anthropomorphic and political. When religion became separated from the state, it lost its historical, communal character and became the concern of individuals and groups. Its domain was transferred from the public to private life, centering on the life purposes of individuals; and it thus exchanged its inner connection with the state, as the ground for and guardian of its purpose in being, for a purely external one, as the guarantor of happiness and escape for its citizens.

It has been rightly observed that in Greece man moved toward the gods and replaced them, while in the Orient God came to man and used him.[9] Those evident and opposing views of man's relationship to God clashed in the Christian doctrinal controversies of the fourth and fifth Christian centuries. Jesus, worshiped as God's son, was considered either to be a man who finally became known for the God he was or a man whom God exalted to divinity; and the Church has never been able to work out to the satisfaction of all Christians the meaning of the credal statement, "Jesus Christ his (God's) only son." The humanism of Greek and Hellenistic religion was a corrective to the theism of the Near East, but alone it could not satisfy the innate human drive to find transcendent values and meaning in life.

The continuing search for values in Hellenistic times led, in the absence of faith, either to reliance on formula or the adoption of new gods and cults to replace the old. Religious practice rested on superstition and belief in miracles, the effectiveness of curses, the healing wonders of Serapis and Apollo, the appearances (epiphanies) of the gods. Those who could not know truth were left only magical avenues to religious satisfaction and commitment. Interest shifted from this life to the next, and Lethe, the river of forgetfulness, became the river of healing. Mysticism and syncretism

---

9. Julius Kaerst, *Geschichte des hellenistischen Zeitalter*, vol. 2, 1, Leipzig, 1909, p. 209.

marked the new religious search, together with astrology, that deadly combination of myth with exact science that postulated a correspondence between the events of history and the movement of the stars and planets. All of this destroyed the historical character of religion, divorcing historical life from any essential connection with religious truth and making religious practice a matter of normalized magical and cultic observance beyond the reach of historical rationality or necessity.

Gilbert Murray summed up the religious transformation that occurred after Alexander in the Mediterranean world in a memorable passage:[10]

Any one who turns from the great writers of classical Athens, say Sophocles or Aristotle, to those of the Christian era must be conscious of a great difference in tone. There is a change in the whole relation of the writer to the world about him. The new quality is not specifically Christian: it is just as marked in the Gnostics and Mithras-worshipers as in the Gospels and the Apocalypse, in Judaism and Plotinus as in Gregory and Jerome. It is hard to describe. It is a rise of asceticism, of mysticism, in a sense of pessimism; a loss of self-confidence, of hope in this life and of faith in normal human effort; a despair of patient inquiry, a cry for infallible revelation; an indifference to the welfare of the state, a conversion of the soul to God. It is an atmosphere in which the aim of the good man is not so much to live justly, to help the society to which he belongs and enjoy the esteem of his fellow creatures; but rather by means of a burning faith, by contempt for the world and its standards, by ecstasy, suffering and martyrdom, to be granted pardon for his unspeakable unworthiness, his immeasurable sins. There is an intensifying of certain spiritual emotions; an increase of sensitiveness, a failure of nerve.

The disillusion of large numbers of men with traditional theologies, with the ability of education to improve the world and with the power of government to create and preserve order led to loss of hope in the world and in organized human effort and threw men back on themselves and their own individual resources. What was lacking was a faith or a "cause"[11] that could give meaning to history and bring order to the chaotic search for values.[12]

Compensating for the widespread "failure of nerve" was the almost

---

10. Gilbert Murray, *Four Stages of Greek Religion*, New York, 1912, p. 103.
11. Edwyn Bevan, "Hellenistic Popular Philosophy," in J. B. Bury, E. A. Barber and E. R. Bevan, *The Hellenistic Age*, Cambridge, 1923, p. 99.
12. Cf. A. D. Nock, "The East conquered the West because it had something to give." *Conversion*, Oxford, 1961, p. 62.

universal trust in technique. Religion, philosophy, art and literature were influenced by the formulism of the period, which offered methods and means to salvation, happiness and beauty rather than descriptions and discussions of their essential nature and character. Religion stressed methods of knowing God rather than efforts to define and refine the conception of deity itself; philosophy was more concerned with making men happy than with probing the enigma of man's life in the world; art and literature strove for emotional effect rather than expression of ideas, as when letter type is arranged to make designs rather than words. The great sculptures of the age—the winged victory of Samothrace, which was probably created to celebrate Demetrius' naval victory over Ptolemy off the coast of Cyprus in 306; the dying gladiator, fashioned to dramatize the horrors of war with the Celts; the Laocoön, intended to portray a horrible death; or the great altar of Zeus at Pergamum expressing the "tumult of the age, the meeting of civilization and barbarism, the conflict of good and evil, the striving with unfamiliar ways of expression,[13]—these were technical masterpieces of effect. The sculptures do not express an ideal of humanity, beauty or purpose. Obsessed with the momentary rather than the timeless, they elicit from the beholder not so much intellectual as emotional participation in exhilaration, pain, horror and change.

Literature, especially as it flourished in Alexandria, emphasized style and subordinated content. What was written became less important than how it was expressed, and in the process heart and feeling were displaced by cleverness and knowing. Menander, the most notable writer of comedy (d. 291 B.C.), rejected mythological themes in favor of drawing vignettes from the contemporary life of Athens. His comedies, however, none of which has survived in its entirety, are conventionalized treatments of decadent life that tell us almost nothing else of the age, even though his elegant and quotable statements brought him applause in his time and preserved his words for posterity. For him and his contemporaries morality became a simple matter of right and wrong without the troublesome and nagging doubts, why and how. The epigrams, most of which are amatory, preserve the passions of the age.[14]

The writing of history in a sense epitomized the Hellenistic period.

---

13. W. W. Tarn and G. T. Griffith, *Hellenistic Civilization* (N6), p. 320.

14. T. B. L. Webster, "New Comedy is social comedy in the modern sense . . . ." *Hellenistic Poetry and Art*, London, 1964, p. 8.

Since all events were considered to be passing and relative, one could ignore the study of history and devote oneself instead to the affirmation of rational, general truth. The writing of history thus became anecdotal, embodying a "sentimental enthusiasm" for the past and divorcing it from any hope for the future. Collecting of data seemed more important than telling the story or developing a philosophy of history. Men prized research and detail more than creative reconstruction, collecting materials of all kinds and publishing them in handbooks. In the absence of compelling wisdom, men devoted themselves to collecting facts, and the widespread want of a sense of historical continuity deepened the Hellenistic inability to form an enduring state. The exceptional histories of Hieronymus of Cardia (in the Thracian Chersonese), Aratus of Sicyon (west of Corinth) who wrote a history of the Achaean League, and above all Polybius (ca. 203–ca. 120 B.C.) stand out from the popular demands of readability at the expense of accuracy and serve to emphasize the general absence of historical concern. One boon Roman conquest would bring was a return to historical writing in the works of Polybius and Livy; and subsequently Christianity would owe its popularity in no small part to the historical perspective it imposed on events.[15]

The sense of belonging and the chance for participating in purposeful community life had, as a result of Alexander's career, shifted from the state and its supporting religion to religion effectively divorced from the state, a breach in political community the ruler-cult did not heal. That shift from the fifth-century Greek ideal of community to the individualism of the post-Alexandrian era, which sought to make men independent of fortune and unhampered by the world in their search for peace of mind, also emancipated them from claims of the community; and it opened to them ways both to fuller and more independent private life and also to the delegation of public responsibilities to willing bureaucrats. Thus the accent in public administration also began to fall on technique and efficiency rather than on morality and ideal purpose, and vocation became a means to individual preferment rather than to service for the community. Service to the state, which had once been a privilege to be accepted in joy and freedom, now became a job deserving remuneration, a specialty requiring specific training.

The ideal Greek city-state, an independent community working

---

15. On early Greek historiography see Robert Drews, *The Greek Accounts of Eastern History*, Cambridge, Mass., 1973.

together to define and achieve its own moral purposes, gave way gradually to a state system composed of specialists working efficiently at state-directed duties. Statecraft became a vocation for the few rather than responsibility for the many, and what had formerly been considered the state's highest duty, the achievement of its own welfare through promotion of the well-being of its citizens, came now to be replaced by the necessity for technical efficiency in the daily routine of a well-functioning bureaucracy. The size of the new states demanded the shift, but the political means available to them—the bureaucratic systems of the East—threatened to destroy the political achievements of the Greek city-state. The development of an administrative system that would preserve the democratic principles of Greece while achieving the bureaucratic efficiency of the East was a problem for the Hellenistic states, for which they found no enduring solution.

Stability within and among the new states was achieved by an equilibrium of forces, a balance of powers, a system of unrelieved tensions. Politics, therefore, became a technical matter of management, and the kings sought means to control tensions rather than relieve them. Those tensions strained the economic, social, political and religious relationships of life.

The economic tension arose between the excessive demands of the foreign, ruling Greeks and Macedonians for a disproportionate share of the labor and natural resources of their subject peoples and the native resistance to foreign exploitation. Emigration of Greek artisans, merchants and politicians from their homeland into the Near East, in search of new economic opportunities, led to a decline abroad in the demand for products from Greece, at the moment when the release of the Persian gold hoards at Susa and Persepolis caused a sharp inflation. Greek prosperity in the East partially ameliorated conditions in Greece, but the riches of Ptolemy simply set in relief both the economic instability in the Greek homeland and the poverty of the native Egyptian workers. Monopolistic and land grant techniques abroad might satisfy the Greek and Macedonian emigrant managers and directors, but at the expense of the natives whose labor was essential to all prosperity and wealth. The equitable distribution of goods began to occupy men's minds as a social problem.

The social tension was both cultural and institutional. The ruling ideal of man was the Greek, and the evidence from the Near East for the spread of Greek language, for name changes from Semitic to Greek, for athletic competitions in newly constructed gymnasia and arenas, and for cities and city-planning in the Greek style, especially in the Seleucid state,[16] points to the strength of Greek influence, supported as it was by Macedonian and Greek political power. The majority of the people, however, no doubt continued to follow their ancestral patterns of life, and the Roman historian, Livy, would later concede that it was impossible for the Macedonian conquerors to live untouched by their new environment.[17] Aramaic remained the popular language, later the official language of the Nabateans in Palmyra and Petra; but the government, at least in the ruling cities, was Greek. The tension between the native cultural and institutional inertia and the foreign drive for change could not be resolved in the Hellenistic era, and it stretched throughout the Roman period until it finally began to snap in the first century A.D. with the Jewish revolts.

Superficially the culture was Greek, but that cultural unity concealed a disparity of political and social opportunity between Greeks and non-Greeks. We know the social life of the time only from the limited records of inscriptions and literature. Since what we know derives from the cities, which were the centers of Greek and Macedonian power, where primarily Greeks and Philhellenes alone had status or opportunity, we remain ignorant of life in the villages and countryside. The economy was essentially agricultural, based on the labor of natives, controlled and manipulated by the upper Greek stratum of society. The Hellenistic state-system enriched a few, who loudly proclaimed the Greek notions of freedom, individualism and self-fulfillment, while paradoxically it impoverished many.

Political stability was undermined from the start by rivalries among the kings, with their attendant military conflicts, and by the fierce struggles among the Greeks at home for independence. These rivalries, erupting in the "Syrian Wars" of the third century, contributed to the steady disintegration of the Seleucid state, territorial heartland of the Hellenistic world, and finally ruined Egypt. Egypt, independent, defensible and prosperous, had become a pivot for Hellenistic economic and political equilibrium, but beginning in the middle of the third century other Mediterranean powers

---

16. Cf. Pliny VI.117, "The whole of Mesopotamia once belonged to the Assyrians, and the population was scattered in villages, with the exception of Babylon and Nineveh. The Macedonians collected its population into cities because of the fertility of the soil." (H. Rackham, Loeb).

17. XXXVII.17.10. Cf. Polybius XXXII.2.6.

began effectively to check Egyptian dominance, until by the first century Egypt became but a private preserve of the Roman army. In 255 at Cos the Ptolemies lost control of the Aegean, and once the native Egyptians became aware of their potential power, after they contributed decisively to Ptolemy's victory over Antiochus at Raphia in 217, they increasingly weakened the Ptolemaic state from within by continued uprisings. As a consequence, the Seleucids and Antigonids, observing the weakness of Egypt, schemed in the second century to partition Ptolemaic overseas wealth between themselves, until their designs were thwarted by the Middle States and Rome.

In the end the Hellenistic monarchs failed to establish both political stability at home and a durable balance of power in the Mediterranean. Only Macedonia under Antigonus Gonatas was a united state. Within the other states the monarchs were unable to unite Macedonians and natives in a viable political structure. They would not admit the natives, whom they considered culturally and perhaps even intellectually inferior to themselves, into leading positions in the bureaucracy or society. They were unable to resolve either the conflicting ideologies of the city-state and oriental monarchy or the complex relationship between the Greek citizen and the oriental subject. The tradition of free Greek economy did not accord well with that of oriental state enterprise, and only the Ptolemies tried to combine the two. These tensions between rulers and ruled, between haves and have nots, bourgeoisie and proletariat, city and country, between competing values and legitimacies—all these increased with time and contributed to Rome's easy defeat of the East. In turn, Rome also failed satisfactorily to solve the same problems. Rome did for a time establish a Mediterranean empire, but Rome could not control the Parthians, Armenians or Jews, and her inability both to bring all the benefits of stable government to the provinces and to create a recognized free society contributed to the breakup of the empire.

One can see that the Hellenistic states shared several common characteristics. Primary among them was the inevitable struggle for viable political form, which was fought to the virtual exclusion of insistent concern with the state's philosophic or social purpose. The question, what should the state be or do, became subordinated to the question, how can it be held together. Alexander's expeditions had brought home forcibly to his generals the Near Eastern conception of the state as the monarch's personal, inherited possession, entrusted to him by his god(s). The Macedonian state, however, also in effect an inherited monarchy, made of its king one noble among equals, accountable for his reign to the army, which acted as the court of final authority in decisions about treason. The Hellenistic kings, whose ambitions were Alexander's and whose power depended upon the unwavering loyalty of their armies, thus strove to keep their military might invincible and, with the exception of Macedonia under Antigonus Gonatas, paid little heed to the purposes of the state as they had been defined by Aristotle in the Greek polis or were suggested by Zeno and the Stoics. Their territories, they asserted, were theirs by right of conquest, and they considered neither the gods nor their defeated servants entitled to decisive roles in state policy. The Ptolemies presided over a vast and profitable corporation; the Seleucids over reluctant, often backward provinces that defied attempts to unite them culturally, economically or politically; the Attalids over a more compact version of Ptolemaic Egypt at Pergamum; and the Antigonids over ancestral but economically impoverished lands. As long as the royal armies could be satisfied and supported, the monarchs reigned securely. But if economic support were denied the army or the morale of the soldiers undermined, the dynastic ruling family faced deposition or annihilation.

A second distinguishing quality of the Hellenistic states, again with the exception of Macedonia, was an absence of national cohesion. To be sure, the Greek and Macedonian rulers never doubted their cultural superiority, but they avowed no political loyalty either to Greece or Macedonia. Cultural rather than political bonds tied them to their Greek homeland. The monarchies over which they presided were thus nationalities ruled by a minority of outsiders rather than national states. Outside Macedonia itself the first strivings of national feeling we can document arose in Egypt after the Ptolemaic defeat of the Seleucids at Raphia (217), when the Egyptians began to exploit their vital contributions to the Ptolemaic economic and military superiority over the Seleucids.[18] There were also, of course, national Iranian uprisings against the Seleucids, but these occurred on the fringes rather than at the center of the Hellenistic world.

The Hellenistic states were, thirdly, territorial. They held this trait in common with their oriental predecessors who had counted under their authority everyone living within ever more precisely defined geographic limits. This was in contrast with the Greek polis, where citizenship was the sign of membership in the political family. The problem in the Hellenistic, territorial state was to incorporate into the Near Eastern conception of

---

18. Polybius V.107.1–3.

residence the Greek idea of citizenship. The great size of these states created problems of administration, law and defense which had been unknown in the Greek world and which were difficult to resolve by a simple transfer to the new states of concerns of citizenship in a polis. The new monarchs were unable to solve these problems partly because their large states furthered the philosophic ideals of universalism and cosmopolitanism characteristic of the age and also because they provided opportunities for political maneuver and power that the new dynasts and their Macedonian and Greek supporters could never have found in Greece or Macedonia. It is probable that the administration of the territorial states followed Persian practices, i.e., that the Greeks and Macedonians left the old administrative system alone as long as it worked and permitted them to skim off for themselves appropriate economic profits. But evidence for the inner workings of the states is meager.

In the fourth place, a major necessity in the successor states was for their rulers to find legitimizing principles to support their dynastic assertions of authority. Foreign, conquered people had to recognize the legality of Macedonian, Hellenistic rule as being based on more than military or assumed cultural superiority. Since the conquered provided the primary labor force and staffing for much of the bureaucratic, administrative structure, their consent to their new overlords could be neither compelled indefinitely nor taken for granted. In addition, those conquered peoples included the Greeks, who were accustomed to accepting reason as the supreme arbiter in life and among whom ideas of freedom and political participation were traditional. They required rational grounds for their political loyalty, even when they were willing to sell themselves as mercenary soldiers to their new overlords.

The need for legitimacy might be satisfied in the cult of the divinized king, who would present himself before the people as the one whose military and political excellence were infallible marks of divinity. Political necessity appears in fact to have been the mother of religious invention. The ruler's excellence was claimed as proof of his divine legitimacy, which entitled him to receive obedience and reverence from his subjects. He became the wise one, who alone knew God's will, and that knowledge carried with it authority to rule as god on earth, as Plutarch would later attribute to Alexander the belief "that he came as a heaven-sent governor to all" men.[19] The popular Cynic and Stoic doctrines of destiny, fate and

---

19. *Moralia*: Fortuna Alexandri, 329 c, ed. F. C. Babbitt (Loeb), 1936, IV, p. 339.

eternal law on the one hand, and of personal freedom on the other, supported the ruler-cult. The ruler in turn adopted various emblems of legitimacy: the diadem (a cloth headband),[20] the signet ring, and the eternal fire, all of which symbolized the necessity for general consent to his divine will.[21]

The cult of the divinized king was developed in all states except Macedonia. It became the basis of kingship and the symbol of absolute sovereignty, without reference to ethnic or religious traditions, even though it was coupled wherever possible with traditional religious dogmas, as in Egypt, where the Ptolemaic king presented himself as one of the pharaohs of Re. The Seleucids fell heir to the religious conceptions of the Mesopotamians and Iranians who for the most part did not worship their monarchs as divine.[22] But the Syrian successors could not shed their Macedonian origins or afford to be outmaneuvered by their Macedonian contemporaries. Antiochus I probably imitated his contemporary, Ptolemy II, in establishing the ruler-cult in Antioch, and the royal titles, *nicator, theos, epiphanes*, confirm the existence of the cult in Syria. The monarchic cult was a strong cohesive force among peoples who traditionally appealed to divinity for truth and guidance rather than to reason. Even in Greece it could be regarded as a logical extension of the crowning of the Olympic victors, who as the finest specimens of Greek manhood offered their crowns of laurel to the gods. Those excellent young men then became gods themselves, and the kings simply followed that example.

Finally, all Hellenistic kingdoms depended for their continued existence on the superior fighting force of Macedonian troops or Greek mercenaries. When all else failed, formal, popular allegiance could be compelled by the best soldiers in the world. Many of those soldiers returned eventually

---

20. Cf. Hans-Werner Ritter, *Diadem und Königsherrschaft*, Munich, 1965. Before Alexander the Greeks had no special royal headdress and no royal ornamentation at all, but in the first decade after Alexander's death, the diadem was the symbol of absolute, unlimited rule over Asia. When Ptolemy Ceraunus assumed the diadem it had lost its significance of rule over Asia and was simply a sign of Hellenistic kingship.

21. For a review of the evidence of the Hellenistic ruler-cult cf. F. Dvornik, *Early Christian and Byzantine Political Philosophy* I, Washington, 1966, pp. 205–77. Cf. C. W. McEwan, *The Oriental Origins of the Hellenistic Kingship*, Studies in Ancient Oriental Civilization 13, Chicago, 1934; A. D. Nock, "Notes on Ruler-cult I–IV," *Journal of Hellenic Studies* 48 (1928), pp. 21–43 (reprinted in A. D. Nock, *Essays on Religion and the Ancient World*, vol. 1, Oxford, 1972, pp. 134–59).

22. Cf. J. Teixidor, *The Pagan God: Popular Religion in the Greco-Roman Near East*, Princeton, 1977.

to their homes in Greece or Macedonia, but large contingents still patrolled the roads and towns of the near Eastern states, receiving for their services grants of land (cleruchies) and special tax exemptions within the states. What prevailed in the end were compulsion and force rather than reason and law, until Roman legal and structural genius forged a Mediterranean empire that could endure three centuries.

The Hellenistic monarchic ideal was closely connected with the realization of an ecumenical culture. The ideal of human virtue was to be embodied in the ideal king who should possess all virtues and whose sovereignty would also be universal. This ideal arose as the distinction between barbarians and Greeks shifted from a national to a cultural basis and the unifying force in the world became cultural rather than political. The monarchic titles already mentioned, savior, victor, beneficent, illustrious, derived from an ideal of ruling superiority that rested on its demonstration in war rather than on any conformity with clearly defined and generally accepted goals of state.

The fact of military conquest and the right of talent to rule mark the Hellenistic view of the state. State unity derived from the ruling dynasty, in which the state found its purpose and strength. Where there was no dynasty there was no state. Unity was imposed from the top rather than implanted at the bottom. The state did not create the dynasty; the dynasty created the state. Oriental dynasties had emerged as the ruling families of definite peoples; Hellenistic dynasties represented the rights and aspirations, purposes and world view of outsiders, not natives. Greece was not the capital of any Hellenistic state, but Greek and Macedonian rulers subjected foreign peoples to the Greek view of life. Hellenistic civilization "had all the marks of a conquering and ruling upper class—except faith in its own wisdom."[23]

What we see in these state systems, then, are the birth pangs of future political organization that would be efficient without oppression, give freedom without anarchy, create order without regimentation, and treat people as citizens rather than subjects. Individualism in philosophy, religion, culture and the state was in search of community; and in the end an eastern ideal of love was to replace those Stoic virtues of withdrawal and duty.[24]

---

23. A. Momigliano, *Alien Wisdom: The Limits of Hellenization*, Cambridge, 1975, p. 149.

24. A succinct summary of Hellenistic culture is provided by M. Rostovtzeff, *Social*

SUGGESTIONS FOR FURTHER STUDY:

Orientation to the vast and complex material is given by W. W. Tarn and G. T. Griffith, *Hellenistic Civilization*, 3rd ed. (London, 1952); M. Hadas, *Hellenistic Culture* (New York, 1959); and by M. Cary, *A History of the Greek World from 323 to 146 B.C.*, 2nd ed. (London, 1951;reprinted 1963).

For philosophy, read W. K. C. Guthrie, *History of Greek Philosophy* (Cambridge, 1965); J. M. Rist, *Stoic Philosophy* (Cambridge, 1969); idem, *Epicurus: An Introduction* (Cambridge, 1972); and A. A. Long, *Hellenistic Philosophy* (London and New York, 1974).

On religion, consult the works of A. D. Nock, especially *Conversion* (Oxford, 1933; paper, 1961), and *Essays on Religion and the Ancient World*, 2 vols., ed. Zeph Stewart (Oxford, 1972). A valuable collection of texts has been edited by F. C. Grant *Hellenistic Religions* (New York, 1953). Helpful is H. I. Bell, *Cults and Creeds in Greco-Roman Egypt* (Liverpool, 1957), to which is appended a brief, basic bibliography.

On the state see the provocative chapter by Mason Hammond, "Hellenistic Leagues and Monarchies" in *City-State and World State in Greek and Roman Political Theory until Augustus* (Cambridge, Mass., 1951).

---

and Economic History of the Hellenistic World, Oxford, 1941, especially the "Summary and Epilogue," vol. 2, p. 1026ff.

V

ROME IN THE EAST

When Antigonus Gonatas died in the spring of 239, the heyday of Macedonian imperialism had passed, for the states of Alexander's successors had proved unequal to their long-term task of government. The Macedonian throne passed to Gonatas' son, Demetrius II (239–229), then in turn to Gonatas' nephew, Antigonus III Doson (229–221), grandson, Philip V (221–179), and great-grandson, Perseus (181–168), before the independent Macedonian state came to its end in defeat by Rome at Pydna. In those seventy years between the deaths of Gonatas and Perseus the other Hellenistic states also increasingly lost their independence before the Roman drive to domination which virtually converted the Mediterranean sea into a Roman lake. Rome's conquest of Carthage in 202, followed by her defeat of Philip V in 197 and Antiochus III of Syria eight years later, made Rome mistress of the sea, inextricably entangling her in the domestic policies and interstate rivalries of the Hellenistic kingdoms. Those Roman victories made the Roman capture of Perseus in 168 and the subsequent quartering of Macedonia into separate, leaderless republics anticlimactic, a matter of thorough housecleaning.

One of the Greeks taken to Rome as hostage after the defeat at Pydna was Polybius. Befriended in Rome by his victorious conqueror, L. Aemilius Paullus, in whose house he lived, he also became closely associated with Paullus' son, Scipio Aemilianus Africanus, with whom he often travelled, and in whose association he recognized the prospects for continued and comprehensive Roman rule in the Mediterranean. He probably watched Scipio's destruction of Carthage in 146. Roman supremacy and institutions awakened Polybius' historical interest, and he determined to subject the Roman achievement to historical and political analysis. "Who," he asked, "is so worthless or indolent as not to wish to know by what means and under what system of polity the Romans in less than fifty-three years have succeeded in subjecting nearly the whole inhabited world to their sole government . . . ?"[1]

As starting point for his account Polybius selected the 140th Olympiad (220–216 B.C.), i.e., the accession to power of three Hellenistic monarchs: Antiochus III (the Great) in Antioch, 223; Ptolemy IV Philopator in Egypt, 221; and Philip V in Macedonia that same year, for he reasoned that from that time the dispersed doings of the world became organically linked, and the Romans had "quite adequate grounds for conceiving the ambition of a world-empire and adequate means for achieving their purpose."[2] The coincidence of two eastern Mediterranean wars with Rome's victory in the Hannibalic war over Carthage, namely, the Greek Social War in which Achaeans united with Philip of Macedon against Aetolians (peace of Naupactus, August 217), and second the war in Asia between Antiochus and Ptolemy for Coele-Syria—this coincidence, reasoned Polybius, emboldened the Romans to cross into Asia. Polybius thus found in Roman expansion a fortunate and necessary organizing power for the confusing political history and decaying political unity of the late third century Hellenistic world. Subsequent historians have been unable to improve his perspective.

A Roman move into Asia had first been made against Illyria (modern Yugoslavia) eight years earlier. At that time the Romans, who had as yet no Hellenic policy[3] and were apparently not anxious to increase their modest economic contact with Epirus or the Greeks of Corcyra, Corinth or Athens, began to suffer ravages both to their mariners and to some of their coastal villages from the organized and state-supported pirates of the Illyrian queen Teuta. After the queen rebuffed the envoys that Rome finally sent in 230 to protest the outrage, and one of them was murdered on the return trip to Italy, the Romans vanquished the Illyrian army at Corcyra in 229 and secured by treaty the following year a guarantee of peaceful navigation in the waters between Italy and Greece.[4] That guarantee lasted only five years before Demetrius of Pharos, to whom the Romans had entrusted the

1. I.1.5.(Loeb).
2. I.3.4–10.
3. Shortly thereafter they sent their first embassy to Greece, Polybius II.12.7.
4. Polybius II.12.3.;M. Holleaux, *CAH* VII, ch. xxvi.

representation of their cause at the Illyrian court, joined the Macedonian king, Antigonus Doson, against them. Unfortunately for Demetrius, his ally Doson died shortly after defeating the Spartans at Sellasia (222); and Doson's seventeen-year-old successor, Philip V, was at war with the Aetolians when the Romans again, within a few months, brought order to the Adriatic (219).[5]

Flickering Roman interest in Greek and Macedonian affairs, however, was ignited by the pact of friendship and alliance Philip V made with Hannibal in 215.[6] That treaty with Rome's most feared adversary aroused Roman hostility toward Philip and started the momentous chain of events, which finally subjected the Hellenistic world to Rome. That chain-reaction, which began with the Carthaginian-Macedonian agreement, came at a moment in Hellenistic affairs that had been developing ever since the death of Antigonus Gonatas nearly 25 years previous, a moment when the eastern kingdoms seemed ready prey to the burning political fears and ambitions of a strong state like Rome.

The Hellenistic world had been disrupted by the wrenching Seleucid struggles both for dynastic order at Antioch and for territorial cohesion in the face of provinces revolting in Asia Minor and Iran. The Laodicean or third Syrian war, 246–241, followed in Asia Minor by the so-called Fraternal war between Seleucus II Callinicus and his brother Antiochus Hierax ("the Hawk"), 238–228, brought anarchy to Asia Minor, including Galatian uprisings and anti-Seleucid politics in Bithynia and Pontus. A sign of the malaise was that in the end not a Seleucid but Attalus, king of Pergamum, restored order to the land.

East of the Caspian Sea, in the district of Parthia (Parthava), the new Parthian, Arsacid dynasty arose about the same time (ca. 240),[7] and still further east the Bactrian and Sogdian provinces declared their independence of the Seleucid king. The final loss of Parthia and Bactria one hundred years later would reduce the Seleucid realm to Syria and Mesopotamia and result in the establishment of an eastern counterbalance to Roman imperialism: the Parthian empire, whose five-hundred-year history, twice the length of

---

5. Cf. J. V. A. Fine, "Macedon, Illyria, and Rome 220–219 B.C.," *Journal of Roman Studies* 26 (1936), pp. 24ff.

6. Polybius gives the terms, VII.9.

7. In late Babylonian documents the Parthian era dates from the first of Nisan, 247 (March–April).

its Seleucid precursor's, would inaugurate the effective and lasting revolt of Iranians against the western conquests of Alexander and his successors. Within that century, however, the Seleucids made several valiant attempts to preserve their faltering kingdom intact.

Seleucid decline was accompanied by gradual Ptolemaic impoverishment and internal uprising. The Ptolemies, as we have seen had been losing their importance at sea ever since their naval defeats at Ephesus (261) and Cos (255). This loss of sea power had reduced their resources for hiring mercenary soldiers and forced them to use a twenty-thousand-man contingent of native troops in the fourth Syrian war to defeat the Seleucids at Raphia (217),[8] which led to later internal, Egyptian uprisings against their Greek and Macedonian overlords. Adding to Ptolemaic distress were the loss of Egyptian commercial outposts in Carthage, Sicily and Italy because of the Roman victories in the Punic wars, and the resulting rise of prices in Egypt due to the scarcity of goods. Ptolemaic difficulties in paying for mercenaries allowed the other Hellenistic states to profit from Ptolemaic decline.[9]

Thus Philip's alliance with Hannibal in 215, after the latter's stunning defeat of the Roman legions at Cannae the year before, came at a moment when cohesion among the Hellenistic states was weak and when incipient decline of the two great Near Eastern kingdoms was evident. Therefore, in the struggle of the Greek leagues against Macedonia, Rome went to the aid of Greece; and the two so-called 'middle states,' Pergamum and Rhodes, pleaded for Roman assistance against Philip and Antiochus, whom they treated as Hellenistic aggressors.

Pergamum, as noted above, had by now achieved order and power in Asia Minor, and Rhodes was on the way to gaining an island league of her own, which she did by 200, following the gradual decay of the Macedonian fleet after the death of Gonatas. The first Macedonian war with Rome had negligible military importance, but its political consequences were substantial. It produced a Roman alliance with Attalus of Pergamum, injected a decisive power in the Greek and Macedonian feuds (the Aetolians agreed to peace with Rome in the winter of 206/5), and placed Philip V among the

---

8. Our account of the battle comes from Polybius V. 79–86. The battle occurred in June while Philip was attacking the Aetolians. Cf. E. A. Bevan, *A History of Egypt under the Ptolemaic Dynasty*, London, 1927, p. 229.

9. Cf. P. M. Fraser, *Ptolemaic Alexandria*, 3 vols., Oxford, 1972, vol. 1, p. 150ff.

enemies of the Roman people. Those major consequences of an insignificant military maneuver would bear fruits within the next four decades. The treaty concluding the Macedonian war was signed in 205 at Phoenice, in Epirus, and brought all of Greece and Pergamum permanently within the orbit of Roman supervision. Henceforward the affairs of Greece would be subject to Roman scrutiny and major decisions eventually to Roman approval.[10]

The first Macedonian war with Rome, prelude to the collapse of the Hellenistic state-system, was followed by two events in the Near East that seemed ominous to Rome and shook to bits the unstable peace of Phoenice. Those events occurred almost simultaneously and immediately following the end of the war. Ptolemy IV Philopator died in the summer of 204 and was succeeded by his five-year-old son, Ptolemy V Epiphanes, under the guardianship of his ambitious and scheming vizier, Sosibius;[11] and Antiochus III returned, most likely in the spring of that same year, from his "triumphant" seven-year expedition (212–205) into eastern Iran, having received from the Parthian and Bactrian princes renewed pledges of allegiance to Seleucid rule. Thereupon, emboldened by his success and doubtless mindful of its effect on his Greek and Macedonian contemporaries, Antiochus assumed the title, 'great.'[12] Still smarting, furthermore, from his defeat at Raphia twelve years before, he now thought it possible, in the coincidence of his own achievement with the obvious Egyptian instability, finally to enforce the Seleucid claim to Coele-Syria; and he received ready encouragement for his action from Philip of Macedon.[13] The Romans, however, had just seized the offensive in the second Punic war (218–201), as in 204 Publius Cornelius Scipio Africanus landed his forces in Africa. That offensive brought victory to Rome at Zama in 202; and that victory, giving Rome confidence in her military superiority, freed her to confront the Hellenistic states energetically.

---

10. Livy XXIX.12. The scholarly discussion is reviewed by Roger B. McShane, *The Foreign Policy of the Attalids of Pergamum*, Urbana, Ill., 1964, pp. 105–16.

11. Polybius XV.25. Cf. F. W. Walbank, "The Accession of Ptolemy Epiphanes: A Problem in Chronology," *Journal of Egyptian Archaeology* 22 (1936), pp. 20–34; Hatto H. Schmitt, *Untersuchungen zur Geschichte Antiochos' des Grossen und Seiner Zeit (Historia,* Einzelschriften, Heft 6), Wiesbaden, 1964, pp. 189–261, especially 236–37.

12. Appian, *Syria*, I.15.61.

13. Polybius III.2.8; XV.20.

Rome's principal threat appeared to be Philip. His humiliation at Phoenice had kindled his determination to rebuild Macedonian naval power in the Aegean and brought him, during the winter of 203/2, to a formal understanding with Antiochus, according to which the two monarchs would divide between them the wealth of Egypt "which both coveted when they heard of the death of king Ptolemy."[14] Philip, who seems to have initiated the agreement with Antiochus, may indeed, as Polybius believed,[15] have envisaged an eastern Mediterranean naval empire, stretching from Cyrene to Byzantium, worthy of the dreams of his ancestor, Demetrius the besieger, only to have lost his nerve for the undertaking when the opportune moment for its inception arrived.[16] As it happened, however, Philip's naval operations and attacks on Aetolian and Byzantine cities united Rhodes, the Greek cities dependent on Black Sea trade, and Attalus of Pergamum against him. Those allies, after an inconclusive naval engagement with Philip at Chios in 201, made a formal, united appeal to Rome late that summer for help.[17] That appeal, for which Attalus seems to have been the spokesman, led to Rome's second war with Macedon (200–197).

Antiochus, meanwhile, on the basis of his agreement with Philip, advanced into southern Syria that same year (201) and in the spring of 200, at Panion (modern Banyas, the Caesarea Philippi of the Gospels, Matthew 16:13 and Mark 8:27), near the headwaters of the Jordan river, defeated Scopas,[18] the mercenary, Aetolian commander of the Ptolemaic forces. That victory brought under Seleucid control most of Coele-Syria ("Samaria, Abila, Gadara and Jerusalem").[19] The Ptolemaic defeat and Rome's knowledge of the Macedonian-Seleucid agreement respecting Ptolemaic dominion no doubt reinforced the Roman decision to accede to the Attalid appeal for help. Rome therefore sent envoys with an ultimatum to Philip in August 200,[20] demanding that he make reparations to Attalus for injuries he had caused him and in addition that he "make war on no Grecian

---

14. Livy XXXI.xiv.5. For opinion about the planned division cf. H. Schmitt, *Geschichte Antiochos'* (N11), p. 254, n. 1.

15. XVI.10.

16. H. Schmitt, *Geschichte Antiochos'* (N11), p. 255.

17. Polybius XVI.24.3; Livy XXXI.ii.1–2.

18. Polybius XVI.18–19.

19. Polybius XVI.39.3.

20. H. Bengtson, *Griechische Geschichte*, Munich, 1950, p. 450.

state."[21] The Roman emissaries then, in an effort to consolidate Greek support against Philip,[22] publicized their demands among the Epirotes, Aetolians and Achaeans, before "they sailed away to meet Antiochus and Ptolemy for the purpose of coming to terms."[23] That Roman embassy to Antiochus probably represents Rome's first formal contact with the Seleucid state.

When Philip, as expected, refused the terms of the Roman ultimatum, the Romans landed an army at Apollonia in Illyria, probably in September 200, and the second Macedonian war began. Antiochus, who mistrusted Philip and feared Rome, remained aloof, leaving Philip with the support only of Thessaly to face Rome alone. The war dragged on indecisively for two years until in 198 the consul, Titus Quinctius Flamininus, who had fought against Hannibal, took command of the allied forces. A man who soon discovered the power of Greek public opinion,[24] Flamininus, the philhellene, became extraordinarily beloved in Greece, and after winning over the Achaean league to the anti-Macedonian cause,[25] he succeeded in occupying Thessaly. Then, in 197, south of Larissa on the slopes of a low Thessalian ridge, Cynoscephalae (Dogs' Heads), his Roman legions outmaneuvered and cut to pieces the Macedonian phalanx, bringing the war to its abrupt conclusion.

The terms of the peace treaty have not been preserved, but the Roman senatorial decree is known: The Macedonians were to free the Greeks of Asia and Europe and restore them to the rule of their own laws: within the year Philip was to yield control of the Greek cities and towns in which he had placed garrisons, and to release all prisoners of war and deserters; he was to surrender all his warships except "five light vessels and his great ship of sixteen banks of oars," and pay an indemnity of one thousand talents of silver, half at once and the other half in ten yearly installments.[26] His army was reduced to a police force with a maximum of five thousand men for

---

21. Polybius XVI.27.2.

22. McShane, *The Foreign Policy of the Attalids of Pergamum* (N10), p. 123.

23. Polybius XVI.27.5. Regarding Roman opposition to Philip, see J. P. V. D. Balsdon, "Rome and Macedon, 205–200 B.C.," *Journal of Roman Studies* 44 (1954) pp. 30–34.

24. E. Badian, *Roman Imperialism in the Late Republic*, Ithaca, 1968, p. 10.

25. Cf. R. M. Errington, *Philopoemen*, Oxford, 1969, p. 86, "cautious willingness to co-operate."

26. Polybius XVIII.44.

internal security only, and his son, Demetrius, was taken to Rome as hostage.[27] The Greeks were delighted, and at the Isthmian games proclaimed Greek freedom, by which, Polybius reports, "all the Greeks inhabiting Asia and Europe became free, ungarrisoned, subject to no tribute and governed by their own laws."[28] Greek freedom, surrendered to Macedonia at Chaeronea nearly one hundred fifty years before, must have seemed restored to Greece by Rome at Cynoscephalae. Only the Aetolians, who shrewdly saw in the victory merely a shift of masters, from Macedonians to Romans, objected to the settlement.

The Aetolians' discontent with what they called the changed Roman attitude toward them, once victory over Philip had been won, combined with their knowledge of Antiochus' ambitions in Asia Minor, guaranteed their renewed war with Rome. Antiochus' march through Asia Minor to the Hellespont in 196, reclaiming the Seleucid possessions of his great great grandfather en route, without regard for Ptolemaic, Rhodian or Attalid sensibilities or claims to them, together with Hannibal's flight to Antiochus at Ephesus the following year was viewed with great alarm at Rome. Still, the Seleucid embassy to Rome the next year, 194, one of several between 196 and 193,[29] might have produced peace, if Antiochus had been willing to withdraw from Europe. But his envoys refused to yield, properly asserting that Rome had no ground to meddle in Asian affairs; and anti-Seleucid ambassadors to Rome from Smyrna and Lampsacus, who remained loyal to Pergamum,[30] ruined the chance for peace.[31] When in addition Antiochus gave his daughter in marriage to the adolescent Ptolemy V in 194/3[32] and appeared therewith to secure control of Ptolemaic territories, the Aetolians found the moment opportune and invited him to liberate Greece. Misled by the Aetolian envoy about conditions in Greece, goaded against Rome by Hannibal, and lured perhaps by the hope of reconstituting

---

27. Livy XXXIII.xxx.

28. XVIII.46.15.

29. D. Magie, *Roman Rule in Asia Minor*, 2 vols., Princeton, 1950, vol. 2, p. 755, n. 50; 948, n. 55.

30. Livy XXXIII.xxxviii.3–5; XXXV.xlii.2.

31. Smyrna, under siege by Antiochus, consecrated a temple to the deified city Rome in 195, "a new cult, hitherto unknown either in Italy or in Greece," a sign of allegiance to Rome. D. Magie, *Roman Rule in Asia Minor* (N29), vol. 1, p. 106.

32. For the date see Bengtson, *Griechische Geschichte* (N20), p. 453.

Alexander's empire for himself, Antiochus accepted the request, with disastrous consequences for the future.

In the autumn of 192 Antiochus, escorted by one hundred warships, sailed with two hundred transport ships, carrying ten thousand infantry, five hundred cavalry and six elephants, from Ephesus to Demetrias in Thessaly. That invasion of Greece brought a Roman declaration of war.[33] The small force Antiochus landed, however, "scarcely sufficient to take possession of Greece if it were undefended, not to mention the necessity of resistance to the Romans,"[34] disheartened the Aetolians; and when the Achaeans and Philip at first remained aloof and then joined Rome against Antiochus, they doomed to failure his war to liberate Greece from the Romans. In the spring of 191 a Roman army trapped and destroyed Antiochus' forces at Thermopylae, while the king with only a few aides escaped to Ephesus. Within the year thereafter the Aetolians had accepted a truce with Rome, Antiochus had lost control of the sea, and in the winter of 190/89, not far from Mt. Sipylus and Magnesia in Asia Minor, in a rain-soaked field of the Hermus river valley, Antiochus' phalanx was out-maneuvered and exposed to destruction by the missiles of the Pergamene cavalry. The Great King, who two years later with a body of troops would be killed in modern Luristan (winter of 188/7), had "opened his reign with an error—the attempt to deal with the foreign situation before he had put his house in order (Raphia, 217 B.C.); and he ended it with a great disaster—his irreparable defeat by the Romans at Magnesia in 190 B.C.[35]

For Rome, the victory was unbelievable, and Appian, writing three hundred years afterward at Alexandria, could still marvel at the event. For " . . . it brought them great confidence in their own good fortune that such a small number, in the first battle and at the first assault, in a foreign country, should have overcome a much greater number, composed of so many peoples, with all the royal resources, including valiant mercenaries and the renowned Macedonian phalanx, and the king himself, ruler of that vast empire and surnamed the Great—all in a single day. It became a common saying among them, 'There was a king—Antiochus the Great!'[36] These

---

33. Livy XXXVI.ii.2.
34. Livy XXXV.xliii.6.
35. W. S. Ferguson, *Greek Imperialism*, New York and London, 1913, p. 187.
36. Appian, *Syria* 37

feelings of strength and superiority no doubt dictated the stiff terms Rome imposed on Antiochus.

Terms of peace were set by the Senate in 189 and delivered to representatives of Antiochus at Apamea in Asia Minor the next year. Antiochus must give up all territory west of the Taurus mountains, renounce hostility against the Romans and their allies and agree to hire no mercenaries and receive no fugitives from lands under Roman rule. He must pay Rome an indemnity of 14,500 talents of silver, five hundred at once, two thousand on ratification of the treaty by the Senate, and an additional one thousand annually for twelve years. In addition he must provide the corn needed by the occupying Roman army, nearly one hundred fifty thousand bushels over twelve years, surrender specified prisoners, including Hannibal (who escaped to Bithynia), restore to Eumenes of Pergamum all the possessions of his father, Attalus, and pay him an additional indemnity of nearly five hundred talents. Finally, he must give his elephants and not keep any in the future, surrender his warships except for ten decked ships of war and send twenty hostages, including his younger son, Antiochus to Rome.[37] The leading role of the Attalid king, Eumenes, in the peace conference at Rome in 189 is fully recorded,[38] and not surprisingly the Romans entrusted to him the chief responsibility for preserving political stability in Asia Minor.[39]

The war and its peace at Apamea were a disaster for the Hellenistic world. The Seleucid defeat allowed the eastern provinces, Parthia and Bactria, successfully to declare their independence of Antioch, and their example was followed by Armenia and Media. The crushing burden of the Roman indemnity led to the death of Antiochus in 187 and perhaps also of his son, Seleucus IV in 175, as they sought funds for Rome from temple treasuries.[40] The Peace isolated the Near East from the West and doomed Greece therewith to poverty and depopulation by suicide,[41] while the Seleucid and Ptolemaic states crumbled to pieces. And finally, the treaty at Apamea delivered Asia Minor to Roman plunderers and slave traders, whose

37. Polybius XXI.42; Appian, Syria 38.
38. Polybius XXI.18–21.
39. Cf. McShane, The Foreign Policy of the Attalids of Pergamum (N10), p. 153f.
40. Cf. Daniel 11:20.
41. M. Rostovtzeff, Social and Economic History of the Hellenistic World, 3 vols., Oxford, 1941:

depredations some decades later would be partially punished by the massacres of Mithridates of Pontus. For the moment, however, Rome did not abuse her power in Asia Minor,[42] though the looting of Ambracia in Epirus augured ill for the Greek future under Roman hands.[43]

Eumenes, dependent as he was on Roman moral support to maintain his position in Asia Minor, attempted in vain to preserve friendship with Rome and with Rome's enemies at the same time. But when he made an alliance by marriage with king Ariarathes IV of southern Cappadocia,[44] just when the pro-Seleucid, Pontic king, Pharnaces, seized the Greek cities, Sinope and Heraclea, on the Black Sea in 183, he had to recognize that Asia Minor was divided into a northern Pontic-Armenian empire and a southern Pergamene-Cappadocian entente, to which Bithynia was also attached. This division of Asia Minor increased Eumenes' alarm at any sign of Macedonian-Seleucid coalition and made him even more dependent on the Roman senate which for the time being refused military assistance.

Elsewhere in Greece and Asia Minor the apprehension that began to spread after Rome showed her hand at Apamea turned all eyes toward Macedonia for possible relief. There, Philip, after his capitulation to Rome at Cynoscephalae, had "never relaxed his attention to the assembling in times of peace of strength which whenever the chance should be given, he could use in time of war"[45] and as a consequence had so increased the resources of his kingdom that his son, Perseus, when he succeeded to the throne in 179, could contemplate independence of Rome. Perseus found an ally in Prusias, king of Bithynia, to whom he gave his sister in marriage, and he took to wife the daughter of Seleucus IV, Laodice,[46] whom the Rhodians brought to Macedonia in their ships.[47] These events seem to have aroused fears at Rome, not so much about Macedonian as about Seleucid intentions; for Rome released Antiochus, Seleucus' brother, who had been kept hostage in Rome since 189, in exchange for Seleucus' son, Demetrius, thus creating the possibility for dynastic struggle at Antioch. Antiochus

42. D. Magie, *Roman Rule in Asia Minor* (N29), vol. 1, pp. 117–18.
43. Livy XXXVIII.ix.13. Polybius XXI.30.9–10.
44. Livy XXXVIII.xxxvii.5; xxxix.6.
45. Polybius XXV.3.9–10; Livy XXXIX.xxiii f.
46. Livy XLII.xii.3–5.
47. Polybius XXV.4.8.

apparently went to Athens, for he was there when Seleucus died in 176/5.[48] The call to war, however, came four years later from Pergamum, when in 172 Eumenes at Rome urged the destruction of Macedonia.[49]

The Roman suspicion—implanted perhaps, reinforced certainly, by Eumenes—that Perseus was planning hostilities against Rome became certainty with news of the unsuccessful attempt on Eumenes' life at Delphi as he was returning home.[50] The senate accused Perseus of masterminding the plot againt Eumenes and began preparations for war. Polybius, in fact, cited that ambush as the beginning of the third Macedonian-Roman war.[51] If Perseus, however, had counted on Greek support in a war against Rome, he was disappointed. The Greeks did not trust him, the Rhodians could not agree to join him against Rome, and the Seleucids, who had recently renewed their treaty of peace with Rome, were at the moment complaining to the Roman senate about the aggressive Ptolemaic attitude toward Palestine, which necessitated their own mobilization for defensive war. When, therefore, in 171, war erupted between Rome and Macedonia, Perseus, like Philip before him, had to face the Romans alone. The decisive battle in a protracted campaign took place near Pydna, some thirty miles south of the capital city, Pella, in June 168, where the Roman legions overcame and massacred the Macedonian phalanx. Perseus fled the slaughter, was captured on the island of Samothrace and taken in ignominy to Rome, where he died in prison.

Thereafter Rome deprived Macedonia of all means for future resistance and took the occasion to settle scores with the rest of the Greek states. She broke Macedonia into four republics, each with its own officials, selected yearly, to take the place of the captured royal dignitaries, and designated no administrative arrangements by which the republics could cooperate as a national state. She permitted three provinces to raise an army to defend the northern frontier, but placed the gold and silver mines under Roman supervision, forbade the import of salt (no doubt an economic sanction), and prohibited the cutting of wood for ships. Those Greeks suspected of supporting Macedonia were punished: the Rhodians, who had interceded with Rome on behalf of Macedon, were deprived of their few mainland

---

48. Appian, *Syria* 45.
49. Livy XLII.ii.1–3, vi.2–5. Appian, *Macedonica* xi.1ff.
50. Livy XLII.xv.3–xvi.5; Appian, *Macedonica* xi.4.
51. XXII.18.8.

possessions and forced to compete commercially with Delos, which Rome subjected to Athens and made a free port; one thousand leading men from Achaea, including Polybius, were deported to Italy; the Aetolian league was dismembered; seventy Epirote cities were destroyed and 150,000 of the population sold into slavery; and even Eumenes, probably because of his leading position in Asia Minor, became suspect in the eyes of the Roman senators. The judgment that "both the growing deterioration of the Roman character and the temporary eclipse of Roman philhellenism were reflected in the settlement"[52] is borne out by subsequent events.

In Egypt Ptolemy V Epiphanes, whose foreign possessions Philip V and Antiochus III had desired to expropriate for themselves, had died in 180, leaving three minor children. The older son, Ptolemy VI Philometor (as he came to be known), was six years old at his father's death. Shortly after 173 when his mother died, he was induced by his guardian ministers, Eulaeus and Lenaeus, to declare war on Antiochus IV Epiphanes in an effort to regain Palestine for Egypt. It was that Ptolemaic hostility about which Antiochus was complaining to Rome at the outbreak of the third Macedonian war. In 170 Eulaeus and Lenaeus marched into Palestine only to be routed at Pelusium by Antiochus, who captured Philometor. Antiochus then, as protector for Philometor, invaded and subdued Egypt except for Alexandria, where in the emergency Ptolemy's younger brother, later known as Ptolemy VIII Euergetes II, had been crowned king.[53]

Hope for the Ptolemies now seemed to rest with Rome. Therefore, three months before the fateful battle at Pydna, envoys from Ptolemy VIII appeared in Rome protesting Antiochus' siege of Alexandria and entreating the Senate "to come to the rescue of a kingdom and a royal pair who were friends of Roman rule." The senators responded by sending to Egypt three representatives, whose mission to "bring an end to the war between the kings" was to become one of the most celebrated of antiquity. The envoys, Gaius Popillius Laenas, Gaius Decimius and Gaius Hostilius, were to go first to Antiochus and then to Ptolemy, declaring that their war was to be concluded and that the one refusing to make peace would incur the enmity of Rome.[54] On their way to Alexandria from Delos, where they had received the news of Pydna, the envoys stopped at Rhodes to rehearse Rome's

---

52. Tarn and Griffith, *Hellenistic Civilization*, p. 32.
53. Polybius XXIX.23.4.
54. Livy XLIV.xix.4–14.

displeasure with Rhodian conduct during Rome's war with Macedon,[55] and they arrived in Egypt in time to meet Antiochus who was returning from Palestine, intending no longer to be regent for Philometor but conqueror of Egypt.

The meeting with Antiochus revealed more than anything the arrogant Roman attitude toward the Near Eastern states. Popillius refused to take the proffered hand of his old friend, Antiochus, until the latter had read the Roman decree that he leave Egypt; and Popillius went so far as to restrain Antiochus from consulting on the matter with his aides by scratching a circle on the ground around the Syrian king, with a rod he was carrying, and declaring, "Before you step out of this circle, give me an answer which I may take back to the Senate." Only after Antiochus acquiesced to the insulting order did Popillius give his hand to the king as an ally and friend.[56] That extraordinary meeting demonstrated the universal Hellenistic respect for Roman power, which had no doubt increased greatly after the Macedonian defeat at Pydna. In his account of the meeting Polybius remarked appropriately: " . . . all was again set right simply owing to the fact that the fate of Perseus had been decided. For had this not been so, and had not Antiochus been certain of it, he would never, I think, have obeyed the Roman behests."

The events of 168, which were a consequence and continuation of the Roman settlement at Apamea twenty years earlier, were to have a profound effect, that could not have been realized at the time, on the Hellenistic world and on Rome. Loss of Macedonian independence signalled the demise of Macedonian power in Syria and Egypt a century later, which was preceded by the decline of Pergamum and the Roman exploitation of Asia Minor. The controlling agent in this Hellenistic political decline and the unwilling heir to the Hellenistic state system, the only power capable of keeping order in the world, was the Roman republic, whose administrative system collapsed under the weight of its new political and military responsibilities throughout the Mediterranean. The shift in the center of power from Antioch to Rome made Parthians and Jews clients of Rome in their struggles against the Seleucids, while the formation of the Parthian empire doomed the Seleucid state even as it created an Iranian counterpoise to

---

55. Livy XLV.x.
56. The story appears in Polybius XXIX.27; Livy XLV.xii; Diodorus xxi.2; Appian, *Syria* 66; and elsewhere.

Rome. Next to this new confrontation of East and West the rise of the small Jewish, Hasmonean state was of parochial interest. Its influence on the world, however, has been enormous; for it provided a religious climate in which Christianity would arise to spread through Europe in the succeeding millennium and a political climate that would nourish Zionism and eventually lead to the creation of the modern state of Israel.

SUGGESTIONS FOR FURTHER STUDY:

Read, in addition to works cited in the Notes, M. Cary and H. H. Scullard, *A History of Rome down to the Reign of Constantine*, 3rd ed. (New York, 1975).

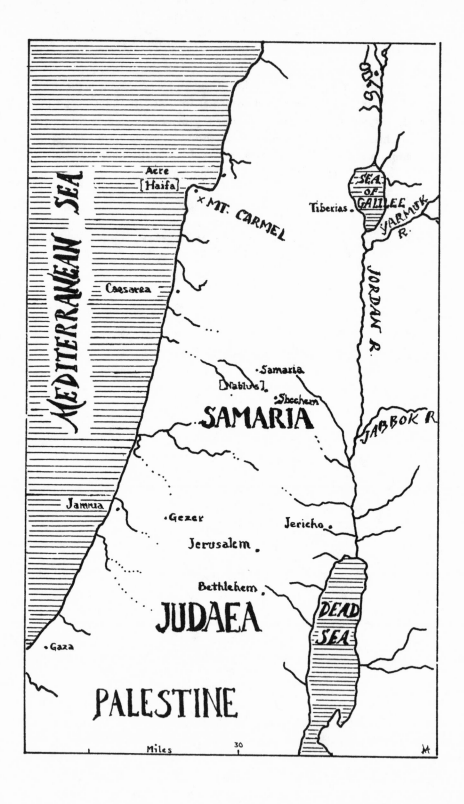

MEDITERRANEAN SEA

Acre
[Haifa]

× MT. CARMEL

Tiberias •

SEA
OF
GALILEE

YARMUK R.

Caesarea

JORDAN R.

• Samaria

[Nablus]

• Shechem

SAMARIA

JABBOK R

Jamnia

• Gezer

Jericho •

Jerusalem •

Bethlehem •

JUDAEA

DEAD
SEA

• Gaza

PALESTINE

Miles   30

VI

THE CONTEST FOR PALESTINE

The history of the Jewish community in Palestine in the Hellenistic period is relatively well known from the books of the Maccabees and the writings of Josephus. Having lived under Persian rule from the end of the sixth century, when a determined group of Jewish exiles returned from Babylon to Jerusalem, until Alexander subjected Palestine to Macedonian control in 332, the Jews had flourished in Judaea[1] as a peaceful temple state. Their interests seem to have been largely internal, social and religious, concerned with the proper service of God and administration of the temple. No vision of a unified political, cultural or religious world troubled their lives, or those of other, non-Jewish communities in Palestine: Samaritans, Edomite Arabs, Philistines and Phoenicians. After the upheavals following Alexander's death in 323, Palestine came under Ptolemaic control in 301, a rule that lasted thoughout the third century, until Antiochus conquered the land in 200. Thereafter the Seleucids dominated Palestine until Judaea secured its independence in 142. By 64 B.C. Syria and Palestine were subject to the dictates of Rome.

During the Hellenistic period Palestine was extensively settled by Greek soldiers, traders and adventurers, who reorganized the ancient towns and cities, especially those on the coast and in the Jordan rift near the Sea of

---

1. Judaea in Persian times, generally the rectangular area marked on the east by the Jordan river and the Dead Sea and extending westward some 32 miles through Bethel 5 miles north of Jerusalem and through Hebron 20 miles south, retained its boundaries unchanged into Hasmonean times. Cf. M. Avi-Yonah, *The Holy Land*, rev. ed., Grand Rapids, Mich., 1977, pp. 13–20.

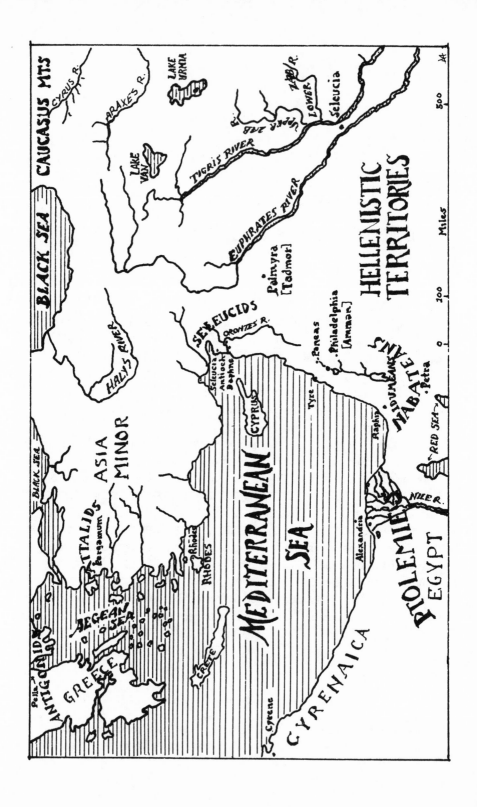

CAUCASUS MTS

BLACK SEA

CYRUS R.

ARAXES R.

LAKE URMIA

LAKE VAN

ZAB R.

LOWER

Selucia

UPPER ZAB

TIGRIS RIVER

EUPHRATES RIVER

HALYS RIVER

ASIA MINOR

BLACK SEA

ATTALIDS
Pergamum

Rhodes

RHODES

SELEUCIDS

ORONTES R.

Seleucia
Antioch
Daphne

CYPRUS

Palmyra
[Tadmor]

Paneas

Philadelphia
[Amman]

Tyre

IDUMAEANS

NABATEANS

Petra

Raphia

RED SEA

MEDITERRANEAN SEA

Pella
ANTIGONIDS

GREECE

AEGEAN SEA

CRETE

Alexandria

PTOLEMIES

EGYPT

NILE R.

CYRENAICA

Cyrene

HELLENISTIC TERRITORIES

Miles

0   200   500

Galilee, according to Greek models. The widespread imitation there of Greek styles in coins, building, and art, as well as the adoption of Greek names attests the pervasive Greek, material influence. Jerusalem, however, remained a Jewish city, managed by a council of elders, whose presiding executive officer was the high priest.[2] The high priesthood was a dynastic position, that had been introduced at Jerusalem after the Babylonian captivity and that claimed descent from the house of Zadok of the Davidic era (ca. 1000–900 B.C.), through the line of Joshua (Jeshua), son of Jehozadak, the priest at the time of the exiles' return from Babylon.[3]

In addition to the high-priestly dynasty a number of other priestly families with experience of the Babylonian captivity were influential in Jerusalem. They were opposed, however, by leaders who had not shared in the religious renewal of those who had gone into exile in Babylon, and the authority of the non-exiles in Palestine was now being threatened and usurped by the returnees. Among these non-exilic, less religiously strict families were the Tobiads from the Transjordan, who married into the leading families of Jerusalem.[4] So well thought of were they[5] that during the reign of Ptolemy II Philadelphus even the high priest, Onias II, gave his sister in marriage to Tobiah. That union strengthened the influence of those in the city who espoused the adoption of Greek humanism, i.e., the Hellenizers, which in turn tended to weaken Jewish feelings of nationalism and strict devotion to Yahwism.

The growing conflict in Jerusalem between the rigorous separatists

---

2. 1 Macc. 12:6; 2 Macc. 11:27.

3. Jehozadak went into exile, according to 1 Chron. 6:15; on Joshua, the priest, cf. Neh. 12:26; Hag. 1:1; Ezra 5:2; Ecclus. 49:11-12. In general consult Emil Schürer, *Geschichte des jüdischen Volkes im Zeitalter Jesu Christi*, 3 vols., 3rd & 4th eds., Leipzig, 1901–11. (References in this book are to *A History of the Jewish People in the Time of Jesus Christ*, 3 vols., Edinburgh, 1924—a reprint of the English translation published in Edinburgh in 1890. A new English version revised and edited by G. Vermes and F. Millar began appearing in 1973. Josephus is cited from the edition of B. Niese; Strabo from the Loeb edition.) The high priests in Jerusalem according to Josephus were Onias I (*Antiquities* xi.8.7. [347]); Simon I (xii.2.4.); Eleasar (xii.2.4.); Manasseh (xii.4.1.); Onias II (xii.4.1–2); Simon II (xii.4.10 [224]); Onias III (xii.5.1. [237–39]). Cf. E. Schürer, *History of the Jewish People*, 1, p. 188, n. 3. On the ruling groups in the Exile see E. R. Bevan, *Jerusalem under the High Priests*, 1904, pp. 5–6.

4. Neh. 6.17–19.

5. Neh. 13:4-9.

(Hasidim) and the Hellenizers was exacerbated after the Seleucid victory at Panion in 200 when the rival Jewish factions sought partisan gains for themselves from the rulers in Antioch at the expense of their opponents and of the Jewish community as a whole. What made these Jewish efforts appealing in Antioch was the financial burden Rome imposed at Apamea on the Seleucids. Antiochus III and his son, Seleucus IV, were desperate for funds to pay the Roman indemnity, and the temple treasuries within their kingdom seemed a providential resource for alleviating their plight. The Seleucid kings seem to have been unable or unwilling to convince their subjects that payment of the royal indemnity to Rome was also in the general welfare, and the officials in Jerusalem were not averse to exploiting the Seleucid economic plight for their own partisan ends.

Thus, when Antiochus IV succeeded to the throne in 175, Jason (Joshua), the high priest's Hellenizing brother, promised Antioch more revenue from Judaea than the high priest himself, Onias III, was paying. Antiochus, apparently persuaded of the advantage of such a simple exchange, made Jason high priest and permitted him to enroll the inhabitants of Jerusalem as citizens of Antioch. The intent was either to make Jerusalem a *polis*, renamed Antioch, and its council of elders a municipal senate, or to give it a Greek quarter, to be occupied by Hellenized Jews (i.e., create a Jewish *politeuma*, "corporation"). The former seems more likely.[6] Jason built a sports stadium and established a body of young athletes, *ephebi*, who walked the city in characteristic Greek mantle and broadbrimmed hat.[7] Once the principle was established, however, that the high priesthood in Jerusalem could be purchased at Antioch, the office was opened to the highest bidder and its religious significance fatally undercut. Jason, as he should have anticipated, was deposed in 171 in favor of a scoundrel, Menelaus, who not only promised the king more money, which he was later unable to pay, but also saw to the murder of the troublesome conservative Onias, perhaps in 170. With that the smoldering fire of rebellion in Jerusalem leaped into flames.[8]

---

6. 1 Macc. 1:11-12; 2 Macc. 4:7-10; V. Tcherikover, *Hellenistic Civilization and the Jews*, Philadelphia, 1966, Appendix III.

7. Jason's Hellenization of Jerusalem is described in 2 Macc. 4:11-15. Cf. E. R. Bevan, *Jerusalem under the High Priests* (N3), p. 79; and *House of Seleucus*, 2 vols., London, 1902, 2, p. 170, n. 2.

8. The author of 2 Macc. gives his judgment on the new developments:

The deep-seated conflicts and rivalries between the generally aristocratic Hellenizers and the more popular, conservative Hasidim were embittered by personal contests among the partisans of Onias and Tobiah, Antiochus and Ptolemy; and all were made critical by the oppressive Seleucid need for funds. With news of Onias' death, mob violence broke out in Jerusalem, and when an armed contingent led by Menelaus' brother, Lysimachus, was unable to quell the uprising, Lysimachus was killed.[9] Menelaus was brought before the king at Tyre and accused of provoking the insurrection, but he obtained acquittal for himself and the death penalty for his accusers by bribing one of the king's relatives, retaining thereafter his high-priestly office.[10] Antiochus' whereabouts before and after this revolt are not known for certain. He was in Egypt in 169 and again in 168 and may have visited Jerusalem each time he returned to Antioch, but the sources are contradictory, and the course of events leading up to his proscriptions against the Jews in 168 is not clearly known.[11]

What is known is that Antiochus attempted to Hellenize the cities of his realm by settling in them Greek immigrants from Asia Minor, in contravention of the treaty of Apamea. In 169 he let himself be proclaimed "epiphanes," the god manifest, substituting on his coins for the former Apollo the enthroned Olympian Zeus and erecting that god's statue in Apollo's temple at Daphne. He reorganized Babylon as a Greek city, equipped with theater and gymnasium, though he did not rename the city; he made Jerusalem a *polis*, renamed Antioch, and named five other Antiochs

---

As a result, the priests no longer had any enthusiasm for their duties at the altar, but despised the temple and neglected the sacrifices; and in defiance of the law they eagerly contributed to the expenses of the wrestling-school whenever the opening gong called them. They placed no value on their hereditary dignities, but cared above everything for Hellenic honours. Because of this, grievous misfortunes beset them, and the very men whose way of life they strove after, and tried hard to imitate, turned out to be their vindictive enemies. To act profanely against God's laws is no light matter, as will become clear in due time. *NEB* 2 Macc. 4:14-17.

9. 2 Macc. 4:39-42.

10. 2 Macc. 4:43-50.

11. The books of 1 and 2 Maccabees record that Antiochus himself made one visit to Jerusalem; according to 1 Macc. 1:20 it was after his first Egyptian expedition; according to 2 Macc. 5:11, after his second. Cf. V. Tcherikover, *Hellenistic Civilization and the Jews* (N6), p. 186ff.

and as many Epiphaneias for himself. The report, therefore,[12] that the king wished all his subjects "to become one people and abandon their own laws and religion" and that "the nations everywhere complied with the royal command," including many in Israel, is corroborated by the evidence.[13]

Antiochus' rebuff in 168 in Egypt by the Roman legate, Popillius, gave rise to a rumor in Jerusalem that he had died.[14] Acting on that report Jason collected a force of supporters and made a surprise attack on Jerusalem to unseat Menelaus. He captured the city and massacred numbers of its inhabitants; but when he proved unable to take Menelaus who had taken refuge in the citadel, Jason was forced to flee as a fugitive to Transjordan in the face of popular resentment against all Hellenizers.

When thereafter Antiochus returned from Egypt,[15] no doubt smarting from his treatment by Rome and in a mood to be outraged by the Jewish uprising in Jerusalem, he took the city by storm, killing many of the inhabitants and selling as many into slavery. The Hasidic insurgents fled into the surrounding hills, where they resorted to the life of guerrillas, and Antiochus invested the city with a garrison of Hellenized Syrians, who installed in the temple their own god, Baal Shamin, "The Lord of Heaven," known in Jewish tradition as the "abomination of desolation."[16] The Jewish Hellenizers, with the support of Antiochus, thus appeared to have prevailed, making Jerusalem a Hellenistic city; and Antiochus decided the time had come to root out the source of all rebellion, the offensive Torah. He therefore ordered that the Sabbath and Temple worship were to be profaned, the image of Zeus Olympius to be erected above the altar, circumcision to be forbidden, the books of the Law to be confiscated and burned, and noncompliance with his proscriptions to be punished with death.[17] Clearly, Antiochus, who may have been dubbed "Epimanes," "madman," for this action,[18] was ignorant of the nature and strength of popular Jewish religious conviction. In addition, he was misled by the Hellenizing Jews,

---

12. 1 Macc. 1:41-42.

13. Cf. W. W. Tarn, *The Greeks in Bactria and India*, 2nd ed., Cambridge, 1951, p. 190ff.; E. R. Bevan, *House of Seleucus* (N7), 2, p. 148ff.

14. 2 Macc. 5:5.

15. 2 Macc. 5:11ff.

16. 1 Macc. 1:54; cf. J. Teixidor, *The Pagan God*, Princeton, 1977, p. 26ff.

17. 1 Macc. 1:44-50.

18. But cf. Polybius, XXVI.1, who reports that Antiochus behaved like a buffoon.

lured by the temple wealth, and precipitous in his action. The result was the Hasmonean or Maccabaean war.[19]

That war was the logical outcome of the Hasidic rebellion, now invested with organized leadership and strategy. According to tradition it began in the village of Modin, midway on the ancient road between Jerusalem and Jaffa, when a priest, Mattathias, refusing to obey a Syrian official who had arrived to compel sacrifice to the new god, killed a compliant Jew together with the official, thereafter demolishing the pagan altar and fleeing with his sons into the wilderness.[20] There he had to abandon the practice of refusing battle on the Sabbath, after the massacre of a large number of the non-resisting pious on the Sabbath day demonstrated the inevitable consequences of steadfast adherence to Mosaic precepts.[21] Freed of their religion, the zealous rebels gained success after success against both their Hellenizing brothers and their Syrian overlords.

When Mattathias died in 166, his son Judas "Maccabaeus," for whom the movement has been named, became field marshall. His triumphs, based as they were on Seleucid preoccupation elsewhere, on his precise knowledge of Judaean topography, and on the conviction that his cause was God's cause, a conviction reinforced among his followers by each military victory, would culminate in the formal rededication of the temple in Jerusalem on December 25, 164, exactly three years from the day when Antiochus had erected there the "abomination of desolation" and dedicated the temple to Zeus Olympius. Undoubtedly Hasmonean ambitions as well as Jewish piety were at work in the war, but it was clearly much more than a "civil war for the high priesthood," even if one takes fully into account a Maccabaean lust for power.[22]

Neither the Seleucid government nor the Hellenizing Jews, entrenched in Jerusalem, had initially paid serious attention to Judas. Antiochus in 167 apparently believed he had settled the problem of

---

19. "Hasmonean" probably derives from a place name, Heshmon; Maccabee, properly applied only to Judas, cf. 1 Macc. 2:4, may have referred to the shape of his head, 'mallet-headed,' from the Aramaic, *maqqaba*, 'hammer' (H. M. Orlinsky in *IDB*, "Maccabees"). On the war, cf. A. Momigliano, "Greeks, Jews and Romans from Antiochus III to Pompey," in *Alien Wisdom: The Limits of Hellenization*, Cambridge, 1975, pp. 97–122.

20. 1 Macc. 2:15ff.

21. 1 Macc. 2:39ff.

22. S. K. Eddy, *The King is Dead*, Lincoln, Neb., 1961, pp. 215–17.

Jerusalem and Judaea and in the spring of 166 held a great festival at Daphne, a suburb of Antioch,[23] presumably to celebrate the re-incorporation of Bactria into the Seleucid state, which had been accomplished by his general, Eucratides.[24] Thereafter, in 165, he had marched eastward to join Eucratides, reducing Armenia as he went and refounding Alexandria on the lagoon between the Tigris and Eulaeus rivers in Chaldaea as Antioch. He was en route to Ecbatana (modern Hamadan) when he died in Kislev (Nov.–Dec. 164) of tuberculosis at Gabae (modern Isfahan).[25] Left behind in Antioch was Antiochus' eight- or nine-year-old son, Antiochus V Eupator, under the guardianship of Lysias, the viceregent and king's relative.[26]

After Antiochus' departure for the east in 165, however, Judas had succeeded in isolating Jerusalem from direct communication with Antioch, and the adverse situation required a Seleucid response. Lysias, therefore, in the spring of 164 marched into Judaea against Judas, but instead of engaging him in combat proposed terms of peace. The change of plan came perhaps in the wake of reports about Antiochus' failing health, and apparently with the advice and help of Menelaus as mediator between himself and the majority of Jews who remained committed neither to the Maccabaean nor Hellenizing factions.[27] This large group of uncommitted, who were perhaps the chief sufferers from Antiochus' decrees, were unable to return to their former lives, freed from Syrian harassment, unless the hated proscriptions were lifted. Menelaus therefore used his influence both with Lysias and with Roman ambassadors who were then passing through Palestine[28] to secure an annulment of the laws, in an effort both to increase his own support among the people and to deprive Judas of the primary reason for his war. The Seleucid officials, however, much as they desired peace and order in Palestine, were wary of rescinding their king's laws in his absence and of abandoning their legal basis for pursuing the insurgent Maccabees. They therefore imposed a two-week deadline, before which all should declare

23. Polybius XXX.25–26.
24. W. W. Tarn, *The Greeks in Bactria and India* (N13), pp. 193–95.
25. Appian, *Syria* 66. Cf. Tarn's map *CAH* VII, facing p. 156.
26. 2 Macc. 11:1.
27. 2 Macc. 11:16-38; Cf. E. Bickerman, *From Ezra to the Last of the Maccabees*, New York, 1962: 116; V. Tcherikover, *Hellenistic Civilization and the Jews* (N6), pp. 213–17.
28. 2 Macc. 11:34-38.

their intentions either to surrender their arms and return home freed of further Syrian persecution or to continue the war.[29] Thereafter, apparently satisfied that the situation was under control, Lysias returned to Antioch. But the plan failed, apparently because widespread suspicion of Menelaus immobilized the uncommitted Jews, and within six months Judas had stormed and taken Jerusalem, leaving to Menelaus only the fortified citadel.[30]

His capture of Jerusalem in 164 made Judas the acknowledged Jewish leader, and from all Palestine Jews appealed to him for help against their Syrian and Greek oppressors, who supported the Seleucid government.[31] Judas and his brothers campaigned throughout the land, inflicting slaughter on their enemies and destroying pagan cultic centers;[32] but when Judas laid siege to the citadel in Jerusalem, Menelaus successfully appealed to Antioch for help,[33] and Lysias returned with a large army to Judaea in the spring of 162. His departure from Antioch, however, allowed a certain Philip, "foster-brother" of Antiochus Epiphanes,[34] to claim the regency for the young Antiochus and this unfavorable development once more compelled Lysias to return to the capital. Before leaving Jerusalem, he again made terms with Judas, dissolving the *polis* at Jerusalem and ratifying the temple status achieved two years earlier, in exchange for which Judas declared allegiance to the Seleucid king.[35] By allowing the Jews, because of Judas' efforts, to observe their own laws, the Syrian government appeared to support the Maccabees. But Lysias, uneasy about the prospects for peace in Judaea, ordered Judas' fortifications in Jerusalem to be destroyed and a Syrian garrison stationed in the citadel. He then had Menelaus, whom he blamed for the failure of the ill-advised Hellenizing program, taken to Beroea (Aleppo) and executed.[36] As successor to the high priesthood, Lysias

---

29. 2 Macc. 11:27-33.
30. The foregoing reconstruction is by V. Tcherikover, *Hellenistic Civilization* (N6), pp. 217-20.
31. Evidence from this time for widespread hatred of Jews is limited to 1 Maccabees 5 and difficult to evaluate. Cf. E. R. Bevan, *House of Seleucus* (N7), 2, p. 182; V. Tcherikover, *Hellenistic Civilization* (N6), p. 209ff.
32. 1 Macc. 5; 2 Macc. 12.
33. 1 Macc. 6:16ff.
34. 1 Macc. 6:14-15; 2 Macc. 9:29; cf. E. R. Bevan, *House of Seleucus* (N6), 2, p. 283.
35. 1 Macc. 6:58-61; 2 Macc. 11:23-26.
36. 2 Macc. 13:3-8.

appointed Alcimus (Hebrew Jakim), a moderate Hellenizer of the Oniad family.[37] When Lysias returned to Antioch, Philip the pretender escaped to Ptolemy and disappeared from history.[38]

The appointment of Alcimus temporarily satisfied the Hasidim[39] because Alcimus was "of the family of Aaron," but it displeased the Maccabees, not least because the highest religious leader of "God's people" had been appointed by a foreign sovereign.[40] In Antioch, meanwhile, a new situation arose to upset the peace Lysias had attained when Demetrius, Epiphanes' nephew, the son of Seleucus IV, arrived from Rome in the summer of 162. (His mother, Laodice, may previously have been Epiphanes' wife; Demetrius and Antiochus V Eupator would in that case have been half-brothers.) He had been hostage there all his life (23 years) and spurred by the news of his uncle's death had finally escaped with the help of Polybius to claim his kingdom.[41] Demetrius arrived in Syria amid popular acclaim and immediately ordered, before he should lay eyes on them, that his cousin, Antiochus, together with the boy's guardian, Lysias, be dispatched by his troops. The execution of that command put Demetrius firmly upon the throne of Syria, and it was to him that Alcimus appealed both for confirmation of his appointment as high priest and for an armed escort to take him to Jerusalem and install him in the temple. Acceding to that request, Demetrius sent Bacchides from east of the Euphrates[42] to Judaea to guarantee proper transfer of authority to Alcimus.

But on every side, Demetrius' assumption of rule was greeted with suspicion and revolt among members of the old regime. Antiochus IV had appointed two brothers from Miletus to important posts in his government: Heraclides as minister of finance, and Timarchus as governor of the eastern provinces with headquarters in Seleucia.[43] After his execution of Lysias, Demetrius dismissed Heraclides, who apparently returned to Miletus only to appear in Rome eight years later against Demetrius. Timarchus, more

---

37. 1 Macc. 7:14; 2 Macc. 14:7. On the timing cf. V. Tcherikover, *Hellenistic Civilization* (N7), p. 487.

38. Josephus, *Ant.* XII IX.7 (386), reports that he was taken and put to death.

39. 1 Macc. 7:13.

40. 2 Macc. 14:3; 1 Macc. 7:5.

41. Polybius XXXI.2; 11ff.; Appian, *Syria* 46–47.

42. 1 Macc. 7:8.

43. Appian, *Syria* 45.

impetuously, proclaimed himself king of Babylon, with the blessing of Rome and the support of Artaxias of Armenia, and set out against Syria. But Demetrius, who enjoyed a stronger position than the upstart governor realized, met him at the Euphrates, and when Timarchus' army defected to Demetrius, the contest was over, and Demetrius was greeted thereafter in Babylonia as savior.[44]

In Cappadocia, Ariarathes V, Demetrius' cousin (son of Antiochis, his father's sister), refusing the hand in marriage of Demetrius' daughter, looked for support against the Seleucid king both to Rome and to Attalus of Pergamum. But Roman support was diplomatic rather than military,[45] and Rome later would not support Ariarathes against Orophernes, his brother, who, with the assistance of Demetrius, was in revolt against him;[46] thus, the eastern potentates were left to squabble among themselves. The Romans did dispatch a commission in 161, headed by the censor, Tiberius Sempronius Gracchus (father of Tiberius and Gaius), to investigate affairs at Antioch, and as a result, the next year, guardedly recognized Demetrius as king.[47] But Roman influence in Near Eastern affairs was out of all proportion to the Roman will to intervene with material or military assistance.

The prestige Rome enjoyed in Palestine is evident in the appeals for Roman alliance made by the Hasmonean princes. Judas' continuing hostility toward Alcimus led Demetrius to dispatch a Syrian expeditionary force from Antioch, headed by the general, Nicanor, to restore order and to compel acquiescence to the new high priest. Nicanor engaged Judas in combat on the 13th of March 161, was defeated and killed,[48] and the day of victory was celebrated annually thereafter in Judaea as Nicanor's Day. In the afterglow of the victory, before Rome could formally recognize Demetrius as king, Judas concluded a pact of friendship with Rome, according to which "the Jewish nation" and Rome promised to support each other in the event of war.[49] The treaty, which in effect recognized Judaea as an independent

---

44. Appian, *Syria* 47.

45. "The world is always half ruled by imagination." E. R. Bevan, *House of Seleucus* (N6), 2, p. 198.

46. Polybius XXXII.10.1–8.

47. Polybius XXXII.3.13; XXXI.33.3.

48. 1 Macc. 7:43.

49. 1 Macc. 8:23-30. On the truth of the report cf. E. R. Bevan, *House of Seleucus* (N6), 2, p. 300 (Appendix L); E. Bickerman, *From Ezra to the Last of the Maccabees* (N27), p. 132ff.

state, did not, however, deter Demetrius from sending Bacchides with an overwhelming force against Judas, and within a few weeks of Nicanor's defeat and death Judas himself lay dead upon the field of battle.

The death of Judas marks a shift in emphasis in the Jewish wars. No longer were they an attempt to restore or preserve Jewish religious practice; that restoration had been accomplished, and proscriptions like those of Antiochus IV were not again introduced in Jerusalem. The new emphasis was on Jewish political independence, the right of Jews to name their high priest and have him accountable to his own people rather than to a foreign power. The conflict continued to center, of course, on the internal Jewish rivalry between the Hellenizers and the purist Hasidim, but that now was part of a nationalist rather than a religious movement.[50] Indeed, it was part of a widespread Near Eastern reaffirmation of indigenous traditions and values and a self-conscious stirring of popular efforts to cast off the oppressive yoke of western domination and exploitation. In this context the possibilities and realities of Roman intervention offered hope of independence to the native-born, a hope that was subsequently stillborn when the consequence of their victory over the Macedonians turned out to be subjection to the Romans.

In Jerusalem, as long as Bacchides commanded the Seleucid troops, Jonathan, Judas' brother and successor, awaited with his followers in the desert hills of Judaea a favorable opportunity to renew the war. The chance came when Alcimus died of a stroke in 160, and Demetrius, without naming a successor to the high priesthood in Jerusalem, recalled Bacchides to Antioch. Jonathan therewith resumed his operations against him. Bacchides once more marched against the Maccabees, was unable to take Jonathan, and concluded that the best hope for political stability was to make peace with him, which he did in 156. Once again, therefore, as in 162, the Maccabees were the acknowledged leaders in Jerusalem, supported by the Seleucids; and Jonathan brought an era of peace to Palestine.[51]

That peaceful interlude in Palestine could not endure amid the turmoil elsewhere in the Near East, which accompanied the decline of the Hellenistic states. In Egypt the Ptolemaic brothers, Philometor and

---

50. Cf. V. Tcherikover, *Hellenistic Civilization* (N6), p. 235. His later observation that "The war of the Hasmoneans against the Greek cities was internally bound up with the foundation of the Jewish state and with its economic development" (p. 247) is apologetic.

51. 1 Macc. 9:73.

Euergetes II, with the mediation of Rome had divided the kingdom between them in 163, Philometor remaining king of Egypt and Cyprus while Euergetes ruled in Cyrenaica (territory fronting the Mediterranean in Northeast Libya) and Libya.[52] Then in 162/1 Euergetes, currying favor with Rome and seeking to outmaneuver his brother, drew up his will, which he published six or seven years later, in which he bequeathed his kingdom to Rome in the event that he should die childless, i. e., through the machinations of Philometor. The latter, however, after Antiochus IV died, turned his attention away from Cyrenaica to Palestine in the hope of reestablishing there the Ptolemaic kingdom of his grandfather. Aided by the dynastic upheavals in Syria as well as by the pro-Ptolemaic sentiments of many in Palestine, he eventually did succeed in being acclaimed king of Asia at Antioch in 145 (cf. below, n. 65).

In Cappadocia, in the civil war between Ariarathes and Orophernes, Eumenes of Pergamum and his son, Attalus, supported Ariarathes against Orophernes, who was allied with Demetrius, and even produced a rival claimant to the Seleucid throne in the person of Alexander Balas. Balas resembled Antiochus IV, whose son he was said to be, and when he demanded the kingdom sometime between 158 and 156, Demetrius found himself fighting a war for survival on two fronts. Demetrius' haughty, demanding nature and his foreign upbringing made him unpopular in Antioch. Polybius reports that "he was much given to drink and was tipsy

---

52. The chief city of Cyrenaica, Cyrene, was well represented throughout the Mediterranean by emigrants, many of them Jews. The Christian New Testament mentions Simon who carried Jesus' cross (Matt. 27:32; Mark 15:21), Lucius in the church at Antioch (Acts 13:1) and others at Antioch (Acts 11:20) as well as some who debated with Stephen (Acts 6:9). There is a tradition that the apostle Mark was a native of Cyrene and that he introduced Christianity into Cyrenaica and Egypt. Jason who wrote a history of the Hasmonean wars during the period 176–160 was from Cyrene; his original five-volume work, written probably between 160 and 152, is abridged in the second book of Maccabees. The celebrated poet, Callimachus, and the geographer, Eratosthenes, who became librarian at Alexandria about 235 B.C., were from Cyrene. The territory was ravaged by the Persians in the seventh century and was in ruins when the Arabs occupied it after A.D. 640. Cf. Alan Rowe, *A History of Ancient Cyrenaica* (Supplement aux Annales du Service des Antiquités de l'Egypte # 12, Cairo, 1948). For the Roman attitude toward Cyrene in the first century B.C., cf. E. Badian, *Roman Imperialism in the Late Republic*, Ithaca, N.Y., 1968, pp. 35ff. and 99ff. On Cyrene as a Hellenistic cultural center, cf. P. M. Fraser, *Ptolemaic Alexandria*, 3 vols., Oxford, 1972, vol. 1, pp. 786–89. Cf. below, Ch. VII, n. 11.

for the greater part of the day,"[53] so that we may conclude the people were ready to accept a new king. No doubt aware of the unrest at Antioch and urged to action by Attalus, Balas appeared in Rome in 153 with Heraclides, the former finance minister of Antiochus IV, who had been ousted from Antioch by Demetrius nine years earlier, to plead restoration of his rightful kingdom. The Senate was favorably impressed with the opportunity for weakening Demetrius,[54] however it may have perceived the legitimacy of Balas' claims,[55] and it gave him authority to go home to regain his father's throne. Balas collected a force in Ephesus and in 152 landed at Ptolemais (modern Acre, south of Tyre ca. 10 miles north of Haifa), where he was hailed as king.[56]

Balas had chosen his port of entry carefully. Safely situated far south of Antioch, it was also easily accessible from Galilee in northern Palestine and thus close to the forces of Ptolemy who was anxious to assist this rival of Demetrius.[57] More than that, however, Ptolemais was within easy reach of the still uncommitted Jonathan and his Maccabean forces, and both Balas and Demetrius recognized the decisive part the Jews could have in the Seleucid contest.

Demetrius apparently reached Jonathan before Alexander Balas did and authorized him as his ally to raise and equip an army, ordering at the same time that the Jewish hostages being held in the citadel of Jerusalem be released. Not to be outdone, Balas offered Jonathan the high priesthood together with the title of King's Friend if he would join him,[58] and he sent Jonathan a purple robe and gold crown as proof of his promise. Jonathan gratefully assumed the high priest's vestments and recruited an armed force[59] but delayed committing his support. Demetrius then attempted to counter Balas' influence by extravagant promises: to reduce taxes, release Jewish prisoners, withdraw the Seleucid garrison from Jerusalem, and allow

---

53. Polybius XXXIII. 19.

54. Polybius XXXI.10.7 "For many decisions of the Romans are now of this kind: availing themselves of the mistakes of others they effectively increase and build up their own power, at the same time doing a favour and appearing to confer a benefit on the offenders."

55. Polybius XXXIII.15; 18.6–13.

56. 1 Macc. 10:1.

57. Appian, *Syria* 67.

58. 1 Macc. 10:2-20.

59. 1 Macc. 10:21.

Jewish troops to follow their own customs, be commanded by Jews, and receive the usual army pay; to subject territories of Samaria to Jonathan's control, devote Ptolemais to support of the temple in Jerusalem and donate an additional fifteen thousand shekels annually from the royal treasury for the same purpose, recognize the Jerusalem temple as an asylum for debtors, and underwrite the cost of repairing the temple, the walls and fortifications of Jerusalem and the fortresses in Judaea![60] But Jonathan realized that for him to support Demetrius would entail an unwanted war with Egypt, and he correctly judged that Demetrius could not withstand the coalition of Balas, Ariarathes, Attalus, Philometor and Rome. He knew that to remain neutral would be to risk the displeasure and reprisal of a victorious Balas, and he therefore gave him his support. Not long thereafter Demetrius fell in battle with Balas in 150, and Alexander Balas became king.

Shortly after his accession to the throne Balas married Ptolemy's daughter, Cleopatra Thea in 150/149, a sign perhaps of Ptolemaic ascendancy in Syria,[61] and one of the honored guests at the wedding in Ptolemais was Jonathan. Balas, in spite of dissatisfaction with Jonathan in Jerusalem, enrolled him among the First Friends of the King and appointed him governor of Judaea. Thereafter "Jonathan returned to Jerusalem well pleased with his success," having achieved within two years the high priesthood of the Jews, the governorship of Judaea,[62] and the highest rank among the Seleucid king's friends. Balas, who was roundly disliked at Antioch, apparently ruled from Ptolemais, for two years later, when he learned that Demetrius, the son of the Demetrius he had overthrown, had arrived in Antioch from Crete to claim the throne, he had to return to Antioch to prevent the takeover.[63]

In the ensuing conflict Jonathan remained loyal to Balas, but Ptolemy, perhaps at the instigation of his scheming daughter, Balas' wife, who had borne Balas a son, Antiochus, believed apparently that the time had come for Egypt to reclaim Coele-Syria.[64] He accordingly joined forces with the younger Demetrius, giving him his daughter, Balas' wife, Cleopatra Thea,

---

60. 1 Macc. 10:29-45; 11:34.
61. 1 Macc. 10:54.
62. *Strategos*, commander, and *Meridarches*, governor.
63. 1 Macc. 10:68.
64. 1 Macc. 11:3,11.

in marriage. The Antiochians acclaimed Ptolemy king;[65] but in the subsequent battle with Balas, Ptolemy was mortally wounded while Balas escaped with his infant son into Arabia. There he was captured, beheaded, and his severed head brought back and exhibited to the dying Ptolemy. "So in the year 145 Demetrius became King."[66]

The young king, then about fourteen years old, was the puppet of Cretan mercenaries whose presence in Antioch the Syrians resented, and he cast about for other support. His wife, Cleopatra, after the death of Philometor, her father, could no longer command the presence of Egyptian forces who now marched at the behest of Euergetes II, her uncle. The young Antiochus, Balas' son, was in the custody of an Arab sheikh, Imalcue,[67] who would be most unlikely to support Demetrius. Demetrius therefore had to hope for assistance from Jonathan. When, then, the Jewish Hellenizers complained that Jonathan was besieging the citadel in Jerusalem, Demetrius responded angrily ordering Jonathan to raise the siege and appear before him in Ptolemais. Jonathan, fully aware of the political forces at play, gave orders to continue the siege, and after collecting some appropriate gifts for Demetrius went to meet him. The result of their meeting was a victory for Jonathan. He received official confirmation of his high position in Judaea, the addition of three districts in Samaria to his lands, and exemption from future tribute to Antioch in exchange for the immediate payment of three hundred talents.[68] Jonathan probably agreed in addition to lift the siege at Jerusalem.

The opportunistic Jonathan, however, was less concerned with propping up a Seleucid dynasty than with making Judaea an independent principality. When, therefore, Diodotus Tryphon, a former general of Balas, revolted against Demetrius and produced Balas' young son, Antiochus, as the rightful heir to the Seleucid throne, Jonathan supported him, claiming that Demetrius had broken his promise to remove the Seleucid garrison from the citadel in Jerusalem.[69] Following the precedent of his brother, Judas, Jonathan also sent envoys to Rome "to confirm and renew

---

65. Cf. Polybius XXXIX.7.
66. 1 Macc. 11:19.
67. 1 Macc. 11:39. Josephus, *Antiquities* XIII.V.1 (131), calls him Malchus; E. R. Bevan, *House of Seleucus* (N7), 2, p. 220, "Yamlik."
68. 1 Macc. 11:20-37.
69. 1 Macc. 11:42-43.

the treaty of friendship."[70] Demetrius marched against Jonathan unsuccessfully, but Tryphon, realizing that Jonathan's support could not be counted on, managed to lure him together with a small force into Ptolemais, where he massacred his troops and imprisoned Jonathan,[71] intending no doubt to bargain with the Jews for his freedom. When, however, leadership in Judaea passed smoothly to Jonathan's brother, Simon, Tryphon had Jonathan executed in 143.[72] Shortly thereafter he also killed the young Antiochus VI and had himself declared king at Antioch.[73]

Power in Syria was thus divided between Tryphon, who ruled generally in the Orontes valley, and Demetrius II Nicator, who was recognized in territories along the coast. Following Jonathan's death, Simon sent envoys to negotiate peace with Demetrius. The result of that parley was a declaration of Jewish independence, and the year 142 B.C. became year one of the Hasmonean era.[74] The next year, when the citadel in Jerusalem capitulated to Simon, Jewish independence was deemed to be complete, in spite of the divided and disputed sovereignty of Demetrius in Syria. Demetrius thereupon looked eastward to his supporters in Mesopotamia and Babylonia, who were calling for his help against the Parthian king, Mithridates.[75] It is possible that the families of both Timarchus and Heraclides (see above, p. 114) were in Media, where they found opposition to Tryphon a means of inducing Demetrius to aid them against Mithridates.[76] Accepting their call, Demetrius set out from Syria in 140, leaving Cleopatra behind to engage in plots against Tryphon, her former husband and murderer of her child.[77] On his successful march through Mesopotamia and Babylonia Demetrius was everywhere acclaimed, but in Media the next year his army was defeated and he was taken captive. The defeat of the Seleucid king in 139 gave Mithridates and the Parthians control of Media and Babylonia.

Demetrius' younger brother, Antiochus Sidetes, so-named because he

---

70. 1 Macc. 12:1.

71. 1 Macc. 12:39-48.

72. 1 Macc. 13:12-24.

73. E. R. Bevan, *House of Seleucus* (N7), 2, p. 230, n. 4; E. Schürer, *A History of the Jewish People* (N3), 1, pp. 176–77.

74. 1 Macc. 13:34-41.

75. Josephus, *Antiquities* XIII.V.11(184–86).

76. A. V. Gutschmid, *Geschichte Irans*, Tübingen, 1888, p. 51f. But cf. E. R. Bevan, *House of Seleucus* (N7), 1, Appendix S.

77. Josephus, *Antiquities* XIII.VII.1(222). Appian, *Syria* 68.

had grown up in the Pamphylian seaport of Side, was living in Rhodes when Cleopatra notified him of his brother's capture and invited him to become her third husband and claim the throne.[78] He accepted by sailing to Seleucia in 138, where he was acclaimed king by the soldiers who rallied in large numbers to his side.[79] Seeking the support of Jerusalem against Tryphon, Antiochus confirmed his brother's earlier declaration of Jewish independence,[80] in addition, perhaps, permitting Jews the right to coin their own silver money; and he gave his attention to defeating Tryphon. In his attempt to regulate affairs in Palestine, however, Antiochus sharply questioned Simon's retention of the cities he had taken, Jaffa, Gezer and the citadel in Jerusalem, and he demanded either their return or their purchase for five hundred talents of silver with an additional five hundred talents in reparations.[81] Failure to heed the demand would mean war.

Simon, claiming ancestral Jewish rights to the captured territory, offered one hundred talents for the troublesome cities, Jaffa and Gezer.[82] The infuriated Antiochus thereupon ordered his governor in Palestine, Kendebaeus, to make war on the Jews while he himself continued his pursuit of Tryphon, whom he finally captured near Apamea in the Orontes valley and forced to commit suicide.[83] Kendebaeus established his headquarters in Jamnia, about 10 miles south of Jaffa, but in a decisive engagement with Simon's sons, John and Judas, he and his army were routed, and John returned victorious to Jerusalem.[84]

Sometime thereafter, in February 135,[85] a certain Ptolemy, son of Abubus, who had married Simon's daughter in an effort to secure for himself supreme power, murdered his aged father-in-law, last survivor of Mattathias' five sons, together with two of Simon's sons. Ptolemy apparently hoped for the support of Antiochus, to whom he sent word of his coup,[86] but his scheme was frustrated by the timely measures of Simon's son, John Hyrcanus, who, when he learned of his father's death, raced from where he was

78. Josephus, *Antiquities* XIII.VII.1(222).
79. 1 Macc. 15:10.
80. 1 Macc. 5:3-9.
81. 1 Macc. 14:5-7; 15:28-31.
82. 1 Macc. 15:33-35.
83. Strabo XIV.5.2(C668).
84. 1 Macc. 16:4-10.
85. 1 Macc. 16:14; E. R. Bevan, *House of Seleucus* (N7), 2, p. 239; E. Schürer, *A History of the Jewish People* (N3), 1, p. 272, n. 1.
86. 1 Macc. 16:18.

in Gezer to Jerusalem ahead of Ptolemy and succeeded to the high priesthood in place of his father. Secure in this office, Hyrcanus then besieged Ptolemy in his fortress near Jericho but gave up his effort for the sake of his mother, whom Ptolemy exhibited atop the wall and threatened to kill unless Hyrcanus retired. Ptolemy had the lady killed nonetheless, and thereafter he fled to Philadelphia (modern Amman) where he vanished from history.[87]

Antiochus, however, now seriously undertook to enforce the demands he had made on Simon and besieged Hyrcanus in Jerusalem for more than a year. Hyrcanus, after Antiochus generously granted the city a seven-day truce for its celebration of the Feast of Booths (Sukkoth), sued for terms, and Antiochus lifted the siege. In return, the besieged surrendered their weapons, agreed to pay tribute for Jaffa, Gezer and the other towns Simon had taken, and in exchange for freedom from a Syrian garrison in Jerusalem paid an additional five hundred talents of silver and gave hostages, including a brother of Hyrcanus. For good measure before he returned home, Antiochus destroyed the strong defensive wall the Jews had erected around the city. Having thus subdued Judaea, Antiochus spent the following three years consolidating his strength in Syria in anticipation of his forthcoming campaign in the eastern provinces of his kingdom.

In 130 he set out for the East at the command of a large army, accompanied by members of the royal family including Demetrius' daughter and son, Seleucus,[88] and a Jewish contingent commanded by John

---

87. Josephus, *Antiquities* XIII.8.1(235).

88. The father of Seleucus is not certainly known. Appian (*Syria* 68) states explicitly that Cleopatra bore Demetrius two sons: Seleucus and Antiochus Grypus; she bore Antiochus one son: Antiochus Cyzicenus. Porphyry, as represented in Eusebius' Chronicle, (*Eusebius Werke*, Josef Karst, ed., vol. 5, Leipzig, 1911, p. 121), tells us that Antiochus had five children, two sons and three daughters, and that he died in 129 in his thirty-fifth year and the ninth year of his reign, his son Seleucus then becoming a prisoner of Phraates. Appian's account seems the more likely to be accurate, especially since Antiochus could scarcely have been twenty-six at the time of his accession to the throne (E. R. Bevan, *House of Seleucus* [N7], 2, Appendix R). The Seleucus mentioned by Posidonius (Jacoby, II B, pp. 1217–18, fr. 32.19) is assumed to be Antiochus' son (E. R. Bevan, 2, p. 245, n. 3; N. C. Debevoise, *A Political History of Parthia*, Chicago, 1938, p. 34, n. 25), but his identity is uncertain. Appian reports (*Syria* 69) that Seleucus assumed the diadem after the death of his father, Demetrius, but he does not report any of the royal family as having accompanied Antiochus on his eastern expedition. If Antiochus took Demetrius' daughter with him on his eastern campaign (Justin XXXVIII.10.9–10), would he have deliberately left behind her older brother? On the other hand, Phraates might well have released Seleucus when he regretted his release of Demetrius, whom he was then unable to recapture; or Seleucus might have

Hyrcanus himself.[89] His intention was no doubt to reconstitute the empire of his great grandfather, Antiochus III,[90] establishing Demetrius, perhaps, as governor in Babylon. But he could not be sure that Demetrius, who had married the Parthian king's (Phraates) sister[91] and become the father of several children, would accept the proposal. Demetrius was unhappy in Hyrcania and had made at least two unsuccessful attempts to escape to Syria. His attitude and intentions were thus a primary consideration in the hopes and plans of both Phraates[92] and Antiochus, each of whom had designs on the other's territory, which included an appropriate manipulation of Demetrius.[93]

Antiochus rallied to his cause those in Babylonia who were dissatisfied with Parthian rule and subdued that satrapy with relative ease before the onset of winter. In quartering his troops, however, he mistreated the villages in Media so that they turned against him.[94] In the spring of 129 Phraates sought terms of peace, but Antiochus demanded total surrender, i.e., withdrawal of Parthian forces to Parthia proper from the satrapies Phraates and his father Mithridates had seized, together with the payment of appropriate tribute to Antioch and the release of Demetrius. Phraates, properly outraged, did release Demetrius, sending him with an armed Parthian escort to reclaim his throne in Syria.[95] He then launched a surprise attack against the Syrians, before which Antiochus fell and his troops fled.[96] That defeat marked the last serious Seleucid attempt to reconquer the East. Phraates now regretted that he had sent Demetrius home, but an uprising of the eastern Sacas that same year prevented his marching on Syria. In his campaign against the Sacas, Phraates compelled the remnants of Antiochus' army to accompany him, but they joined the Sacas, when the latter began to

---

escaped after Phraates' death. Our confusing sources reflect the turbulence and uncertainties of this period in Syrian history.

89. Josephus, *Antiquities* XIII.8.4 (251–52).

90. Justin XXXVIII.10.6.

91. Appian, *Syria* 67.

92. Justin XXXVIII.9.10.

93. See the literature cited by N. C. Debevoise, *A Political History of Parthia* (N88), pp. 30–32.

94. Diodorus XXXIV.17.2.

95. Appian, *Syria* 68; Justin XXXVIII.10.7.

96. The spring of the year 128. Cf. Diodorus XXXIV.15.

prevail in the fighting, and contributed to their victory and Phraates' death in 128.[97]

That victory saved Syria temporarily from Parthian invasion and gave Demetrius the opportunity to rule. But he was disliked in Syria and was foolhardy enough to plan war against Egypt at the urging of his former mother-in-law, Cleopatra II, sister and wife of Ptolemy Euergetes, who sought for herself the supreme command of Egypt.[98] To counter that threat, Euergetes found in 129/8 an Egyptian to claim the Syrian throne on the pretext of being an adopted son of the popular Antiochus Sidetes. Naming him Alexander,[99] Euergetes had him escorted to Antioch. There the Syrians, "refusing no man for their king, if they might but be freed from the insolence of Demetrius," acclaimed him king;[100] but they nicknamed him Zabinas, "the bought one."[101] In his decisive battle against Demetrius, Zabinas routed the latter's army, forcing Demetrius to flee. He fled to Ptolemais, where on orders of his former wife, Cleopatra Thea, he was barred from the city. Taking sail to Tyre, where he hoped to take refuge in the temple, he was killed by an assassin as he stepped off the ship in 126/5.[102]

Thereafter the Seleucid state succumbed to internal dynastic strife increased and embittered by Seleucid and Ptolemaic intermarriage, which involved each dynasty in the domestic feuds of the other. The elder of Cleopatra's sons by Demetrius, Seleucus V, reigned briefly only to be replaced by his brother, Antiochus VIII Grypos (hooknosed?), when Seleucus refused to be his mother's puppet. Euergetes gave his daughter by Cleopatra III, Tryphaena ("the magnificent"), to Antiochus in marriage and helped him establish himself over Zabinas, who suffered decisive defeat in 123 and ended his life with poison.[103] When Grypos then also sought to escape maternal direction, Cleopatra offered him a cup of poison which he,

97. Justin XLII.1; N. C. Debevoise, A Political History of Parthia (N88), p. 37.

98. Cleopatra was previously the wife of Euergetes' older brother, Philometor, to whom she had borne Cleopatra Thea, Demetrius' wife.

99. According to Porphyry in Eusebius, Chronicle (N88), he was a pretended son of Balas.

100. Justin XXXIX.1.

101. Diodorus XXXIV.22.

102. Justin XXXIX.1.

103. Diodorus XXXIV/XXV.28. Eusebius, Chronicle (N88), p. 122.

forewarned, forced her to drink herself in 121/20.[104] He ruled thereafter four years before his half-brother, Antiochus IX Cyzicenus (from Cyzicus, where he had been educated), son of Sidetes, made war against him (ca. 116 B.C.) and forced a division in Syria: Grypos in the north and Cyzicenus in Palestine and Phoenicia. That division, which was effected about 112, left the Jews virtually independent in Palestine, since Cyzicenus shortly after gaining the throne "lapsed into drunken habits, crass self-indulgence, and pursuits utterly inappropriate to a king."[105]

The last years of Seleucid independence, before Pompey's "settlement" in 64, were filled with insurrections, competing claimants to the throne and political chaos, as the central districts of Seleucid power followed the outlying districts in reverting to native control. Pontus had come under the control of Mithridates, Armenia under that of Tigranes, Mesopotamia that of the Parthian Mithridates, and Palestine that of the Jews and Nabataeans, while Syria was divided among three members of the royal house. So disrupted and disordered was the central government that its takeover by the Armenians in 83 came as relief, and the last Seleucid kings even appealed to Rome to be enthroned in Egypt, the land of their mother Selene (see below, p. 129), no doubt to escape the physical dangers and political disarray in Antioch and Syria.[106] When Selene herself met her death at Seleucia on the Euphrates at the hand of Tigranes in 69, the Seleucid vision of one world vanished with her.

SUGGESTIONS FOR FURTHER STUDY:

M. Avi-Yonah, *The Jews of Palestine* (New York, 1976); W. Stewart McCollough, *The History and Literature of the Palestine Jews from Cyrus to Herod, 550 B.C.–4 B.C.* (Toronto and Buffalo, 1976); George F. Moore, *Judaism in the First Centuries of the Christian Era*, 3 vols. (Cambridge, Mass., 1927–30); M. Rostovtzeff, *Social and Economic History of the Hellenistic World*, 3 vols. (Oxford, 1941).

---

104. Justin XXXIX.2.
105. Diodorus XXXIV/XXXV.34.
106. Josephus, *Antiquities* XIII.13.4; 14:3; 15.1(365–71; 384–86; 387–91). Appian, *Syria* 69.

VII

THE END OF THE HELLENISTIC STATES

The collapse of the Ptolemaic kingdom followed within a century that of the Seleucid. The history of Egypt in the second half of the second century is that of Euergetes II, known as the younger Ptolemy, and his wives, Cleopatra II and III. His mother, Cleopatra I Thea, was a daughter of Antiochus III, and Antiochus IV Epiphanes was thus his uncle. He married not only his sister, Cleopatra II Cocce in 144, but also in 142 her daughter by his older brother Philometor, Cleopatra III Euergetis. The introduction through Antiochus' daughter of Seleucid blood into the Ptolemaic house gave Egypt more than a century of powerful and domineering queens, who far excelled their insignificant husbands. These women seem to have been the driving forces for stability and order in the declining Ptolemaic state.

When in 163 Egypt was divided between Philometor and Euergetes II, Philometor became a contender for Palestine; and the death of Antiochus IV Epiphanes early that same year offered him the chance to renew Egyptian efforts to claim Coele-Syria. Ptolemaic partisans in Syria, as we have seen, welcomed Philometor at Antioch in 145; but when he died before September of that same year, and his son shortly thereafter, Euergetes found himself in command of all Egypt yet unable to pursue his brother's initiative in Syria. For by this time the native Egyptians, long resentful of their Macedonian and Greek overlords and overconfident in their own powers to effect changes in the government, were increasingly demanding expulsion of the foreigner and provoking civil wars.

Consequently, Euergetes' long reign (145–116) was torn by dynastic dispute that encouraged public partisanship, popular uprising, and left Egypt exhausted. Dubbed Kakergetes ("Evildoer") by his contemporaries,

Euergetes has been judged "the wickedest of all the Ptolemies."[1] That judgment is probably too harsh, just as the counter-suggestion that he dreamed of constructing a "national Graeco-Egyptian monarchy"[2] is too grand. Euergetes appears to have been politically astute, but he invited the opprobrium heaped upon him by the Greek intellectuals when he expelled them from the country for openly objecting to his policies. Their expulsion brought cultural life in Alexandria to its nadir.[3]

Euergetes seems also to have used excessive military measures in his determination to suppress unrest in the land. Polybius reports that the king, "being frequently troubled by seditions, exposed the populace to the onslaught of the soldiers and destroyed them."[4] His grisly murder of his son Memphites, whose dismembered corpse he presented to Cleopatra II, the boy's mother, on the eve of her birthday in December 131, reveals the lengths to which he would go for revenge and political ends.[5] His obesity became proverbial, earning him the sobriquet, Physkon ("stuffed gut").[6]

The first years of Euergetes' reign were certainly scandalous enough to arouse the hatred of his subjects, but his later years were relatively free from dynastic strife, resulting no doubt from his more orderly conduct of affairs in the kingdom, as he sought to satisfy the insistent expectations of his competing and vituperative wives, Cleopatra II and III, who bore a deadly hatred toward each other. The revolt of his wife, Cleopatra II, which forced him to flee to Cyprus in 131 and led him to ship home from there the dismembered corpse of her son, Memphites, ended in his armed return to

---

1. E. R. Bevan, *A History of Egypt under the Ptolemaic Dynasty*, London, 1927, p. 325.

2. W. W. Tarn and G. T. Griffith, *Hellenistic Civilization*, 3rd ed., London, 1952, pp. 205–06.

3. Cf. P. M. Fraser, *Ptolemaic Alexandria*, 3 vols., Oxford, 1972: 1, p. 86ff.

4. Polybius XXXIV.14.7.

5. Diodorus XXXIV/XXXV.14; Justin XXXVIII.8.13–15.

6. Plutarch, Moralia 200 F, reports that Scipio Aemilianus Africanus (185–129 B.C.) "was sent out by the Senate . . . as an inspector of cities, peoples, and kings; and when he arrived at Alexandria and, after disembarking, was walking with his toga covering his head . . . he uncovered amid shouting applause. The king (Euergetes) could hardly keep up with them in walking because of his inactive life and his pampering of his body, and Scipio whispered softly to Panaetius, 'already the Alexandrians have received some benefit from our visit. For it is owing to us that they have seen their king walk.'" Scipio's visit probably took place in 140/39. Cf. Justin XXXVIII.8; Athenaeus, *The Deipnosophists* XII 549e.

Egypt and the annihilation of Cleopatra's army. Euergetes was said thenceforth to have had a change of heart and to seek remedy by acts of kindness for the hatred people bore him.[7]

Cleopatra's lust for power, however, drove her to that scheme for a Seleucid takeover of Egypt which in turn led to her flight to Syria and ended in the defeat and death of Demetrius II. When in 124 Cleopatra returned to Egypt, she and her brother-husband were ostensibly reconciled, no doubt restrained from attempting to murder each other by powerful Egyptian factions and Roman influence. When Euergetes died on June 28, 116, Cleopatra probably survived him and may have lived another six to eight months before she fell victim to the fierce hatred of her daughter and rival for the throne, Cleopatra III Euergetis.[8]

These intertwined Seleucid and Ptolemaic dynastic feuds form a complicated and dreary conclusion to Seleucid and Ptolemaic history. After Euergetes' death, Cleopatra III of Egypt had to name one of her sons to the throne. She preferred the younger, Ptolemy X Alexander, but the Alexandrians forced her to associate the elder, Ptolemy IX Soter (Lathyros, "Chick-pea"), who was then governor in Cyprus, in rule with herself. Soter accordingly returned to Alexandria and married his sister, Cleopatra IV, while his younger brother went as governor to Cyprus. The mother, however, detecting hostility toward herself in her daughter, Soter's wife, forced Soter to divorce her and to marry her younger sister, Cleopatra V Selene ("the moon"). Thereupon Cleopatra IV went to Cyprus, raised an army, and sailed to Syria, where she gave her hand in marriage to Antiochus IX Cyzicenus, to whom she brought "as a dowry the army of Antiochus Grypos which she had induced to desert."[9] The war between the Seleucid half-brothers, Grypos and Cyzicenus, now became also the death struggle between the Ptolemaic sisters, Tryphaena and Cleopatra IV, both of whom were murdered between 112 and 111.

In 108/7 Ptolemy Soter fled to Cyprus to escape the machinations of his mother. In Egypt he left his wife, Selene, and her two sons; and Ptolemy Alexander forthwith returned from Cyprus to share the rule in Egypt.

---

7. Diodorus XXXIV/XXXV.20.
8. W. Otto and H. Bengtson, *Zur Geschichte des Niederganges des Ptolemaerreiches* (Abh. bayer. Akad., N.F. 17, 1938), pp. 125–36. The evidence for the last days of Cleopatra II is circumstantial and its interpretation controversial. Cf. Fraser (N3), 2, p. 218, n. 250.
9. Justin XXXIX.3.

Cleopatra Euergetis and Soter then vied for Syrian and Palestinian political support against each other—Soter appealing to Cyzicenus and Cleopatra III to Grypus who became Selene's husband. The alliances accomplished nothing of consequence, and in 102 the Ptolemaic forces returned home from Palestine whence they had marched in support of the Jewish Alexander Jannaeus. Cleopatra III died the next year, perhaps at the hand of her son, Alexander,[10] Grypus died five years later, and Cyzicenus who married Grypus' widow, Selene, met his death the next year (95) in battle with Grypus' son, Seleucus VI Epiphanes Nicator. In 98 Ptolemy Apion, a son of Euergetes II, had died having willed his kingdom of Cyrenaica to Rome; and twenty-two years later Rome would create a province of Cyrenaica, valuable because of its strategic location five hundred miles from Egypt on the sea and also because of its monopoly in the production of silphium "a wild plant . . . refractory to civilization," which was "used as a condiment and as a remedy for every kind of ailment," perhaps also as an aphrodisiac.[11]

Ptolemy Alexander, who was heartily disliked in Alexandria, especially after his mother's murder, died in 88, and his older brother, Soter, once more returned to Alexandria as king. His later reign was beset with native uprisings, the precise causes of which remain unclear. Nevertheless, his rebuilding of temples at Denderah, Karnak and Edfu reveals the considerable financial resources of the Egyptian economy. Soter's foreign policy was one of watchful waiting until the future of Rome, which was at that time torn by the Italian wars of Marius, Sulla and Lucullus at home and the bloody conflict with Mithridates VI in Asia Minor, would become clear.

When Soter died in 80, his daughter, Berenice III, widow of his brother, Alexander, who had been associated with her father on the throne ever since his return to Alexandria from Cyprus eight years earlier, became queen. But Alexander, a son of her former husband by another wife, had grown up in Pontus and gone with Sulla to Rome. Sulla therefore, in an effort to dominate Egypt, dispatched him, as the sole surviving male heir to the Ptolemaic throne, to Egypt, where he married Berenice. Unwilling,

---

10. Justin XXXIX.4–5.

11. Charles H. Coster, *Late Roman Studies*, Cambridge, Mass., 1968, Ch. V, "The Economic Position of Cyrenaica in Classical Times," reprinted from *Studies in Roman and Social History in Honor of Allan Chester Johnson*, P. R. Coleman-Norton, ed., Princeton, 1951, pp. 115–16.

however, to share rule with a powerful and popular wife, Alexander had her murdered, a deed for which he paid with his own life at the hands of an Alexandrian mob.

The death of Egypt's last legitimate heir seemed to support the claim of Selene's sons, Antiochus XII (Asiaticus) and his younger brother (whose name is not known), to the Ptolemaic throne; but the Alexandrians in nationalistic spirit produced two sons of Soter by a concubine, whom they installed in Cyprus and Alexandria as rulers. The king in Alexandria, Ptolemy XII, they called Nothos ("the bastard"), but he became known as Auletes because of his pride in playing the flute. [12] His troubled reign, during which he sought acceptance by the Alexandrians who hated him because he assiduously tried to bribe Rome into recognizing his royal position, finally ended when he died in 51, on the eve of Rome's last convulsive upheaval before the establishment of stable rule under Octavius Caesar. [13]

The protracted and bloody disintegration of the governments in Syria and Egypt had earlier inflamed the ambitions of John Hyrcanus in Palestine for a restoration of the ancient, Davidic kingdom of Israel, a goal in pursuit of which he did not scruple to employ foreign mercenaries. [14] The death of Antiochus Sidetes, whom Hyrcanus had accompanied at the head of a Jewish contingent against the Parthians, in the spring of 128, seemed to foreclose any possibility of Seleucid conquest in Palestine. How or when Hyrcanus returned to Jerusalem from Media is not known, though he obviously escaped the disaster of Antiochus' defeat. Upon his return, however, he embarked on a campaign of conquests that led him eastward across the Jordan, where he captured the ancient city of Madeba, northward against the Samaritans at Shechem, whom he defeated and whose temple he destroyed, and southward against the Idumeans (Edomites, southeast of the Dead Sea), whom he forcibly converted to Judaism for reasons that are unkown. [15] As for the Seleucids, "he no longer paid them the least regard, either as their subject or their friend," [16] and late in his reign [17] he suc-

---

12. Strabo XVII.I.11 C 796.
13. Dio Cassius XXXIX.12–16. Cf. P. M. Fraser (N3), 1, pp. 124–26.
14. Josephus, *Antiquities* XIII.8.4 (249).
15. Josephus *Antiquities* XIII.9.1 (257–58); XV.7.9 (254).
16. Josephus *Antiquities* XIII.10.1 (273).
17. E. Schürer, *A History of the Jewish People in the Time of Jesus Christ*, 3 vols., Edinburgh, 1924: 1, p. 283, n. 22.

cessfully besieged Samaria and "demolished it entirely,"[18] taking the strate-gically located Scythopolis in the process. At his death in 105/4, after what had been generally considered to be a happy life and successful rule, he left the kingdom to his widow instead of one of his five sons.[19]

But the oldest son, Aristobulus, managed to seize control of the government and declare himself king, jailing in the process three of his brothers along with his mother and letting her starve to death in prison. He also permitted himself to be tricked by jealous men at court into killing his favorite brother, Antigonus, remorse for which may have contributed to his own death after a year's rule. Said to be a lover of Greeks and a man of candor and modesty, he extended the conquests of his father in Galilee, where, as his father had done in Edom, he forced the inhabitants, Ituraeans,[20] to become Jews.

After Aristobulus died, his widow, Salome Alexandra, released his three brothers from prison and took as husband the oldest, Alexander Jannaeus. He had been brought up in Galilee, out of sight of his father, Hyrcanus, who hated (feared?) him, and that fact has been cited to account for Jannaeus' cruel behavior and profligate life.[21] Certainly, however one accounts for his cruelty, Jannaeus exploited the opportunity presented by the dying Ptolemaic and Seleucid states, before the Roman legions had come to Syria, to enlarge the Jewish state to its greatest extent since the time of David nine centuries earlier. He captured all the coastal cities between the Egyptian border and Mt. Carmel, except for Ascalon which maintained its independence; and east of the Jordan he subjected to his rule the Greek cities, except Philadelphia (modern Amman), that Pompey would later take from Jerusalem and reorganize along with Scythopolis into a federation known as the Decapolis. Like his father Hyrcanus, Jannaeus employed Greek mercenaries for his conquests, but unlike his father he did not scruple to use them against his own people when they rebelled against him.[22] His cruelty, including the crucifixion in his presence of eight

18. Josephus *Antiquities* XIII.10.3 (281).
19. Josephus *Antiquities* XIII.10.7; 11.1 (299–300; 302), "Hyrcanus had left her to be mistress of all" (302).
20. Ituraea in northern Galilee seems to have extended northward into the Beqa' valley of Antilebanon. The inhabitants were called variously Syrians and Arabs.
21. S. Zeitlin, *History of the Second Jewish Commonwealth*, Philadelphia, 1962, p. 321.
22. Josephus *Antiquities* XIII.13.5 (372–74).

hundred men whose wives and children he slaughtered before their eyes as they died, struck such terror into his subjects that eight thousand are said to have left the land to escape his hand.[23]

The military activities of Jannaeus affected not only Seleucids and Ptolemies but also the Arabs, especially those south of the Dead Sea, the Nabataeans, whose capital city was Petra. The Nabataeans began to acquire enormous wealth, when, at the beginning of the second century B.C., the Seleucid conquest of Palestine deprived Egypt of the incense trade from Arabia and made it a Nabataean monopoly. That monopoly established Petra as the hub for the exchange and transport of wares that came overland from Arabia or by ship from the Red Sea and the Gulf of Aqaba. Those wares, mostly spices, were shipped from the vicinity of modern Aqaba by caravan: to Egypt by way of Rhinocolura (modern El Arish), to Palestine, to Syria *via* Philadelphia and Damascus, to Mesopotamia via Damascus and Palmyra, and to Greece and Italy through the port cities Gaza and Ascalon. The expansion of the Hasmonean state east of the Dead Sea and at Gaza, which Jannaeus captured in 96, thus threatened to sever this trade network; and inevitably the Nabataean king, Obodas 9 (ca. 96–87), and Jannaeus came to blows. Obodas was successful in recapturing his way stations in the Negev and in restoring his trade route to the coast,[24] and henceforward Hasmonean politics were to be fatefully intertwined with those of their southern neighbors and competitors, the Idumeans and Nabataeans. Meanwhile the power of Rome came ever nearer. In 133 Rome received the bequest of Pergamum, in 102 established military and naval bases in Cilicia, in 96 received the bequest of Cyrenaica, and in 85 negotiated a peace treaty with king Mithridates VI Eupator of Pontus.

Jannaeus, who in spite of the terrors and intrigues of his reign must be reckoned a man of unusual ability and vision, was unable, following the Jewish tradition about Israel as God's holy people, to chart a political course through the crosscurrents of Hellenistic ideas about the human state and form of government in Palestine that would satisfy a majority of Jews. "A Jewish High Priest could not be a Hellenistic king, and the two conceptions had to be separated."[25] The Jewish state had indeed become a Hellenistic

---

23. Josephus *Antiquities* XIII.14.2 (380–81).

24. Cf. Manfred Lindner, *Petra und das Königreich der Nabatäer*, Munich, 1970, pp. 88–90. Cf. M. Rostovtzeff, *Caravan Cities*, Oxford, 1932.

25. V. Tcherikover, *Hellenistic Civilization and the Jews*, Philadelphia, 1966, p. 265.

state like all others and appeared to many Jews to be losing its central purpose as God's people in the world. Jannaeus struck coins with bilingual inscriptions in Hebrew and Greek; Greek names, games, baths and procedures were commonplace; and Greek ways of thought permeated Palestine. The growing conflict within Jerusalem between the politicians and the pious had first broken out during the reign of Hyrcanus, when a group of scholars known as Pharisees (separatists), openly opposed the Hasmonean government,[26] and Jannaeus was to spend the greater part of his reign combating them. Only in his last years did he begin to seek an accommodation, when the movement had received large popular support; and he recommended to Salome that she should be reconciled with them. After his death in 76, his widow did come to terms with the Pharisees, and their voice in the counsels of government began thereafter to prevail.[27]

The Pharisaic movement represented the struggle of Judaism against accommodation to Hellenism. The Pharisees insisted on the centrality of revealed religion against any enthronement of Greek humanism, but they also recognized the power of Hellenic *paideia* ("education") in the understanding and preserving of truth; and they firmly believed that the distillation of religious tradition was a preventive against infringing the revealed commands of God. They considered the best security against sinning to be a thorough knowledge of the Torah and tried, accordingly, to "make a fence for the Torah" to keep the unwary from approaching the precipice of disobedience. They succeeded finally in imposing upon their religion both a studious respect for tradition and a legal framework for living, both of which persist to varying degrees in modern Judaism, Christianity and Islam. That enlightened legalism is less to be scorned than respected, however alien and ridiculous to modern thought it may seem, for it takes seriously the demands of religious observance and holiness and reckons soberly with the problems of knowing truth.

In this respect Pharisaism was superior to its rival Sadduceeism, which insisted that "only what is written (in the Torah) is authoritative." That

---

26. Josephus *Antiquities*XIII.10.5–6 (288–98).

27. Cf. E. Schürer, *A History of the Jewish People in the Time of Jesus Christ* (N17), div. 2, vol. 2, pp. 1–28; V. Tcherikover, *Hellenistic Civilization and the Jews* (N25), pp. 253–65; 491, n. 27; E. Bickerman, *From Ezra to the Last of the Maccabees*, New York, 1962, pp. 153–65.

comfortable doctrine limits religion to a well described "routine of conventional decencies,"[28] and it was in fact the persuasion of the upper classes in Jewish Palestine. Within their recognized religious limits, however, the Sadducees were strict and far more severe in penal legislation than the Pharisees,[29] for they thought that men bring about their own adversity or prosperity and are not objects of any supernatural determinism. One sees in them the upstanding aristocrats for whom religion is a solace and pastime, the leaders of long-established and well-organized religious communities. Both groups, Pharisees and Sadducees, disappeared with the Jewish state in the first Christian century, but their basic religious outlooks are as prevalent today as they ever were.

Salome Alexandra, at Jannaeus' death, became the 64-year-old regent of a state in which the Pharisees assumed authority and lived as lords.[30] She ruled nine years, during which the Pharisees took revenge on their enemies, while her older, less active son Hyrcanus II officiated as high priest, and her younger, ambitious son Aristobulus II gradually gained the support of the Sadducees and strategic control of the country. When she died in 67 war erupted between Hyrcanus, who claimed the right of the firstborn to rule, and Aristobulus, who with the strong support of the Sadducean nobility now had possession of the strongest fortifications in the state. The results of that civil war were to be Roman military intervention for the first time in Palestine and the spectacular rise to power of the Idumaean, Antipater.

Hyrcanus at first reached a compromise with his brother, according to which he abdicated the throne and high priesthood and retired as a private man to enjoy his estate.[31] But now Antipater, the ambitious governor of Idumaea, who suspected Aristobulus of hostility against him, determined to use the weak and gullible Hyrcanus as a pawn in his own schemes for power. He persuaded Hyrcanus that he should flee from Aristobulus, who had designs on his life, to the Nabataean king, Aretas, at Petra. His argument was that Hyrcanus, the older of the two brothers, was obligated to rule Judaea and therefore, whether he wished it or not, embodied a constant challenge to his brother's tenure in office. The argument finally persuaded

---

28. E. R. Bevan, *Jerusalem Under the High Priests*, London, 1904, p. 125.

29. Josephus *Antiquities* XX.9.1 (199), "The Sadducees are very rigid in judging offenders above all the rest of the Jews." Cf. XIII.10.6 (297–98).

30. Josephus *Antiquities* XIII.16.2 (409).

31. Josephus *Antiquities* XIV.1.2 (6).

the reluctant Hyrcanus of his brother's evil intentions against him, and, after receiving assurance from Aretas that he would indeed be secure in Petra, Hyrcanus journeyed thither accompanied by Antipater. The Idumaean then persuaded Aretas that he should restore Hyrcanus to his throne, in exchange for which Hyrcanus would return to Aretas twelve cities east of the Jordan valley and in the Negev that his father, Jannaeus, had taken from the Nabataeans.[32]

These agreements having been reached, Aretas accordingly marched against Aristobulus and defeated him, forcing him to take refuge with the priests in the temple at Jerusalem, where he was besieged. By this time, however, the Romans had reached Syria, whither they had been drawn by war first with Pontus and then with Armenia, and a new era was about to open in Near Eastern history (cf. below, pp. 151ff.). In 64 the Roman senate confirmed Pompey's arrangements making Syria a province, therewith bringing the hopelessly divided Seleucid state mercifully to its formal end and depriving the Nabataean king of Damascus.[33] Inevitably the appeals of Hyrcanus and Aristobulus to the Roman imperialist, Pompey,[34] that he arbitrate their claims to rule, brought an end to Jewish independence as well; and the Hellenistic era in Near Eastern history was left gasping its last breath in Egypt. Pompey brought to Syria a conception of *pax Romana* and a plan for rule according to Roman legal practice that substituted a Roman attempt at government for the aggressive and exploitative policies of the Macedonian overlords. He also provided an easy entrance for the caravan

---

32. Josephus *Antiquities* XIV.1.4 (14–18).

33. M. Gelzer in *Pompeius*, 2nd ed., Munich, 1959, p. 97ff., shows that Pompey imitated Alexander the Great in founding cities in Asia, facing the Roman senate with a series of *faits accomplis* and following "the grand policy of the first Seleucids in founding cities and Hellenizing the land." Cf. Stefan Weinstock, *Divus Julius*, Oxford, 1971, p. 37, n. 1, who cites the evidence that "Pompey's dream was to become a second Alexander." Pompey left his pro-quaestor in Syria with two legions while he returned through Cilicia to Amisus. He spent the winter of 63/2 organizing the Roman provinces of Bithynia-Pontus and Syria into a form that was to last as long as the empire. His general principle was to subject territories with a Mediterranean coastline to Roman rule and to leave inland countries under native rule. Thus, Armenia, Cappadocia and Galatia were left under the control of client kings. The great bend in the Euphrates became the eastern limit of Roman expansion, except during Trajan's reign.

34. Cf. E. Badian, *Roman Imperialism in the Late Republic*, Ithaca, N.Y., 1968, pp. 77–79, 81.

trade from the East into the expanding Roman world of the West.[35] His settlement has therefore rightly been celebrated as inaugurating a new political and cultural era in Syria and the Near East.[36]

In Palestine, however, where the quarrels of the Hasmonean family ground to their bitter end, Roman intervention brought only partial satisfaction and political settlement. Pompey's quaester, M. Aemilius Scaurus, who had arrived in Damascus from Armenia in 65, marched into Judaea to investigate the civil war and there received the ambassadors of Aristobulus and Hyrcanus, both of whom sought Roman support and offered for it bribes of 400 talents.[37] Scaurus considered Aristobulus the more likely to make better use of Roman assistance and therefore decided in his favor, warning Aretas to return to his land unless he wished to be treated as an enemy of the Roman people. Two ears later, however, Pompey, who saw the matter as but one part of the total Near Eastern problem for Rome, took time to investigate the situation further. When he arrived in Damascus in 63 he received three Jewish delegations: one each from Hyrcanus and Aristobulus representing their claims to the throne as well as their charges against each other, and a third from the Jewish people, strongly Pharisaic in its viewpoint, who desired to remove the Hasmonean usurpers, abolish the kingship altogether and give their sole allegiance to the legitimate priest of their God.[38]

Pompey, who had planned an expedition to the Red Sea, no doubt to investigate the extent and lucrativeness of the Nabataean trading monopoly, bade the Hasmonean brothers accompany him from Damascus while he considered enroute their complaints and claims. The combined delegations set out with the Roman army, but when they reached the upper Jordan valley, Aristobulus, disappointed in his hopes and mistrusting Pompey's intentions, deserted and fled to his fortress, Alexandrium, twenty miles

---

35. Cf. M. Rostovtzeff, *Caravan Cities* (N24): 29.

36. M. Gelzer (N33), pp. 110–11, "For the first time in her history Rome undertook to regulate the administration of newly conquered lands according to comprehensive plan." This was an attempt to govern; it was a bow to Greek culture. Edmund Bouchier, *Syria as a Roman Province*, Oxford, 1916, p. 22, observes that "Pompey wisely recognized that direct Roman rule was necessary if Syria was not to revert to barbarism." He relied for government primarily on the towns "which already had a definite municipal organization, and for remoter districts on the native princes."

37. Josephus *Antiquities* XIV.2.3. (29–33).

38. Josephus *Antiquities* XIV.3.2 (41).

north of Jericho. Unwilling to sustain there a Roman siege, he fled further toward Jerusalem. Pompey pursued him as far as Jericho, where he received the news that Mithridates of Pontus had died and the thirty years' war in Asia Minor was over. Secure in that knowledge Pompey abandoned his planned Nabataean expedition and proceeded directly to Jerusalem in pursuit of Aristobulus.

In Jerusalem the Hasmonean gave himself up, promising to surrender the city in exchange for a cessation of hostilities. But when the city would not open its gates to Pompey's general, Gabinius, Pompey imprisoned Aristobulus and prepared to besiege it. At the sight of the Roman army the majority of Jerusalemites relented and allowed the Romans to pass through the gates. A small group that supported Aristobulus, however, determined to resist and fortified themselves in the temple, located on the eastern hill of the city which was joined to the rest by a bridge over the Tyropoeon valley.[39] There Pompey besieged them three months until his forces breached the wall and massacred the defenders in the late autumn of 63. Pompey entered the temple precinct and its most holy place, which, except for Antiochus Epiphanes a century earlier, none but the high priest had ever seen; and having satisifed his curiosity[40] he left to give his attention to settling the affairs of Judaea. Hyrcanus he restored to the high priesthood, Jerusalem he made tributary to the Romans, and to the cities of Syria and Palestine taken by Jannaeus and his father Hyrcanus he restored independence, making them dependencies of the new Roman province of Syria. Stationing Scaurus with two legions in Syria, Pompey then departed for Cilicia and Rome, taking with him Aristobulus, his two daughters and his sons, Alexander and Antigonus. Alexander managed to escape almost immediately together with a large number of Jewish prisoners. Two years later, in his triumphal procession in Rome, Pompey exhibited among other notable prisoners the one-time Hasmonean prince to an enthusiastically admiring crowd.[41]

The province of Syria was henceforth ruled by a Roman governor, who from 57 onwards had the authority as proconsul to hold the governorship for two years. We know the names of these governors and a little about their

39. Josephus Antiquities XIV.4.2 (58).
40. Tacitus, Historia, V.9.
41. Appian, Mithridatic Wars, pp. 116–17. Pompey's commemorative tablet is given by Diodorus XL.4.

activities.[42] Gabinus, the first Syrian governor of consular rank, was an able leader of independent spirit. He attempted to bring the Roman system of tax-farming under his own control and regulation and to make the powerful Jewish political organization of Palestine strictly accountable to Roman government. To that end he deposed Hyrcanus, subjected Judaea to heavy taxation, broke it up into five administrative districts[43] and rebuilt several Greek cities that had been destroyed by Jannaeus. In Egypt, which had committed a corps of cavalry to Pompey's campaign in Palestine, he restored Auletes to the throne, after the latter had been banished by the Alexandrians in favor of his oldest daughter, Berenice IV,[44] and in Armenia he adopted a firm policy against Parthian intervention in order to guarantee the flow of Roman profits from trade with the East.

His successor, the avaricious M. Licinius Crassus, exacted more than eight thousand talents from the temple in Jerusalem[45] before he lost his life in battle at Carrhae (Haran on the Belikh river) in 53, in pursuit of the supposed inexhaustible wealth of Parthia.[46] The Roman defeat at Carrhae, in the first major confrontation between east and west since Alexander's conquest three centuries earlier, dealt a severe blow to Roman pride even as it opened Syria to the Parthian armies, thus jeopardizing the Near Eastern "settlement" that had been effected by Pompey. The new Roman governor, Cassius, prepared Antioch for siege, but internal Parthian strife at Ctesiphon, across the Tigris river from Seleucia, required the Parthian forces to withdraw from Syria and return home in 50 B.C. Syria was thus delivered

---

42. Scaurus propraetor 63–62; Marcius Philippus propraetor 61–60; Lentulus Marcellinus propraetor 59–58; Aulus Gabinius 57–55; M. Licinius Crassus 54–53; C. Cassius Longinus 53–51; M. Calpurnius Bibulus 51–50; Vejento 50–49; Q. Metellus Scipio 49–48; Sextus Caesar 47–46; Caecilius Bassus 46; C. Antistius Vetus 45; L. Statius Murcus 44; C. Cassius Longinus 44–42; Decidius Saxa 41–40; P. Ventidius 39–38; C. Sosius 38–37; L. Munacius Plancus 35; L. Calpurnius Bibulus 32–31; Q. Didius 30. The names are given by E. Schürer, *A History of the Jewish People in the Time of Jesus Christ* (N17), div. 1, vol. 1, pp. 326–70. Cf. further Glanville Downey, *A History of Antioch in Syria from Seleucus to the Arab Conquest*, Princeton, 1961, and its abridgment in *Ancient Antioch*, Princeton, 1963, Ch. IV, "The Coming of the Romans." Cf. Appian, *Syria* 51; Josephus; Dio Cassius XXXIXf; Plutarch, "Crassus," "Caesar."

43. Josephus *Antiquities* XIV.5.4. (91); *War* I.8.5 (170).

44. Strabo XVII.I.11 C 796.

45. Josephus *Antiquities* XIV.7.1 (105).

46. Cf. N. C. Debevoise, *A Political History of Parthia*, Chicago, 1938, pp. 78–95, with bibliography in n. 36.

from one storm only to be buffeted by another: the destructive political and economic waves set in motion by the Roman civil war, which swept away from Syria and Palestine great chunks of wealth and undermined political stability.

The Roman confrontation with Parthia in 53, which came after a century of senatorial attempts to accommodate the parochial, Roman city-state government to the demands of nascent empire, exposed the futility of those attempts. Just as the imperial Roman exploitation of Asia Minor came in the wake of the Macedonian defeat at Pydna in 168, so Pompey's arrangements in Syria a century later opened the way to the Roman challenge of Parthia. These military and political actions derived from Roman confidence in the superior effectiveness of the Roman legions. That superiority had become obvious after the Roman subjection of Hannibal at Carthage (Zama) in 202, Philip at Cynoscephalae in 197, Antiochus III at Magnesia in 189, and Philip at Pydna; and it had transformed the traditional, Roman citizen militia, which had been conscripted only in time of danger to the Republic, into a necessary and permanent instrument of imperial policy. In the army's wake, throughout the Mediterranean, followed traders, entrepreneurs and political magistrates, who found the economic fruits of Roman conquest bountiful and sweet.

But the costs to Rome of her success were high. The Roman tax-farmers (publicans), who grew rich by collecting more from their provinces than they had to deliver to the Roman treasury, engendered hatred for Rome wherever they went. The destruction and razing of Carthage, Corinth and Numantia in 146 were shameless exercises in terrorization. Rome reluctantly created the provinces of Macedonia, Carthage, Asia and Gaul between 146 and 121 because of the necessity for continued Roman intervention in those areas to preserve order. This, however, required that the number of magistrates legally permitted to administer the provinces had to be increased and their terms of office lengthened, a necessity that strained the capacity of the Roman political and administrative machine. In addition, Republican Romans could control provincial administrators only with difficulty, and the necessity for creating standing, professional armies to keep peace in the provinces not only made the traditional Roman citizen army impractical and obsolete, it also created a powerful threat to the Roman senate. These new, professional soldiers, who, like those of Alexander more than two centuries earlier served away from home for long periods of time, owed their loyalty not primarily to the senate but to their own military commanders, to whom they looked both for remunerations during their terms of service and for proper retirement benefits (usually land allotments) after their discharge. Furthermore, Roman victories flooded

Italy with prisoners of war who provided the state with cheap, slave labor, enabling the newly rich senators and knights to buy up small Roman farms and transform them into large estates worked by slaves, while the former owners moved into cities, seeking employment. The Gracchan attempts in 133 and 122 to restore land to the small farmers and thereby to sustain the citizen militia ended in failure; and after 90 B.C. the Social War, which extended Roman citizenship south of the Po river, made city-state government impossible and pitted the two political factions of the state, the *populares* ("demagogues") and *optimates* ("best people") in fierce struggle against each other. The consequence was the transformation of the Roman republic into Roman empire, which is associated with the career of Julius Caesar, who was born July 13, 100 B.C., and died on March 15, 44 B.C.[47]

One can see in retrospect that the collapse of the Ptolemaic, Seleucid and Jewish states was an inevitable consequence of parochial feuding in the face of powerful outside demands for world order. Rome sought peace and stability after a century of internal strife, and the Parthians required a respite from foreign wars to set their political house in order. To both these states the independent territories of Syria and Palestine, in spite of their economic attractiveness, were political and military nuisances, as Pompey had made clear by his "settlement." The rise of Rome and Parthia thus brought the Hellenistic era to its inglorious end, bringing a new confrontation between the Near East and the West, while it gave the native eastern spirit a chance to assert itself. Roman rule in Syria would bring peace to that troubled region as Parthian control in Mesopotamia would bring prosperity. In Rome a new form of government was being fashioned, drawing on the lessons of earlier territorial, city-state and monarchic rule, on the Alexandrine and Roman wars of conquest, and on Stoic and emerging religious insights. With its vision of one world, the new Roman government would bring to the Mediterranean world two centuries of order and prosperity.

SUGGESTIONS FOR FURTHER STUDY:

S. Lieberman, *Hellenism in Jewish Palestine* (New York, 1950); G. F. Moore, *Judaism in the First Centuries of the Christian Era*, 3 vols. (Cambridge, Mass., 1927–30); Ronald Syme, *The Roman Revolution* (Oxford, 1939); E. Badian, *Roman Imperialism in the Late Republic* (Ithaca, N.Y., 1968); G. W. Bowersock, *Augustus and the Greek World* (Oxford, 1965).

---

47. The political situation in Rome is summarized by Matthias Gelzer, *Caesar, Politician and Statesman*, P. Needham, trans. (from the German original, 1959), Cambridge, Mass., 1968, pp. 1–26.

VIII

ROME AGAINST PARTHIA

The unblushing annalist of Roman greatness, Livy, who lived from 59 B.C. to A.D. 17, believed that Scipio's astonishing defeat of the great Antiochus at Magnesia in 190 B.C. made the Romans masters of the world,[1] and it seems probable that in Livy's day the celestial and terrestrial globe, which had often been represented in art and mentioned in Greek literature, had indeed become a political symbol for Roman world mastery.[2] That symbolic use of the globe probably owed much to the career of a man whom Livy seems to have considered less than good for Rome, Julius Caesar, who with his practical genius perceived better than any of his contemporaries Rome's inescapable political responsibility for world order and introduced into the government administrative reforms that prepared the way for Roman empire.[3]

Convinced of the Roman right to rule, Caesar had planned to avenge the spectacular insult to Roman honor, which the Parthians inflicted in 53 B.C. in their defeat of Crassus,[4] by a fully developed Roman offensive

---

1. "in hac victoria quae vos dominos orbis terrarum fecit" 37.45.8.

2. The evidence is cited by S. Weinstock, *Divus Julius*, Oxford, 1971, p. 42ff. The Sasanian crown or diadem, worn in combination with a ball, may be an expression of the Roman symbol. Cf. the figures in G. Rawlinson, *Seventh Great Oriental Monarchy*, 2 vols., New York, 1876, vol. 1, pp. 66, 67.

3. Cf. M. Cary and H. H. Scullard, *A History of Rome*, 3rd ed., New York, 1975, pp. 276ff. Also n. 1, p. 622 on sources.

4. Plutarch tells the story, "Crassus" XX–XXV.

campaign through Armenia to Ctesiphon against the Parthian king;[5] and he apparently intended to justify this proposed campaign and his actual military expeditions by adopting for himself the title "liberator."[6] Caesar's view of the purposes of Roman government may indeed have inspired the later Augustan belief that Roman conquest brought "freedom, security and concord at home" and abroad, for Caesar inaugurated as policy the Romanization of the formerly politically isolated provinces[7] and forged a bond of loyalty between the Roman ruler and his subjects that would prove its durability and receive widespread popular acclaim in the days of Augustus Caesar fifty years later.[8]

Caesar's murder in 44, however, began the Roman Civil War, which would end fourteen years later with Octavian's naval victory over Antony in the bay of Actium on the northwestern shore of Acarnania in Greece. That conclusive battle would also bring to its end the Roman Republic and herald the beginning of the Augustan Principate.[9] The social unrest in Rome, of which the so-called civil war was but a final phase, had lasted a century, from the tribunate of Tiberius Gracchus, 133. It had been a period of widespread social turbulence, during which the face of the world had been fatefully altered. Slave uprisings in Sicily, Sardinia and Asia Minor revealed the seriousness of Roman labor problems; the rulers of Pergamum, Cyrenaica and Bithynia, unable to contemplate further fruitful independence for their kingdoms, had bequeathed them to Rome; the Pontic empire of Mithridates VI Eupator, who ruled from 120 to 63 B.C., had collapsed under continued Roman pressure; flourishing organized piracy had been swept from the eastern Mediterranean; Pompey had "settled" affairs in Syria, Palestine, and Asia Minor to the economic profit of Rome with the establishment of increased order and security in the East; the Jewish Commonwealth had foundered in internal strife; and the Iranian reaction against

5. Dio Cassius 43.51.1; Appian, *Bella Civilia* 2.110.459. Cf. R. Syme, "Some Notes on the Legions under Augustus," *JRS*, 1933, p. 28, n. 101; Justin 42.4.6.

6. S. Weinstock, *Divus Julius* (N2), pp. 142ff.

7. G. H. Stevenson, *Roman Provincial Administration*, 2nd ed., Oxford, 1949, pp. 91ff.

8. "Caesar's policy of gradually breaking down the distinction between Italians and provincials, and of converting the Roman empire from a military dominion into a mere commonwealth, was his most important contribution to Roman statesmanship, and on this question he gave a lead which his successors could not ignore." M. Cary and H. H. Scullard, *A History of Rome* (N3), p. 278. Cf. S. Weinstock, *Divus Julius* (N2), p. 259.

9. John M. Carter, *The Battle of Actium*, New York, 1970.

three centuries of western domination had assumed formidable proportions in the shape of an aggressive and militarily elusive Parthian kingdom.

The Hellenistic inheritors of Alexander's conquered territory had played out their final political and military cards, leaving the contest for political supremacy in the Mediterranean to be decided between a poorly organized Iranian kingdom of vassal states and the strongly centralized, efficiently organized and well-meaning Roman state which claimed the authority and power for world rule. Alexander's mantle had come to rest on Roman shoulders, and Romans would now attempt the world government which Macedonian kings and conquerors before them had been unable to effect.[10]

The Augustan view of the world, however, was politically developed far beyond that of Alexander and his contemporaries, drawing as it did on three centuries of western imperial experience in the Mediterranean Near East. The newly organized and consolidated Augustan state, when compared with the Greece torn by rivalries during Alexander's lifetime, no doubt made Augustus seem a fortunate military successor to the Macedonian general. He profited from Roman experience with some of her own conquering generals abroad, who returned home laden with honor and supported by fiercely loyal troops to usurp the power of government; that was a duplication of Hellenistic history that could not be tolerated in a "just" state. Augustus sensed, as Antigonus Gonatas two centuries before him had declared, that political power is best used as a public trust for the well-being of the ruled; and the new Caesar made good government a mark of his rule. To that end he shared responsibilities for the state with well-chosen administrators and generals, in the conviction that shared authority is more beneficial to a state than outright dictatorship. Beyond that, moreover, recognizing that the costs of Roman conquest and its related peace-keeping operations were far greater than their economic benefits to the state, Augustus concluded with rare insight that Rome had probably reached its optimum territorial size. His testamentary advice to Tiberius, in which he expressly urged that the empire be kept within the bounds he had set for it, was read to the Senate after his death in A.D. 14;[11] and it became thereafter axiomatic that Rome would not expand beyond the northern and

---

10. Cf. W. M. Ramsay, *The Social Basis of Roman Power in Asia Minor*, Aberdeen, 1941, pp. 5–6, 48ff.

11. Dio Cassius 55.33. Tacitus, *Annals* 1.11.

eastern river boundaries of the Rhine, the Danube and the bend of the Euphrates.

That self-imposed territorial limitation, which took account of the costs of conquest and a widespread popular longing for peace, was also a shrewd recognition of the unlikely chances for repeated, decisive, Roman victories like those of the two centuries just elapsed. A new power had arisen in the East that compelled Roman respect, however unwillingly or deprecatingly Rome might give it. That respect is probably best recorded in the apocalyptic vision of the four horsemen of war, bloodshed, famine and death (Revelation 6:22ff.) who would bring divine judgment on the world. The unknown author's choice of image suggests widespread fear of the horse nomads from the East, represented in his day by the Parthians, and later by the Huns, Mongols and Turks.[12]

Parthian history, which spans half a millennium from about 250 B.C. to about A.D. 250, unfortunately is episodic, recorded for us by prejudiced Greeks, Romans and Muslims for whom Parthian civilization was devoid of major interest and important only as an adjunct to their own. For that reason, no doubt, the classical accounts of Parthian history written by Arrian and others have not survived. Moreover, almost nothing is extant in Pahlavi, the official language of the Parthian state. Too little Parthian archaeology has been undertaken, and the meager information from numismatic evidence scarcely provides an outline for historical development. Parthians and Romans began their advances into Hellenistic territory within a few years of each other, the Romans into Illyria in 228 B.C., and Arsaces of Parthia into Hyrcania east of the Caspian Sea about ten years earlier. The Roman advance is well documented, that of Arsaces remains obscure. Both states would be seriously stalled by revolutions in the third Christian century, and both would emerge from that chaos with renewed political vigor and changed political face: Rome under the Dominate of Diocletian, and Persia under the rule of the Sasanid kings.

The beginnings of Parthian history can be seen only dimly. The Greek historian, Strabo, a native of Pontus who lived from about 63 B.C. to A.D. 21, believed that the Parthians, whom he called Parni nomads, had migrated after the death of Alexander into the old Persian province of

---

12. For references to the Parthians in Roman literature see N. Debevoise, *A Political History of Parthia*, Chicago and London, 1938, pp. 208–12.

Parthava (modern Khurasan) from the steppes of central Asia (modern Russian Turkestan).[13] Strabo's contemporary, Pompeius Trogus, a native of Gaul, whose work has been preserved for us by Justin, added that the insurgents were Scythian exiles who, under the leadership of Arsaces, had invaded Parthia during Rome's first war with Carthage; and he tells us that Arsaces, "no less memorable among the Parthians than Cyrus among the Persians, Alexander among the Macedonians, or Romulus among the Romans," established a dynastic kingdom.[14] This scanty and contradictory evidence does not permit more precision about Parthian origins. It seems clear, however, that the new immigrants supplanted the original inhabitants of Parthava (Parthia) and in the process adopted their language. The Parthians of history are those immigrants into the old Persian province of Parthava, who arrived there sometime after and perhaps as a result of Alexander's Persian conquest.

Late in the third century B.C. the Syrian kings, Seleucus II and Antiochus III, attempted with moderate success to compel Armenian and Iranian submission to Antioch;[15] but the Seleucid disaster at Magnesia early in the second century, followed as it was by fresh revolts against Antioch in Armenia, Palestine and eastern Iran, allowed the Parthian king, Mithridates I, who ruled from 171 to 138, after the death of Antiochus IV Epiphanes in 163, to wrest control of Media from his Syro-Macedonian overlords. He had probably begun his rule at Nisa in northeastern Iran, but his residence city, called Hecatompylos (hundred-gated), presumed to be near Damghan some thirty miles northeast of Tehran, remains undiscovered. From the Median highlands in the summer of 141 Mithridates moved esily into Mesopotamia to capture the Greek emporium, Seleucia on the Tigris, and by the time he died three years later, the Parthians had made the bend in the Euphrates river their western boundary, restricting the Seleucids to Syria.

The Parthian threat to the feeble Seleucid state in the west was moderated by continued forceful nomadic incursions into Parthia from the

---

13. Strabo XI.9.1–3 (C515).
14. Justin 41.1–6; cf. J. Wolski, who considers Arrian's account inferior to the Strabo-Justin tradition,"The Decay of the Iranian Empire of the Seleucids and the Chronology of Parthian Beginnings," *Berytus* 12 (1956–57), pp. 35–52.
15. Cf. Polybius V.55.

east, that required constant Parthian vigilance and exertion.[16] One such irruption prevented Mithridates from exploiting his capture of Seleucia; but he seems nevertheless, in the wake of Jewish independence in 142, to have considered his capture of the Seleucid king, Demetrius, during the winter of 140/39, legitimate grounds for his own claim to Seleucid Mesopotamia. Certainly the death in Media early in 128 of Antiochus VII Sidetes, the last Seleucid king and general to attempt forcible submission of Parthia, gave Mithridates' son and successor, Phraates II, reason to claim Syria for his own. Both he and his uncle and successor, Artabanus, were prevented from executing that claim by renewed wars against nomadic incursions from the east. In those wars both kings lost their lives, Phraates against the Sacae in 128 and Artabanus against the Yueh-chi in 123. These royal deaths, within five years of each other, together with extensive territorial losses in eastern Iran produced such turmoil within the Parthian state that many vassal kings and governors were emboldened to proclaim their independence of the Arsacid crown. Hyspaosines, the governor of Charax, a Greek city at the mouth of the Tigris river, was able to establish a dynasty that would control the district of Characene until the second century A.D.[17]

The revolts also produced, however, one of the ablest kings of Parthian history, Mithridates II (ruled 123–97). His predecessors, Phraates and Artabanus, had successfully deflected the Sacae southward into India, and Mithridates could therefore devote his efforts to regaining former subject territories in the west and consolidating the Parthian kingdom. He retook Mesopotamia without difficulty, annexing in 121/20 as a Parthian vassal territory the kingdom of Characene, which would remain loyal to the Parthian state for two hundred years, and toward the end of his life[18] he made some conquests in Armenia. The precise nature of the Parthian-Armenian relationship, however, remains obscure, for the two peoples, who may have been branches of the same ethnic group, seem to have intermarried extensively. Mithridates managed to take as hostage the young Armenian

---

16. Polybius XI.39.5 speaks of the "relapse into barbarism" that would occur if the nomads were allowed into Bactria.

17. S. A. Nodelman, "A Preliminary History of Characene," *Berytus* 13 (1960), pp. 83–122. Charax of Hyspaosines became known as Charax Spasinu to distinguish it from Charax in Media. Cf. W. W. Tarn, *The Greeks in Bactria and India*, 2nd ed., Cambridge, 1951, pp. 53–54.

18. Justin 42.2.7.

prince who would later become known as Tigranes I the Great, and the Armenian royal family eventually became a branch of the Arsacid dynasty. By the time Nero became emperor of Rome (54–68) the Armenian-Parthian relationship was so close that the Parthians believed their claims to Armenia outweighed any that Rome might bring forward.

Mithridates appears to have been the first Parthian ruler to adopt the title "king of kings" on his coins,[19] an assertion that not only recalls the earlier Assyrian and Achaemenid royal claims,[20] but also points to the loose Parthian confederation of vassal kingdoms that comprised the Parthian empire. How the confederation cohered or functioned is not known precisely. The Arsacids apparently had won royal status from the nobility, but their royal power[21] depended on both approval by the priests who controlled vast tracts of land and on continued good will of the vassal kings who could withhold tribute and military contingents in time of war. Furthermore, the Greek cities, foundations of Alexander and his successors, were often independent communities, governed by their own elected senators, and tributary to the Arsacid king but otherwise free. The Arsacids' declaration on their coins of friendship for Greece, Philhellene, reveals their economic dependence on Greek enterprise, manpower and cultural tradition. Necessary as this admission may have been, however, for maintaining the Parthian confederation, it earned the Arsacids the contempt of their Iranian successors, who numbered Parthians among the Hellenistic usurpers of legitimate Iranian authority.

In 94 B.C. Mithridates, thinking apparently that he had made an ally of Armenia, allowed Tigranes, whose father had died, to return home and ascend his father's throne. But Tigranes disappointed the expectations of his would-be benefactor, for in less than a year he married the daughter of the Pontic king, Mithridates VI Eupator, forming an alliance that he hoped

---

19. Cf. M. A. R. Colledge, *The Parthians*, New York, 1967, p. 33. A dedicatory inscription from Delos, dated to the late second century B.C., reveals that the Parthian king was known in Greece as "king of kings." N. Debevoise, *A Political History of Parthia* (N12), p. 41, n. 53.

20. Cf. A. T. Olmstead, *History of Assyria*, New York, 1923, p. 606. For the Assyrian claim see D. D. Luckenbill, *Ancient Records of Assyria and Babylonia*, Chicago, 1926, vol. 1, p. 73; for the Achaemenid see Darius Besitun Inscription 1 in R. G. Kent, *Old Persian*, 2nd ed., New Haven, Conn., 1953.

21. Strabo XI.9; Ammianus Marcellinus XXIII.6.

would enable him to recover from Parthia his father's losses and to share with the Pontic king the territory of Cappadocia. That allied effort in Asia Minor aroused the old Roman fears of Syrian power and set in motion the chain of diplomatic events that would bring Parthia and Rome to blows.

Another link in that chain had been forged four decades earlier. Attalus III, the last king of Pergamum, had died childless in 133, leaving his kingdom to Rome.[22] Whatever the deceased monarch's motives may have been,[23] Rome, lured by expectations of large revenues from the royal lands, accepted the bequest and thereby became responsible for maintaining order in that turbulent land. Costs of that responsibility came due almost immediately when Roman legions had to suppress the insurrection of a pretender to the throne, Aristonicus, who claimed to be an Attalid, called himself Eumenes III, declared the will of Attalus III to be fraudulent, and rallied to his cause the discontented serfs, slaves and mercenaries of Pergamum, with the plan of establishing a Utopian Sun-State in which social classes would be abolished and all people would be equal in all respects.[24] His ragtag Asiatic army did in 131 destroy the Roman consul P. Licinius Crassus[25] and his force, but the next year the Romans suppressed the uprising and in the following year (129) established the province of Asia in place of the kingdom of Pergamum. Then, to spare themselves further costs in Asia, the Romans placed their allies, Mithridates V of Pontus and Ariarathes VI of Cappodocia respectively, in control of the central (Greater Phrygia) and eastern (from the Halys river to the Taurus mountains) districts of Asia Minor. At Mithridates' death in 120 B.C., the Romans repossessed Greater Phrygia and added it to their province of Asia.

Mithridates VI (lived ca. 132–63 B.C.), ascended the Pontic throne as a boy of eleven years. He did not regard favorably the loss of the Phrygian territory and would later launch the most vigorous opposition Rome encountered from Asia. But for the time being he was unable to oppose

---

22. For relevant inscriptions cf. N. Lewis and M. Reinhold, *Roman Civilization*, 2 vols., New York, 1966, vol. 1, pp. 321ff.

23. Cf. M. Rostovtzeff, *Social and Economic History of the Hellenistic World*, Oxford, 1941, vol. 2, pp. 806–07.

24. W. W. Tarn and G. T. Griffith, *Hellenistic Civilization*, 3rd ed., London, 1952, pp. 122, 125.

25. Father-in-law of Gaius Gracchus and "the wealthiest Roman of his day ": M. Cary and H. H. Scullard, *A History of Rome* (N3), p. 204.

Rome. Carefully biding his time, therefore, between ca. 112, the year he murdered his mother and took charge of the affairs of state, and 93, the year he joined with Tigranes to partition Cappadocia, he established authority over northern Asia Minor, annexing the Crimea and extending his influence into the hinterlands of Thrace, Scythia, and Sarmatia on the northern shores of the Black Sea.[26] When, then, his assaults on Cappadocia aroused objections from Rome, Mithridates was ready to fight. The Romans demanded that the Cappadocian prince, Ariobarzanes, whose father's murder had been arranged by Mithridates, be placed on the throne, since "he seemed to have a better title to the government of that country than Mithridates,"[27] and they sent Sulla, proconsul of Cilicia, to Cappadocia to effect their will. Plutarch's comment that Sulla was ordered to Cappadocia under the pretense of reestablishing Ariobarzanes in his kingdom, but in reality to keep in check the restless movements of Mithridates,[28] probably summarizes Roman policy accurately. Sulla accomplished his mission in Cappadocia, but in the process was drawn into conflict with troops of Tigranes. That brought him within reach of the Parthians.

The Parthians, too, opposed the Armenian-Pontic alliance, and, finding their goals to coincide with those of Rome, they sent an ambassador to Sulla, proposing a formal Parthian-Roman association. Sulla, with Ariobarzanes in tow, met the Parthian envoy at the Euphrates river. Plutarch's account of that meeting, written probably in the first decade of the second century A.D., is one of the revealing anecdotes of antiquity. "During Sulla's stay on the banks of the Euphrates," says Plutarch, "there came to him Orobazus, a Parthian, ambassador from king Arsaces, as yet there having been no correspondence between the two nations. And this also we may lay to the account of Sulla's felicity, that he should be the first Roman to whom the Parthians made address for alliance and friendship. At the time of which reception, the story is that having ordered three chairs of state to be set, one for Ariobarzanes, one for Orobazus, and a third for himself, he placed himself in the middle, and so gave audience. For this the King of Parthia (Mithridates II) afterwards put Orobazus to death. Some people commended Sulla for his lofty carriage towards the barbarians; others again

---

26. Appian, *Mithridates*, 15.
27. Appian, *Mithridates*, 10.
28. Plutarch, "Sulla" 5.

accused him of arrogance and unseasonable display."[29] Sulla may have congratulated himself on his clever maneuver in making the Parthians appear willing to become Roman tributaries, but, if Plutarch can be trusted, the Parthian offence at this Roman attitude of contemptuous superiority inaugurated centuries of Parthian hostility and warfare against Rome. The immediate consequence was an alliance between the Parthian, Armenian and Pontic kings, the bloody purge in 88 B.C. of some 80,000 Italian residents from 'Asia,' and the resulting start of the so-called Mithridatic wars between Rome and Mithridates VI of Pontus.[30]

When in Parthia Mithridates II died in 87, there ensued more than a decade of Parthian dynastic struggle, upon which Tigranes of Armenia capitalized to overrun northern Mesopotamia and Media, to conquer "all the Syrian people this side of the Euphrates as far as Egypt,"[31] and to take Cilicia. He even assumed the Persian title, King of Kings, deported Greeks from Cilicia and Cappadocia into Mesopotamia, and brought Arab traders into Armenia that he might profit from their mercantile connections and experience.[32] In Babylonia neither Gotarzes, who had been satrap of satraps under Mithridates, nor the aged Parthian king Sinatruces, who died in 70/69 B.C., was able to regain control of the territories ruled by Tigranes or, consequently, to participate in the "Mithridatic" wars of the Pontic king against Rome.

The first Mithridatic war, fought between 89 and 84, began with Mithridates' massacre of the Italian residents in Asia mentioned above. That blood bath, which coincided with a critical period of social war in Rome, revealed Roman weakness in Asia Minor, the anti-Roman sentiments of the Greeks resident there, and the hatred nurtured generally in Asia against the Italian buccaneers. But more than that, the massacre awakened the Roman senate to the need for governing the Roman provinces responsibly. It dragged the senate unwillingly into world rule. In Asia, the plunder taken by Mithridates was so great that he freed the Asians from tribute for five years. Emboldened by success, he prepared to invade Macedonia and Greece, where his agents had taken control of Athens and murdered the

---

29. "Sulla" 5, Modern Library translation; cf. Josef Dobíaš, "Les premier Rapports des Romains avec les Parthes," *Archiv Orientální* 3 (1931), pp. 215–56.

30. Appian, *Mithridates*, 22–23.

31. Appian, *Syria* 48.

32. Plutarch, "Lucullus" 14.

Italian residents on the island of Delos. None of his gains in Asia and Europe, however, could compensate for his alienation of sympathies in Italy from his cause; the supposed advantages of brutality and barbarism were, as they always are, illusory. In 87, perhaps before the death of the Parthian Mithridates, Sulla set out for Asia by way of Greece and Macedonia, and in the summer of 85, in the wake of Roman victories in territories claimed by Mithridates, he negotiated a peace in which Mithridates agreed to give up his conquests in Asia Minor in exchange for being recognized king of Pontus and a friend of Rome.

The heavy expense of the war had cost Mithridates the allegiance of the cities in Asia Minor, which now surrendered to Sulla, who held them to account for their participation in the massacre of 88. Many lost their freedom and were compelled to pay taxes to Rome, collected by the increasingly avaricious *publicani*. Sulla then departed for Rome, leaving behind a subdued but vengeful Mithridates, who after Sulla died in 78 began preparations for another war. Again he sought support from the Parthians, and again they held back. When the final Mithridatic war broke out in 74, therefore, the Pontic king bore its brunt, while the Parthians moved only feebly at the end against Rome in Mesopotamia.

Mithridates invaded Bithynia in 74, perhaps at the request of his newly won Spanish ally (the alliance was probably concluded in the summer of 75),[33] the exiled Roman general Sertorius, who had been abetting the Cilician pirates in their decade-long disturbance of commerce in the western seas, to weaken Pompey's offensive in Spain.[34] But more likely Mithridates' attack was an effort to preserve access to the Bosporus by preventing the Romans from taking Bithynia, which its last king Nicomedes IV, being childless, had earlier that same year bequeathed to them.[35] In Spain, however, Sertorius' murder in 72 by a dissident and jealous commander enabled Pompey quickly thereafter to settle affairs. His drive against the pirates ended in 67 with a successful clearing of the seas after three months.

---

33. T. R. Holmes, *The Roman Republic*, 3 vols., Oxford, 1923, vol. 1, p. 383.

34. Cf. A. Schulten, *Sertorius*, Leipzig, 1926.

35. On this war see D. Magie, *Roman Rule in Asia Minor*, 2 vols, Princeton, 1950, vol. 1, pp. 323ff. For sources see in general T. Rice Holmes, *The Roman Republic*, 3 vols., Oxford, 1923. On the chronology of the war against Sertorius cf. Holmes, vol 1, pp. 369–75 and especially pp. 379–84.

In Asia Minor, the Roman general, L. Licinius Lucullus, compelled capitulation of the fortified Pontian towns, and by 70 had subjected Asia Minor to Rome, Mithridates having taken refuge with Tigranes of Armenia who refused to surrender him to Lucullus.

In 69, therefore, Lucullus, acting without authorization from the Roman senate to make war against Tigranes, crossed the Euphrates into Armenia and captured Tigranocerta.[36] Thereafter, still in pursuit of Tigranes, he marched north toward Artaxata, the Armenian capital situated in the Araxes river valley; but his troops, complaining of the strictness of his discipline and the rigors of the Armenian winter, stopped short of the city and refused to go further. Lucullus regretfully retired with his army to Nisibis for the winter, and Mithridates made good his return to Pontus. Lucullus was later prevented from vigorously prosecuting the war against Mithridates by the refusal of Rome to send reinforcements,[37] which were deployed instead against the pirates. When Pompey swept the seas of this nuisance, the grateful senate commissioned him to settle affairs in the eastern Mediterranean as well, and he promptly sent Lucullus home.

Meanwhile the situation in Parthia had changed. At his death in 69 Sinatruces had left the Parthian throne to his son Phraates III, who hoped to regain the Parthian territories taken by Tigranes. Phraates therefore was in no haste to help when Tigranes and Mithridates solicited his aid against Lucullus, and he temporized when Lucullus demanded that he either help the Romans or remain neutral.[38] In 66 Pompey did secure Phraates' promise of neutrality; but when, in that same year, the younger Tigranes, whose two brothers had been killed by their father,[39] took refuge with Phraates, he offered Phraates an irresistible opportunity to recapture the Parthian districts previously lost to the Armenians. This chance disappeared, nevertheless, when Pompey's easy defeat of Mithridates, as well as his

---

36. The site of the city is disputed. Strabo XVI.1.23 (C 747) and Tacitus, *Annals* 15.4–5, place it close to Nisibis, but the evidence from other classical writers seems to place it elsewhere. The matter receives detailed discussion by T. Rice Holmes, *The Roman Republic* (N35), vol. 1, pp. 409–25, who concludes the possible existence of two sites named Tigranocerta, one near Mardin (Tell Ermenek) and one 40 miles northeast of Diarbekr (Meiafarkin).

37. Appian, *Mithridates* 91

38. Appian, *Mithridates* 87.

39. Appian, *Mithridates* 104.

reputation in Asia for justice and good faith, persuaded the Armenian king that further resistance to Rome would be both foolish and futile, and he and his son, the latter apparently with Phraates' blessing threw themselves on Pompey's mercy.

Pompey then entered upon the political necessities of military victory by making the first of several fateful decisions that are commonly called his settlement of the East.[40] He pardoned the Armenian king for aiding Mithridates of Pontus against Rome and confirmed him in his kingship, while depriving him of his conquests in Syria and giving the districts of Sophene and Gordyene (generally, the territory extending eastward from modern Malatya to Lake Van and south to the present Syrian border) to his son. To Phraates, whom he seems to have mistrusted, Pompey restored Adiabene (bounded by the Tigris and Lower Zab rivers and extending northward along the Tigris to the vicinity of modern Mosul), but not Gordyene which Phraates also claimed. When the younger Tigranes expressed resentment at his share in the settlement, Pompey had him seized and then assigned the districts of Sophene and Gordyene to the Cappadocian king, Ariobarzanes. Thereupon Phraates demanded the return of Gordyene, the establishment of the Euphrates as the boundary between Parthia and Rome, and the release of his son-in-law, the younger Tigranes. Pompey responded to "king" Phraates, reserving the title "king of kings" for Tigranes, by assigning Gordyene finally to the Armenian king, the elder Tigranes, and refusing to release Tigranes junior. The effect of Pompey's decisions in Armenia was thus to ensure the continuation of the breach between Tigranes and Phraates and to create an Armenian buffer and theater of war between Rome and Parthia.[41]

The arrangement ordered by Pompey did not satisfy Phraates, who disputed with Tigranes the boundary between their kingdoms. Both men appealed to Pompey, Tigranes that Rome should help her friends and Phraates that Rome should welcome the Parthians as allies; but Pompey, now engaged in Syria, was unwilling to adjust a boundary line which he considered drawn to Rome's advantage. The kings thus began to realize that Rome was a greater enemy to either of them than they were to each other.[42]

---

40. Appian, *Mithridates* 114–15; D. Magie, *Roman Rule in Asia Minor* (N35), vol. 1, ch. 15.

41. Plutarch, "Pompey" 38.

42. Dio Cassius 37.7.

What that realization might have meant for Parthian-Armenian relations is not known, for Phraates was murdered by his sons Orodes and Mithridates a few years later in 58/7 B.C., and Orodes dispatched his brother not long thereafter in the winter of 55.

By then, Pompey's easy triumph in the east together with the continuing internecine strife in Parthia had convinced the Romans that the time was ripe for removing the Parthian threat to the Roman peace. Accordingly, the senate appointed the ambitious, wealthy M. Licinius Crassus, who was over 60 years of age, proconsul of Syria. Arriving in the east in the spring of 54 he took over from his predecessor, A. Gabinius, command of the Roman army, which with the addition of his forces now consisted of about seven legions (that is, about 42,000 men); but he seems to have allowed his plundering instincts to disorder his military judgment. He spent his first year capturing and garrisoning Greek cities in western Mesopotamia and despoiling the temples of Yahweh at Jerusalem and of Atargatis at Hierapolis-Bambyce (modern Membij, ca. 50 miles northeast of Aleppo), instead of planning his loudly vaunted expedition against the Parthian kingdom.

Crassus made blunder after blunder. His knowledge of Mesopotamian geography was woefully vague; his ignorance of Parthian tactics in war was reprehensible; and his intelligence with respect to Orodes was vastly inferior to Orodes' knowledge of him.[43] The parochial Roman faith in the invincible Roman legion had yet to experience the effect of Parthian mounted archers and heavy-armored cavalry against foot troops.[44] The famous exchange between the Parthian envoys and Crassus sums up the situation. Orodes' messenger to Crassus, in an effort to learn Crassus' intentions but also perhaps to incite him to battle, taunted him with being too old for combat. Crassus in reply snapped that he would answer the Parthian envoys at Seleucia, to which the chief envoy, tapping the palm of one hand with the fingers of the other, answered, "Hair will grow here before you see Seleucia." Finally, in choosing to advance against Seleucia by the most direct route through the open plains of Mesopotamia, rather than along the Euphrates or Tigris rivers, Crassus needlessly gave the Parthian cavalry strategic superiority, exposing his vulnerable legions to the deadly Parthian archers.

---

43. Plutarch, "Crassus" 17–18.
44. Cf. most recently A. M. Ward, *Marcus Crassus and the Late Roman Republic*, Columbia, Mo., 1977, p. 207.

Among his allies Crassus numbered Abgar, king of Osrhoene (Edessa),[45] an Arab sheikh, Alchaudonius, and the new Armenian king Artavasdes. They probably supplied contingents of cavalry as well as tactical counsel in dealing with the enemy. The Parthian cavalry was under the command of Suren, while Orodes waited with his infantry in Armenia, no doubt to keep the Armenian king in check. In the spring of 53 Crassus crossed the Euphrates at Zeugma (near modern Jerablus) and was told that the Parthian horses were in retreat toward Seleucia. The Roman historian Dio Cassius[46] believed that Abgar deceived Crassus into pursuing Suren in order to destroy him, as Procopius would later blame Arab perfidy for Belisarius' defeat by the Sasanian Persians at Callinicum;[47] but the attribution of western military defeats in the Near East to Near Eastern treachery is an ancient explanation of doubtful merit.

The Roman forces engaged the Parthian cavalry on the plain near Carrhae (Haran) and were disastrously defeated.[48] Crassus himself was killed two days later in a scuffle that broke out when Parthian officers tried to lead him to their camp for drawing up on paper the terms of peace, and the Romans suspecting treachery more than likely misread what was happening and resisted.[49] The ill-fated expedition thus cost the Romans 20,000 slain and 10,000 prisoners of war whom Orodes settled far from Syria in Margiana (Merv or Mary in Turkmen S.S.R.), where they married native women and became Parthian subjects.[50] The gains for Orodes were acknowledgment of the Euphrates as the legal boundary with Rome, and an alliance with the Armenian king, Artavasdes, who gave his sister in marriage to Orodes' son Pacorus. The two monarchs, indeed, were reportedly enjoying a performance of Euripides' "Bacchae" when news of the Roman defeat at Carrhae reached them.[51] Beyond that, however, the Parthians had successfully challenged Roman authority in the east; and in the future some disaffected peoples like the Jews in Palestine would look to

45. J. B. Segal, *Edessa*, Oxford, 1970, p. 10ff.
46. Dio Cassius 40.20.
47. Procopius, *History of the Wars* I.18; Kawar, "Procopius and Arethas," *Byzantinische Zeitschrift* 50 (1957), pp. 39–67, 362–82.
48. Cf. Plutarch, "Crassus" 22ff.; Dio Cassius 40.20ff.
49. N. Debevoise, *A Political History of Parthia* (N12), p. 92.
50. Ibid.
51. Plutarch, "Crassus" 33.

the Parthians as deliverers from Rome, while others like the Armenians would turn to the Romans as saviors from their Parthian overlords. As it happened, the Parthians were unable to pursue their military advantage because of internal difficulties at the capital, which cannot be properly assessed. Suren was executed, perhaps because he posed a threat to Orodes; and Pacorus, who led an uninspiring expedition to Syria in 52, was recalled to Seleucia in the summer of 50. The Romans, too, appear to have paid as little heed to their defeat as the Parthians did to their victory, and the murder of Caesar, three days before his intended departure on a full-scale Parthian offensive, saved both states from a military showdown until the ill-advised and abortive campaign of Trajan a century and a half later.

The Roman civil war did temporarily deliver Syria, Palestine and eastern Asia Minor to both the Parthian Pacorus and a defecting Roman general, Quintus Labienus. The latter, who had been the envoy of Cassius[52] to Orodes, preferred, after Cassius' death at Philippi in 42, to cast his lot with the Parthians rather than face the proscriptions that followed in the wake of Cassius' defeat. Thus, seizing their opportunity in the spring of 40, when the Roman world was suffering the divisive struggles among the triumvirs Lepidus, Octavian, and Antony who was in Egypt with Cleopatra, the Parthians invaded Syria as far as Antioch. There they sent Labienus north to subdue Cilicia and southern Asia Minor, while Pacorus reduced Syria and Palestine except the island fortress of Tyre. In Jerusalem, in exchange for a promise of one thousand talents and five hundred Jewish women, Pacorus installed as king, Antigonus, nephew of the high priest Hyrcanus I, and took Hyrcanus captive to Parthia. Herod, who had been appointed tetrarch by Antony, escaped the Parthians to his fortress at Masada; and his brother, Phasael, when captured by Antigonus committed suicide.[53] The following year Antony renewed his campaign against Parthia, and within two years his general Publius Ventidius Bassus out-maneuvered and defeated Labienus and Pacorus, both of whom were slain. Jerusalem fell the next year (37) and Herod was made king of the Jews. This defeat of the Parthian forces brought an end to Parthian dreams of westward expansion. Thereafter for Rome and Parthia the theater of diplomatic and

---

52. One of Caesar's assassins who had fled from Antony to the East.
53. Josephus, *Antiquities* xiv. 13; *Jewish Wars* i. 13. 1.

military conflict became Armenia, over which Romans and Persians would struggle intermittently until the Arab conquest.

Antony's dream of Parthian conquest, however, did not die, and the blood bath in Parthia following the accession of Phraates IV early in 37 B.C., together with Phraates' subsequent murder of his father, Orodes, who had abdicated in his favor, led Antony to believe his dream might be realized. His ambitions were aroused further when a Parthian fugitive, Monaeses, persuaded him that Parthia was ripe for revolt and that with Roman help he, Monaeses, might be crowned king and become vassal to Rome. So determined on war was Antony that Monaeses' subsequent change of heart did not deter him. Unwilling to assault the Parthian fortifications at Apamea, across the Euphrates from Zeugma, Antony marched north to Artavasdes of Armenia, whom he met perhaps near modern Erzerum, and who persuaded him to attack the Parthian vassal state of Media before striking at Parthia itself. Fortified with that advice, Antony marched nearly three hundred miles against Phraaspa,[54] the capital of Media Atropatene, whence, unable to take the city or to exact from the Parthians surrender of the Roman standards, he managed finally to return to Armenia, having lost more than twenty thousand men. That was as close as Antony came to taking Parthia. Although he marched against Artaxata, the Armenian capital, two more times, his war against Octavian brought him to naval defeat at Actium and his suicide along with that of Cleopatra shortly thereafter.

In Parthia, the despotic rule of Phraates finally produced an uprising that forced him to flee the country, leaving his throne to the leader of insurrection, a certain Tiridates. Phraates took refuge with the Scythians,

---

54. Phraaspa is usually identified with Takht-i-Sulaiman, 42 miles southwest of Mianeh, on the basis of Strabo XI.13.3 (C 523) and Dio Cassius XLIX.25. Cf. H. Rawlinson in *Journal of the Geographical Society*, vol. 10, pp. 113–17, cited by G. Rawlinson, *The Sixth Great Oriental Monarchy*, London, 1873, p. 201, n. 4. R. N. Frye, *Heritage of Persia*, New York, 1963, p. 259, n. 23, points out that Takht-i-Sulaiman, Shiz of the Arabs, has been claimed for both the Parthian Phraaspa and the Sasanian Ganzaka. He believes on the basis of V. Minorsky, "Roman and Byzantine Campaigns in Atropatene," *Bulletin of the School of Oriental and African Studies* 11 (1944), p. 268, that Phraaspa and Ganzaka are two distinct sites and that Phraaspa is to be located north of Miandoab. S. A. Matheson, *Persia: An Archaeological Guide*, London, 1972, pp. 102–03, suggests the same location for Phraaspa. Takht-i-Sulaiman was excavated in 1959 by H. H. Van der Osten and R. Naumann, whose preliminary report appeared in *Teheraner Forschungen*, 4 vols., Berlin, 1961–75, vol. 1.

who restored him to his throne, but not before Tiridates abducted Phraates' youngest son and escaped to Syria, where he delivered the young hostage to Octavian who was en route from Egypt to Roman Asia. Octavian returned to Rome with Tiridates and the boy, and when Phraates insisted that both be returned to him, Octavian refused to give up Tiridates but returned Phraates' son on the understanding that the Parthian monarch would in exchange return the Roman standards taken from Crassus and Antony. Those standards were not finally returned until 20 B.C. when they were handed over to Tiberius, whom Octavian, now Augustus and at the time visiting the East, had delegated to receive them. Their return excited jubilant celebration at Rome. Augustus himself thought the recovery worthy of mention in the record of his achievements, making it appear that the Parthian king in returning those trophies had become a vassal of Rome: "I compelled the Parthians to restore to me the spoils and standards of three Roman armies and to ask as suppliants for the friendship of the Roman people."[55] The exaggerated claim, however badly it misrepresented the Parthian attitude, did underscore the peace that prevailed between the two states for half a century.

Antony's downfall had been due to his preoccupation with Cleopatra[56] and the Near East. His divorce of Octavia, Octavian's sister, so that he might marry Cleopatra, and the publication of his will, in which he declared not only his wish to be buried at Cleopatra's side but also that her thirteen-year-old son by Julius Caesar, Caesarion, was Ceasar's legitimate heir, thus making Octavian, Caesar's adopted son, a usurper, fed rumors that Antony intended to crown Cleopatra queen of Rome and to transfer the capital to Egypt. Those rumors mobilized Roman public opinion against Antony and for Octavian. Consequently at Actium Antony's forces deserted him, and his death with Cleopatra in the summer of 30 delivered Egypt into the hand of Octavian, who dispatched Caesarion and made Egypt a Roman province governed by a prefect over whom he retained direct supervision.

When, therefore, after his march through Palestine, Syria and Cilicia, Octavian returned in the late summer of 29 to Rome, he was "acclaimed the Prince of Peace," the bringer of repose to a world wearied by civil strife. It had become clear to all that peace required all power to be centered in one

---

55. *Res Gestae* 29.1.
56. Cf. M. Grant, *Cleopatra*, New York, 1973.

man.[57] In keeping with its adulation the senate two years later gave Octavian the new name, Augustus. In the years following, this fortunate, unpretentious and persistent man forged a unified Greco-Roman empire that determined the shape of Near Eastern life for the next three centuries.[58] During his long rule he fixed the boundaries of Roman empire, guaranteed the continual flow of trade, established politically stable and lucrative Roman provinces, and across the Roman frontiers sought to insure dynasties of kings who would be Roman clients "linking together his royal allies by mutual ties of friendship of intermarriage, which he was never slow to propose."[59] His successes in these enterprises may be taken as evidence that he satisfied the widespread longing for peace with which the Hellenistic era had ended.

His conception of Rome in the East became apparent early and did not change. On the island of Rhodes in 30 B.C., before he departed for Egypt in pursuit of Antony, Octavian had accepted the friendship offered without supplication, excuse or flattery by Antony's client, Herod, and confirmed him as king in Judaea.[60] In Armenia later that year he had tried without success to establish a client kingdom by refusing to be drawn into an Armenian or Parthian campaign against Artaxes, whose father Artavasdes, and brother, Tigranes (II), Antony had captured. Cleopatra had put Artavasdes to death, and Augustus took Tigranes with him to Rome. Ten years later, he placed Tigranes on the Armenian throne; but even though the Roman-trained youth could not maintain his country as a Roman client state, Augustus was satisfied that the Roman frontier was not violated.

In Egypt, after Augustus' departure in 30 B.C., his prefect, the poet G. Cornelius Gallus, began to extend the province into Upper Egypt beyond the first cataract of the Nile, until in 25 B.C. he was halted by the Ethiopian queen, known as Candace. Her envoys to Augustus three years later, after an inconclusive campaign by the consul B. Petronius against her, accepted the border with Rome just south of the first cataract, where it remained for three centuries.[61] With the encouragement of Augustus Cornelius' successor, Marcus Aelius Gallus, attempted an invasion of Arabia

57. Tacitus, *Annals* 1.1,2; *Historia* 1.1.
58. Cf., e.g., G. W. Bowersock, *Augustus and the Greek World*, Oxford, 1965, p. 140.
59. Suetonius, "Augustus" 48.
60. Josephus, *Antiquities*, XV.6.6 (187–193); *Jewish Wars* I.20.1–2 (387–92).
61. Strabo XVII.1.53–54 (C 819–821).

Felix (kingdom of the Sabaeans, roughly modern Yemen). The expedition, reinforced by contingents from Palestine, whom Strabo, because the campaign failed, labeled traitorous, succeeded in opening to Roman trade the strait of Bab-el-Mandeb and access thereby to East Africa and India.[62]

In Asia Minor Augustus subdued the unruly tribes of the central plateau and upon the death of the Galatian king Amyntas created in 25 B.C. the imperial province of Galatia, including Galatia proper, parts of Phrygia, Lycaonia, Pisidia and perhaps Pamphylia. As part of his program to inspect every province of the empire,[63] Augustus made a trip through the eastern provinces in 22–19, when he placed Tigranes II on the throne in Armenia, and twice appointed his confidant and (in 23) successor-designate, M. Vispanius Agrippa, as inspector general of the East, once in 23–21 and again in 17–13. To help Rome in forecasting annual income, but no doubt also to regulate provincial tax collecting, Augustus instituted procedures for taking a regular census in the provinces.[64] In addition he encouraged the building of temples to Augustus and Roma in the provinces and instituted provincial councils to choose high priests for them.

By the time Augustus died at Nola (ca. 15 miles east of Naples) in September A.D. 14, the Mediterranean sea had indeed become a Roman lake whose Near Eastern shores were administered as Roman territories for the advantage of Rome. A line connecting Melitene (modern Malatya) with Aeliana (one mile west-northwest of Aqaba) marks the eastern frontier, beyond which Augustus declined to rule but intended to control. The settlement he achieved endured in its basic form until the beginning of the fourth Christian century.

Augustus' successors, the Julio-Claudian dynasty (A.D. 14–68), continued their founder's policy of maintaining Roman authority in the East with as little cost as possible. They were aided by the near anarchy in Armenia and Parthia, and they reaped the economic benefits of bringing the Arab Nabataean trade network under their own control. The ruined cities of Syria and Transjordan, namely, Bosra, Philadelphia-Amman, Jerash,

---

62. Strabo XVI.4.23–24 (C 780–782).
63. Suetonius, "Augustus" 47.
64. His legate P. Sulpicius Quirinius took a census of Syria in A.D. 6; cf. Luke 2:2, and L. R. Taylor, "Quirinius and the Census of Judaea," *American Journal of Philology* 54 (1933), pp. 122–33. See E. M. Smallwood, *The Jews under Roman Rule*, Leiden, 1976, pp. 568–71 for a complete review of the evidence.

Gadara and others, attest the prosperity bestowed on the land by Roman order and Arab commerce. To facilitate trade from the East through Parthia, Rome established a trading center at Palmyra (biblical Tadmor), on the modern desert road between Homs in Syria and Abu Kemal on the Euphrates at the Iraqi border. The Parthian point of departure for this route, which today is followed by the oil pipe line from the Euphrates to Tripoli in Lebanon, was Dura, near Abu Kemal; and the thriving trade which passed over that route allowed both Dura and Palmyra to enjoy opulent riches during the first Christian century.[65]

When Nero ascended the Roman throne in the autumn of A.D. 54, he had to respond to a new Parthian advance into Armenia that had begun two years earlier. The Arsacid Vologases I, who ruled from 51/2 to 79/80, had placed his brother Pacorus in command of Media[66] and was in the process of subduing Armenia as a province for his other brother, Tiridates. Vologases had already captured the important cities of Tigranocerta and Artaxata before he was forced to withdraw by a new threat from the nomads in the east. In 54 Tiridates was again in Armenia, and when that news reached Rome, the eastern legions were alerted for an invasion of Parthia, and the career soldier Cn. Domitius Corbulo was summoned from Germany to assume command of the Roman forces. He was instructed to tell Vologases that Rome would accept Tiridates as king of Armenia only if Tiridates were to be crowned by a representative of Nero, i.e., to admit that he held Armenia as a gift from Rome, not from Parthia. Otherwise, Corbulo would invade Armenia. Vologases, to avoid immediate war, or "to rid himself of suspected rivals under the name of hostages,"[67] handed over some members of his family to Corbulo; but Corbulo prepared for the invasion.

Vologases put down an uprising, led by his son Vardanes, and thereafter in 58 declared that his brother Tiridates would rule Armenia for Parthia and not for Rome. A revolt of Hyrcania (southeast coastal district of the Caspian Sea), however, whose ambassadors vainly besought Rome for aid against Vologases, left that monarch occupied in the east, unable to support

---

65. M. I. Rostovtzeff, "Dura and the Problem of Parthian Art," *Yale Classical Studies* V (1935), pp. 293ff.

66. N. Debevoise, citing Josephus, *Antiquities* XX.74, unaccountably places Pacorus in Media Atropatene (modern Azerbaijan in northwest Iran). But Josephus says "Media." Cf. G. Rawlinson, *The Sixth Great Oriental Monarchy* (N54), p. 262, n. 2.

67. Tacitus, *Annals* 13.9.

his brother in the west. The Armenians wavered in their allegiance, appealing now to Rome and now to Parthia for aid, though as Tacitus informs us,[68] they were tied geographically and socially more closely to the Parthians whose alliance they preferred. Corbulo invaded Armenia in the winter of A.D. 57/58; Artaxata capitulated in 58; and when Tigranocerta fell two years later Armenia reverted to Roman control. Nero thereupon named Tigranes V, grandson of the last king of Cappadocia, to be king over a greatly reduced Armenia, separating it from its territories bordering Iberia to the north, Pontus to the west and Commagene to the south to make the new province more manageable; and Corbulo withdrew to govern Syria.[69]

Tigranes, however, was not content to rule over a reduced Armenia, and in 61 he invaded the Parthian district of Adiabene to the southeast, between the Lower and Upper Zab rivers. That raid revived Vologases' determination to enforce his brother's claim to Armenia, which he did by besieging Tigranocerta. A food shortage, however, and Corbulo's threat to invade Mesopotamia unless Vologases gave up the siege induced Vologases to intercede directly with Nero for the recall of Tigranes and reinstatement of Tiridates. When that request was denied, Corbulo and the new Roman general appointed to take charge of affairs in Armenia, L. Caesennius Paetus, invaded Mesopotamia. The young commander, however, in an effort to hasten what he considered to be Corbulo's slow conduct of the war, ravaged Armenia; then having rashly furloughed his troops for the winter, he was compelled to engage Vologases, who forced the Roman legions to capitulate and evacuate Armenia. Corbulo, who had not arrived from Syria in time to extricate Paetus from defeat, agreed to withdraw his forces from Mesopotamia if the Parthians would retire from Armenia. Vologases accepted the proposal, since Tiridates was once more established there as king. But the Parthian envoys, who in the spring of A.D. 63 proposed to Nero that Tiridates should be invested with the rule of Armenia by Nero's representative in the east, were sent home with gifts and the demand that Tiridates be crowned in Rome, so that Rome should not appear to have been forced to conclude an unfavorable peace.

The emperor ordered an additional legion to be sent to reinforce

68. Tacitus, *Annals* 13.34.
69. Tacitus, *Annals* 14.26.

Cobulo who again invaded Armenia, where in the summer of A.D. 63 he was met by a Parthian delegation seeking peace. This time Tiridates agreed to go to Rome; and since Corbulo, on Armenian territory, in command of an undefeated Roman army, could make peace on mutually agreed terms without any appearance of capitulation to the eastern powers he accepted the proposal. Tiridates thereupon removed his royal insignia, placed them at the foot of Nero's statue imported for the occasion, and left one of his daughters hostage with Corbulo, until he should have travelled to Rome, received investiture as king of Armenia from Nero, and returned a Roman vassal to Artaxata. Then, after a trip to the east to visit his family, Tiridates set out on his nine-month, overland journey to Rome, an expedition financed by the Roman treasury and conducted in conformance with Zoroastrian religious regulations.[70] In Rome in A.D. 66, amid great public rejoicing, Nero replaced Tiridates' turban with the diadem of sovereignty and thereafter closed the doors of the Temple of Janus, signifying that the Roman state was everywhere at peace.[71] Rome had satisfied the demands of protocol and enjoyed the spectacle of Armenian and Parthian submission; nevertheless a Parthian would now sit on the Armenian throne, and Near Eastern resistance to the West had once again achieved its goal.[72]

But Rome had not abandoned her efforts to control the East. Her war against the Jews, culminating in the destruction of Jerusalem by Titus in A.D. 70, was part of her accepted responsibility for preserving order in the provinces. That Vologases, however, should have found it desirable or necessary to congratulate Titus on his victories over the Jews[73] attests the uneasy truce between Rome and Parthia, for Jews and Parthians had a history of cooperation. The Palestine Jews had earlier united with the Parthians to destroy Seleucid power, a destruction finally accomplished by the Romans, and until the end of Arsacid rule most Babylonian and many Palestinian Jews shared with Parthians the goal of excluding Rome from the Near East.[74]

---

70. Pliny, *Naturalis Historia* xxx.16f.

71. Suetonius, "Nero" 13.

72. On Near Eastern reactions against Hellenism cf. S. K. Eddy, *The King is Dead*, Lincoln, Neb., 1961; Pierre Grimal, *Hellenism and the Rise of Rome*, New York, 1968, ch. 4.

73. Josephus, *Jewish Wars* VII.v.2 (105–06).

74. See also J. Neusner, *A History of the Jews in Babylonia*, I. The Parthian Period, 2nd printing revised, Leiden, 1969, pp. 23–27.

But Rome was not to be excluded. The emperor Vespasian's defeat of the Jewish uprising led him to annex other frontier kingdoms to Rome as provinces. Augustus had annexed Egypt (31 B.C.), Galatia (25 B.C.), and Judaea (A.D. 6); Tiberius had added Cappadocia (A.D. 17) and Commagene, incorporating Cilicia into the province of Syria; Claudius had restored Judaea to his friend Herod Agrippa, but on the latter's death in 44 had to let the territory revert to its provincial status; he also returned Commagene to its king, Anitochus IV. Nero incorporated eastern Pontus into Galatia, and Vespasian recreated the province of Commagene, while also garrisoning the newly created province of Lesser Armenia. Thus Nero's crowning of Tiridates to be king of Greater Armenia in A.D. 66 satisfied Parthia, the one Near Eastern power capable of organized, effective war against Rome, and gave Rome the chance to organize and incorporate as provinces the troublesome buffer states on her eastern frontier.[75]

This settlement of the outstanding Roman dispute with the Parthians, coupled both with subsequent Parthian efforts to defend their eastern frontier against the nomadic Alans from beyond the Caucasus and Roman efforts to keep peace elsewhere—in Palestine, Asia Minor, Europe and Rome—removed Parthia from the topical concern of Roman historians. Our knowledge of Parthia thus suffers a gap until the reign of Trajan (A.D. 98–117).[76]

The Spanish-born Trajan, who as a man of 22 had accompanied his father to Syria and who seems to have considered himself another Alexander, undertook to extend the Roman frontiers beyond those that had been traditionally accepted since the reign of Augustus. Trajan's motives are disputed;[77] but his conception of good government, revealed as it is in his letters to the younger Pliny (C. Plinius Caecilius Secundus), who was his special commissioner to review and revise municipal affairs in Bithynia, probably influenced Trajan's decision to extend Roman rule into what he thought was an anarchic and therefore greatly weakened Parthian state. Besides his own ambition, which was doubtless decisive, Trajan's desire to

---

75. G. W. Bowersock, "Syria under Vespasian," *JRS*, 1973, pp. 133–40.

76. The sketchy evidence for Parthian history in the interim is summarized by N. Debevoise, *A Political History of Parthia* (N12), 213–18; cf. also G. Rawlinson, *The Sixth Great Oriental Monarchy* (N54), Ch. XVII. F. A. Lepper, *Trajan's Parthian War*, Oxford, 1948, and its review by M. I. Henderson, *JRS*, 1949, p. 121ff.

77. Cf. F. A. Lepper, *Trajan's Parthian War* (N76), pp. 22–23.

dominate the trade routes from southern Arabia through Palestine and Syria and from the Persian Gulf through Babylonia and Mesopotamia, led him to carry out his Near Eastern campaigns. In 105–106 he annexed Nabataea as a Roman province, with Bostra as its new capital and Arabia Petraea as its new name, and in 113 he set out to annex Armenia, whose client king Axidares had been unseated by the Parthian king Chosroes (Persian Khusraw). Armenia fell to Trajan without difficulty the following year, and he incorporated it into a new province with Cappadocia.[78] The next year (115) he occupied Ctesiphon, but a Parthian counterattack in 116, perhaps coordinated with Jewish revolts in Cyrenaica, Egypt and Cyprus, which spread through Palestine and Syria, together with Trajan's failing health, forced him to start home; and he died in Cilicia in the summer of 117.

To govern Trajan's Parthian conquest would have required a military commitment Rome could not afford, and Trajan's successor, Hadrian, therefore surrendered all claims to Parthia. He seems also to have allowed Greater Armenia to revert to its client status, but he did retain Arabia as a Roman province. Hadrian's surrender of Parthia was likely also part of the cost required to subdue the Jewish uprising in Palestine that had broken out at the end of Trajan's life. That revolt led finally to the Roman destruction of Jerusalem, its paganization as Aelia Capitolina, and the renaming of the Judaean province as Syria Palaestina in 135.[79]

The Parthians quickly reoccupied Assyria and Mesopotamia, adopted their former respectful attitude toward Rome and rallied behind their king, Chosroes, who had honorably restored the traditional Parthian-Roman frontier. Apart from an incursion of some Alans in 136, through the Caucasus into Armenia, Media Atropatene (Azerbaijan) and Cappadocia, which was repulsed in the west by the Roman governor of Cappadocia, Arrian, Alexander's historian, and bought off in the east by the Parthian king Vologases, the reigns of Hadrian (117–138) and Antoninus Pius (138–161) enjoyed peace in the east.

When Marcus Aurelius (161–180) succeeded to the Roman throne in 161, however, the Parthian king deposed the Roman puppet in Armenia in favor of one Tigranes, and at once invaded Syria and Palestine. Rome responded to the assault by placing her Syrian legions in the field, and

---

78. D. Oates, *Studies in the Ancient History of Northern Iraq*, Oxford, 1968.
79. Cf. E. M. Smallwood, *The Jews under Roman Rule* (N64), pp. 428–66.

within two years her generals had restored Rome's client king to the Armenian throne and peace to Syria. Thereafter, the victorious Roman general and native Syrian, Avidius Cassius, marched down the Euphrates river to Babylon, crossed to the Tigris, and captured the Greek city of Seleucia and its Parthian counterpart across the river, Ctesiphon, in 166. He even marched into the Zagros mountains and laid claim for Rome to Media. But his army contracted a virulent and contagious disease (some think it was smallpox), which they took to Italy with devastating decimation of the population.[80] Parthia, nevertheless, lost to Rome Mesopotamia between the Chabur and Euphrates rivers and for the rest of the second century avoided hostilities with Commodus (180–192).

The third century was filled with anarchy both in Rome and Parthia, which led to the downfall of the Arsacid dynasty and the rise of the Sasanian, and to the removal of the Roman capital to Byzantium (Constantinople) at the beginning of the fourth century. The Parthians were unable to withstand the Romans, Severus (193–211) and Caracalla (211–217), or to stabilize their own kingdom. Domestic rebellions, which may possibly have been observed with satisfaction at Rome, beset the Parthian state, ravaged Syria, disrupted trade, and led Palmyra to try creating "a caravan empire," until Parthia finally succumbed (ca. 227) to the rival Persian dynasty of the Sasanians, headed by Ardashir. But the western Roman power was never able henceforth to maintain a boundary east of the bend in the Euphrates river. The Near Eastern forces of reaction and independence had become invincible.

SUGGESTIONS FOR FURTHER STUDY:

The Parthian history of George Rawlinson, *The Sixth Great Oriental Monarchy* (London, 1873), remains the best available and is both readable and useful, drawing heavily on the Roman history of Dio Cassius, a praetorian prefect of Alexander Severus (Roman emperor from 222–235). Rawlinson's work was revised by Neilson C. Debevoise, *A Political History of Parthia* (Chicago and London, 1938), a work which has not been superseded. W. W. Tarn, *CAH*, vol. 9, ch. 14 (1932), traces Parthian history to the death of Crassus; he includes an excellent bibliography.

The Parthians, by Malcolm A. R. Colledge (London and New York, 1967), contains a good bibliography, as well as excellent photographic plates and archaeological material. The brief surveys in A. Bausani, *The Persians* (London, 1971; Italian original, 1962);

---

80. Ammianus Marcellinus 23.6.23–24; Eutropius, *Breviarium ab urbe condita* 8.6.

R. Ghirshman, *Iran* (Harmondsworth, 1954), and R. N. Frye, *The Heritage of Persia* (New York, 1963), contain needed perspective. Roman history is admirably presented with exemplary notes in H. H. Scullard's revision of M. Cary's *A History of Rome*, 3rd ed. (London and New York, 1975). For sites in the Roman empire, mostly west of the Levant, see Richard Stillwell, *The Princeton Encyclopedia of Classical Sites* (Princeton, 1975).

Michael I. Rostovtzeff, "Dura and the Problem of Parthian Art," *Yale Classical Studies* V (1935): 155–304, contains a bibliography on Parthian ruins, and an unsurpassed review of Parthian artistic creation. Cf. the recent survey by Malcolm A. R. Colledge, *Parthian Art* (Ithaca, 1977).

IX

ROME AND THE JEWS

Perhaps the most troublesome of Rome's eastern responsibilities was the eccentric Jewish state in Palestine. Pompey in 63 had reduced the Jewish state to the condition of a Roman client kingdom under Hyrcanus as high priest and ethnarch, but no longer king. To insure Jewish submission to Rome Pompey had razed the walls of Jerusalem and its temple enclosure, imposed Roman taxation, detached from the Jewish state both western Idumaea and the coastal cities from Raphia in the south to Dora in the north (south of Mt. Carmel), and created the loose federation of independent cities known as the Decapolis: Scythopolis, Pella, Dion, Gadara, Hippos, Abila, Philadelphia, Rephana, Gerasa and Canatha.[1] The location of these cities, at the junctions of trade routes in Palestine, as well as their attachment to the new Roman province of Syria, when considered in the light of their subsequent prosperity under Roman protection, shows Pompey's shrewd sense of economic and political realities and his determination to reduce Palestine to a harmless enclave in the Roman empire, while at the same time letting it appear to be politically semi-independent.

But since a threat to Jewish independence was also a threat to peace in Palestine, there were those in Rome who insisted that complete Jewish subservience to Roman control was prerequisite to peace in the East. But opinion was divided. Thus Jewish independence was compromised fifteen year later, in 48, perhaps at the command of Gabinius in Syria, when the Idumaean Antipater was made governor of the Jews; but the following year

---

1. Cf. A. H. M. Jones, *Cities of the Eastern Roman Provinces*, 2nd ed., Oxford, 1971, pp. 456–57; Josephus, *Antiquities* xiv.iv.4 (74–76).

A ROMAN SEA

MILES→ 0 500

Caesar, doubtless guided by Pompey's earlier policy, restored to Hyrcanus his secular authority as ethnarch and made him a friend and ally of the Roman people, at the same time, nevertheless, granting Antipater Roman citizenship and an administrative position under Hyrcanus. Caesar also restored the seaport of Joppa to the Jews, giving the Jewish state a chance for economic growth, and before he died he authorized the rebuilding of Jerusalem's walls. Pompey's strategy thus became official Roman policy.

When Caesar left Syria, Antipater, assuming his role as Rome's representative in Palestine, appointed his own son Herod military governor of Galilee, with the task of forcing submission there to Roman rule. Rome could not have hoped for a better servant than Herod. So energetic and effective was Herod in stamping out guerrilla warfare that he earned the praise of the Syrian governor, Sextus, which propelled him into his long career of rule in Palestine. That career was to be marked by his vigorous and opportunist support of whatever Roman leader could bring order to Palestine, and to be sanctioned by his marriage in 37 B.C. after a five-year engagement to Mariamne, the granddaughter of Hyrcanus, a liaison that Herod hoped would place him in the Hasmonean priestly succession. Against the Parthian attack of 40 B.C. Herod acquitted himself so well that Rome conferred on him the office of king, a position he was not able to realize effectively until three years later when he captured Jerusalem and subsequently became known to posterity as Herod the Great, perhaps through a misreading of Josephus, who with his description *ho megas*, may have meant only to set Herod, 'the elder,' apart from Herod Antipas.[2]

Herod's rule, however, was that of a secular monarch, an outsider lacking all spiritual authority among the Jews, who refused to accord him either loyalty or confidence.[3] His problems became evident when he had to appoint a high priest in Jerusalem. Hyrcanus had earlier been captured by the Parthians and subsequently handed over to his nephew and rival for the priesthood, Antigonus, who disqualified him for the office by cutting off his ears. But after Herod stormed Jerusalem in 37 B.C. Antony had Antigonus executed. That left Mariamne's brother, Aristobulus, next in line for the high priesthood; and Herod reluctantly appointed him late in 37 when it beame clear that his initial appointment of Ananel, a priest from

---

2. Josephus, *Antiquities* XVIII.V.4 (130–36).

3. On Herod's reign cf. M. Grant, *Herod the Great*, New York, 1971; Stewart Perowne, *The Life and Times of Herod the Great*, New York and Nashville, 1956.

Babylon, displeased his friend Antony. But Herod arranged the drowning of Aristobulus early in 35 and then reappointed Ananel. Four years later, when in 30 B.C. he was summoned to meet Octavian at Rhodes after the latter's defeat of Antony at Actium, Herod before leaving for Rhodes dispatched the aged Hyrcanus, thereby declaring that he would appoint to serve at his pleasure whomever he desired as high priest. Thereafter, confirmed in his position as king of Judaea by Octavian, Herod, in 29, suspecting his wife Mariamne of conspiracy, publicly accused her of marital infidelity and had her murdered too, a deed that was to torment him for the rest of his life. The next year he ordered the execution of her mother, Alexandra, as part of his gradual purge of the Hasmonean family. His deep suspicions leading to family vendettas did not prevent him, however, from bringing prosperity and architectural beauty to Palestine. So successful was he that Pliny the elder, marvelling at Herod's work, felt justified in calling Jerusalem "the most outstanding city in the East."[4]

When Herod died in Jericho, probably of arteriosclerosis, in the spring of 4 B.C., he left the throne to his son, Archelaus, designating Antipas, the latter's brother, tetrarch over the districts of Galilee (west of the Sea of Galilee) and Peraea (across the Jordan river and south of the Yarmuk), and making Philip their half-brother tetrarch over Paneas, Batanaea, Trachonitis and Auranitis (Hauran), east of the Sea of Galilee and the Jordan rift. Headquarters for Philip's government was Paneas (Caesarea Philippi; Panion); for Antipas' government it was Tiberias.[5] Augustus, upon whose approval Herod's will depended, modified it to make Archelaus equal to his brothers as ethnarch over the southern districts of Samaria, Judaea and Idumaea. Archelaus, however, was a weak and inefficient ruler, accused by Jews and Samaritans alike of treating them barbarously.[6] Consequently, in A.D. 6 Augustus summoned him to Rome for an inquiry into his behavior, and finding him unfit for rule banished him to Gaul, where he died. Augustus then, abandoning Pompey's strategy, created the Roman imperial province of Judaea, under his personal control, comprising the former three territories of Achelaus. He kept Antipas in Galilee, where he ruled until he

---

4. Pliny, *Naturalis Historia* v, 70.

5. Cf. G. A. Smith, *Historical Geography of the Holy Land*, London, 1903, pp. 475, 447f.

6. Josephus, *Jewish Wars*, II.vii.3 (111–12).

was deposed in A.D. 40, and Philip in the Hauran, where he ruled until he died in 34.

The emperor subjected the Judaean, provincial governor, known initially as 'prefect,' to the legate of Syria, whom he allowed to hear appeals directly from the Jews and to intervene in Judaean affairs whenever he thought it necessary or advisable; and he made Caesarea the administrative center of the new province. The Jewish Sanhedrin (council) in Jerusalem[7] remained responsible for the proper government of Judaea, but its members were appointed subject to the consent of the Roman authorities, who thereby insured that Roman policy would prevail. The Sanhedrin governed according to Jewish law, but sentences of death may have required ratification by the Roman governor.[8]

The Romans in the first century were committed to protecting Jewish religious freedom, but they could not tolerate Jewish nationalism, which erupted repeatedly against Rome in the province of Judaea, finally in open revolt in the years 66–70. One cannot deny that the Jews were needlessly provoked. Pilate, who was governor in Judaea from 26 to 36, secretly imported Roman standards into Jerusalem on the eve of the Jewish Day of Atonement, expropriated funds from the Jewish temple treasury for necessary public works[9] and circulated coins stamped with designs he knew to be offensive to the Jews. The emperor Gaius (ruled 37–41) ordered a statue of himself to be erected in the innermost cella of the Temple in Jerusalem, and only his assassination prevented that order from being carried out.

In Alexandria, too, the substantial Jewish population suffered needless provocation. Denied Alexandrian citizenship and considered to be resident aliens in Egypt, the well-organized community agitated for Greek citizenship because it was prerequisite to Roman citizenship. The animosities between the Greeks, who perceived the Jews as desiring the benefits of citizenship without being willing to shoulder its burdens, and the Jews, who saw themselves as being unfairly classed with the uneducated Egyptian natives, led to intrigues and persecutions of various kinds. The

---

7. On the composition and functions of the Sanhedrins cf. H. Mantel, *Studies in the History of the Sanhedrin*, Cambridge, Mass., 1961, Ch. II and V.

8. Cf. the explicit statement in the Gospel of John 18:31, but compare the Jewish stoning of Stephen, apparently without Roman approval in Acts 7:58-60. See the discussion in Mantel, *History of the Sanhedrin* (N7), Appendix B, pp. 307–16.

9. Josephus, *Antiquities* xviii.iii.1–2 (55–62).

friction was ignited to fire in 38 A.D., when the prefect of Egypt, A. Avillius Flaccus, who had been appointed by Tiberius and feared he would be recalled to Rome by the new emperor, Gaius (popularly known by his nickname Caligula "Baby Boots"), issued an edict restricting the Jews of Alexandria to residence in a single quarter of the city. The ensuing riots were not quelled until the next emperor, Claudius, in a *Letter to Alexandria*, published in the city in November 41, along with its other provisions restored to the Jews their former position in the city and ordered them to accept their civic status and religious privilege without agitating for further rights or encouraging the immigration into Alexandria of other Jews from Egypt or Syria. The emperor's perception of the Jews as a selfishly disruptive force in the empire foreshadowed the official Roman view that was to result in the destruction of Jerusalem.[10]

But Caligula, in spite of his needless provocations of the Jews, also eased political tensions in Palestine. He placed Herod's grandson, Julius Agrippa, in charge of the tetrarchy of the Hauran after Philip's death in 34, making him king; and when Antipas journeyed to Rome to secure the same status for himself, Caligula found him guilty of treasonable associations with Parthia against Rome, banished him to Gaul and incorporated his territories into Agrippa's kingdom.

Claudius, who succeeded Caligula on the throne, confirmed Agrippa in his kingdom and added to it the province of Judaea, thus restoring all of Herod's territory and more to his grandson as a client king of Rome. Agrippa was a popular ruler who, in spite of his extravagance, preserved order in Palestine and maintained favor with Rome. When, however, he

---

10. On Roman administration in Egypt see H. I. Bell, *CAH* X, ch. 4; A. C. Johnson, *Roman Egypt: An Economic Survey of Ancient Rome* (vol. 2 in *An Economic History of Ancient Rome*, ed. T. H. Frank, 5 vols., Baltimore, 1933–40); P. M. Fraser, *Ptolemaic Alexandria*, 3 vols., Oxford, 1972, vol. 1, "Epilogue." On the Jewish revolt in Alexandria see Philo, *In Flaccum*, ed. H. Box, Oxford, 1939, and *Legatio ad Gaium*, ed. E. M. Smallwood, rev. ed., Leiden, 1970; E. M. Smallwood, *The Jews under Roman Rule*, Leiden, 1976, ch. 10. On Claudius see A. Momigliano, *The Emperor Claudius and His Achievement*, Oxford, 1934, rev. ed., New York, 1961. E. M. Smallwood, *Documents Illustrating the Principates of Gaius, Claudius and Nero*, Cambridge, 1966. The texts are conveniently presented in C. K. Barrett, *The New Testament Background*, New York, 1961, pp. 44–47, 136–38. For maps and sites cf. Y. Aharoni and M. Avi-Yonah, *Macmillan Bible Atlas*, New York and London, 1968. M. Avi-Yonah, *The Holy Land from the Persian to the Arab Conquests, A Historical Geography*, Grand Rapids, 1966.

died of appendicitis in 44, leaving a sixteen-year-old son, Agrippa II, at school in Rome, Claudius decided to reconstitute the Roman province of Judaea, adding to it Galilee and Peraea and reserving for the young Agrippa only the northern and northeastern territories formerly under the commands of Antipas and Philip.

The return of Palestine to direct Roman rule led to Jewish terrorist activity, as Jewish hopes for national independence seemed ever further from realization. Their longing for deliverance from Rome produced fanatics who preached a salvation to be achieved both by miracle and by sword; and Roman officials were soon driven to desperate measures to preserve order. But the procurators did as much to cause unrest as they did to preserve order. Tacitus[11] accused Antonius Felix, a freedman and procurator of Judaea from 52–59, of stimulating disloyal acts by his ill-timed remedies and of believing "he could do any evil act with impunity" because his brother, Pallas, was secretary to the emperor.[12] Felix, Tacitus tells us, "indulging in every kind of barbarity and lust, exercised the power of a king in the spirit of a slave." He went so far as to seduce Drusilla, sister of Agrippa II and granddaughter of Antony and Cleopatra, from her husband and marry her himself (cf. Acts 24:22-26) so that he might become "the grandson-in-law, as Claudius was the grandson, of Antony."[13] Lucceius Albinus, procurator from 62–64, is accused by Josephus of being a villain, guilty of bribery, extortion, expropriation of private property, encouragement of "seditious practices," and general maladministration;[14] and his successor, Gessius Florus (64–66), in whose time war broke out, Josephus asserts was even worse. Finally, the intractable Jews and provocative procurators so enraged each other that many Jews emigrated, and in the summer of 66 the long-smoldering hostilities between Jews and Romans erupted in widespread fighting.

Rebellion against Rome began in Herod's Greek city of Caesarea, where, Josephus reports, Florus instigated the uprising to protect himself from having to answer for his crimes before his Jewish accusers in Rome.[15]

---

11. Conveniently available in an edition of Moses Hadas in the Modern Library, Random House, Inc., New York, 1942.

12. Tacitus, *Annals* xii.53–4.

13. Tacitus, *Historia* v.9.3.

14. Josephus, *Jewish Wars* ii.xiv.1.2 (272–77), but cf. *Antiquities* xx.9.1–5 (197–215).

15. Josephus, *Jewish Wars* ii.14.3 (282–83).

In a property dispute Florus accepted eight talents from the Jews to prevent the building of shops on a vacant lot next to their synagogue. Florus, however, instead of preventing the construction, simply absconded with the money, leaving "the sedition to take its full course, as if he had sold a license to the Jews to fight it out."[16] The precise causes of the fighting are not clearly known, but the large and wealthy Jewish population in Caesarea had long demanded a share in the government; more than that, however, extremists among the Jews desired to be rid completely of Roman government. Thus, in a series of incidents only casually related to each other, Judaea and Rome drifted into total war.

The fighting broke out in the wake of disintegrating Roman authority and spread throughout the country when rival factions of the population—Jewish terrorists known as 'dagger-men' (*sicarii*, from the dagger, *sica*, they concealed in their clothing), Herodians, Greeks and Romans—exploited the turbulent confusion to take reprisals against their adversaries. In September 66, to restore order, Cestius Gallus, the Roman legate of Syria, dispatched a huge army to Judaea and laid siege to Jerusalem. When, however, by mid-November, he had not been able to take the city, he withdrew his army to Caesarea, at the cost of more than five thousand dead. That huge loss guaranteed Roman retribution at the earliest opportunity.

In preparation for the certain Roman offensive, the Jews established a revolutionary government which appointed generals and organized the country into six military districts, one of which, Galilee, was entrusted to Josephus. The Roman emperor, Nero, when Gallus died early in 67, appointed Vespasian and his son Titus to quash the rebellion in Judaea. The Romans invaded Galilee, forcing its surrender before winter, and Vespasian kept Josephus, who had surrendered in exchange for his life, prisoner until the war ended. The next year, 68, Vespasian subdued most of Judaea and in June was preparing to besiege Jerusalem when he learned of Nero's death, which brought to an end the Julio-Claudian dynasty and opened a year of civil war in Rome. That upheaval at Rome, in addition to revealing the Roman army's power to make and unmake kings, a power that would not be exploited until more than a century later, also gave the Jews in Palestine a year's respite from combat—a respite they squandered with in-fighting—until Vespasian resumed the war in the summer of 69. When he became

---

16. Josephus, *Jewish Wars* ii.14.4 (287–88)

emperor later that summer, he gave command of the war in Judaea to Titus, who in the spring of 70 began his siege of Jerusalem. By September the city had fallen in flames, and most of its walls were razed.

The Roman capture of Jerusalem marked the war's effective end. Within three years the last of the rebels holding out at Herod's fortresses— Herodium, ca. 4 miles southeast of Bethlehem; Machaerus (modern Mkaur), east of the Dead Sea; and Masada, west of the Dead Sea, south of Engedi (modern es-Sebbe)— were subdued and their strongholds reduced. Vespasian founded a new city Flavia Neapolis (modern Nablus) north of Jerusalem, near ancient Shechem and Samaria, raised the capital, Caesarea, to the rank of first colony, exempting its citizens from the property or poll tax known as *tributum capitis*, and rebuilt Joppa. Ostensibly to pay for the war he required all Jews in the empire to remit to Rome annually the half-shekel tax they had formerly paid for the support of the temple in Jerusalem. This tax, known as the *didrachmon* (two drachmae) or Jewish Tax[17] meant that Jews had henceforth to pay for their religious privileges in the Roman state.[18]

The destruction of the Temple was decisive for Judaism and for Christianity as well. For Judaism it meant the cessation of animal sacrifices and Temple services, apparently also the end of the high-priestly office. For Christianity it defeated the Judaizing segments of the Church in Jerusalem that were tempted to establish a religious dynasty among Jesus' brothers or insist on the requirements of Jewish law for converts to the new faith. The Jewish Sanhedrin moved from Jerusalem to Jamnia (Jabneh, modern Yebna), where it may have been the nucleus of a rabbinic school that arose there, with the approval of Vespasian,[19] to become the center of Jewish learning. Josephus' account of the Jewish war ends with the events of the years 72–73, and those of the following four decades in Judaea must be reconstructed from scraps of evidence among the classical and Church historians. Apparently the settlement of Vespasian and Titus created a generation of Roman order and relative peace in Palestine.

Trajan's Parthian campaign (115–117), however (see above, p. 166f.) seems to have encouraged Jews in Egypt, Cyrenaica, Cyprus,

---

17. Josephus, *Jewish Wars* vii.vi.6 (218).

18. Cf. E. M. Smallwood, *The Jews under Roman Rule* (N10), p. 515.

19. H. Mantel, *History of the Sanhedrin* (N7), xiii (235–53); E. M. Smallwood, *The Jews under Roman Rule* (N10), pp. 348–50.

Palestine and Mesopotamia to believe the time had come to throw off the Roman yoke and establish a Jewish state. There is no conclusive evidence that the widespread Jewish revolts were coordinated, that they helped decisively to save Parthia from Roman conquest and domination, or that their goal was the formation of an independent Jewish state, though all three suppositions seem likely. [20]

The Jewish uprising in Egypt and Cyrenaica began against the Greeks and became a revolt against Rome when Trajan, surmising the serious nature of the insurrection, dispatched from Parthia his general, Q. Marcius Turbo, with a force to restore order. The revolt, conjectured to have been "Zionist" in seeking a return of Jewish exiles from North Africa to Palestine, [21] left extensive property damage in Cyrene, though less elsewhere, and required almost a year to suppress. By the time of Hadrian's accession to the throne in the fall of 117, Turbo had restored order to Egypt and Cyrenaica. The revolt in Cyprus, mentioned only by Dio, resulted in the banning of Jews from the island. In Mesopotamia the Jews apparently joined with the Parthians in resisting Trajan and were consequently driven from that province by Trajan's Libyan general Lusius Quietus, who was rewarded for his efforts with the governorship of Judaea, which he exercised until recalled to Rome and executed by order of the senate in 118. [22] Quietus' appointment to govern Judaea was probably Trajan's effort to preclude the incipient resurgence of Jewish nationalism in Palestine. But that some hostility also existed between Jews and Parthians is attested by stories like that of the Jewish brothers, Anileus and Asineus, [23] to whom the Parthian king granted authority in the Nehardea district of Babylonia from ca. 20–35. [24]

Roman suppression of the Jewish revolts, during the last years of

---

20. For historical accounts see Dio Cassius lxviii.32.1–3; Eusebius *Historia Ecclesiastica* iv.2.1–4. For discussion of the evidence cf. A. Fuks, "Aspects of the Jewish Revolt in A.D. 115–117," *Journal of Roman Studies* 51 (1961), pp. 98–104; E. M. Smallwood, *The Jews under Roman Rule* (N10), pp. 389–427. On Jewish goals see J. Neusner, *A History of the Jews in Babylonia*, 5 vols., Leiden, 1965–70, vol. 1, pp. 76–79.

21. E. M. Smallwood, *The Jews under Roman Rule* (N10), p. 397.

22. Cf. M. Cary and H. H. Scullard, *History of Rome*, 3rd ed., New York, 1975, p. 428.

23. Josephus, *Antiquities* xviii.9.1–9 (310–79).

24. See J. Neusner, *A History of the Jews in Babylonia* (N20), vol. 1, pp. 53–59. On the location of Naarda cf. F. A. Lepper, *Trajan's Parthian War*, Oxford, 1948, p. 128, n. 1.

Trajan's reign, restored order everywhere but in the province of Judaea. There the drive to national independence produced a leader, long known as Bar Cochba, "son of a star" (cf. Num. 24:17ff.), but in documents from the Judaean desert as "Simon bar Cosiba, Nasi (leader) of Israel," or, after the revolt failed, bar Coziba, "son of lies."[25] He probably sensed in Hadrian's Hellenizing tendencies and his ban on the practice of circumcision a resurgence of the spirit of the Seleucids, especially that of Antiochus Epiphanes IV, and in his abandonment of Trajan's eastern gains a sign of Roman decline. The revolt, identified as Bar Cochba's, lasting from the spring of 132 to the fall of 135, began as a coordinated Jewish effort and ended in guerrilla warfare, when the Romans imported their legions into the province and their leader, C. Julius Severus from Britain. The war was finished when the Jewish headquarters at Bethar (Khirbet el-Yehud, near Battir southwest of Jerusalem)[26] fell, probably in August 135. In the wake of that defeat, Hadrian converted Jerusalem into a Roman city with colonial status, named after himself (Publius Aelius Hadrianus), colonia Aelia Capitolina, had temples of Jupiter constructed on the Jewish Temple site in Jerusalem and the Samaritan Mt. Gerizin, banned Jews from Jerusalem except for a service of lamentation one day a year, and changed the name of the province from Judaea to its earlier designation Syria Palaestina.[27] Hadrian's measures ended Jewish national militancy while leaving Jews free in the exercise of their religion;[28] and it may be considered a vindication of Pompey's original settlement.

The century in Palestine after Hadrian's death was generally peaceful and prosperous. Roman rule was firm and orderly, Parthian power was on the

---

25. Cf. P. Benoit et al., *Discoveries in the Judaean Desert* II, *Les Grottes de Murabba'at*, Oxford, 1961, Nos. 24, 43, 44; Y. Yadin, *Bar Kokhba: The Rediscovery of the Legendary Hero of the Last Jewish Revolt against Imperial Rome*, London and New York, 1971, pp. 124–39, 175–81. Sources: Dio Cassius lxix.12–14; cf. Eusebius, *Historia Ecclesiastica* iv.6; Appian, *Syria* 50. Cf. J. A. Fitzmyer, "The Bar Kochba Period," *Saint Mary's Theology Studies* I, 1962, pp. 133–68. The material is conveniently assembled and translated in Y. Yadin, *Bar Kokhba* (N25), pp. 255–59.

26. M. Avi-Yonah, *Map of Roman Palestine*, 2nd ed., London, 1940, p. 10. Original publication in *Quarterly of the Department of Antiquities of Palestine*, Vol. V (1935), pp. 139–93; Y. Yadin, *Bar Kokhba* (N25), p. 193.

27. Cf. Herodotus I 105; II 104, 106; III 5, 91; IV 39; VII 89.

28. Cf. H. Mantel, "The Causes of the Bar Kokhba Revolt," *Jewish Quarterly Review* 58 (1968), pp. 224–42, 274–96.

wane, and the Jews were financially unable to support another revolt, the less so because of Roman taxation that rose with the current inflation. Members of the Jewish population, whose submission to Roman domination scarcely concealed their resentment of it, were forbidden to reside in Aelia Capitolina or its environs, and they migrated in large numbers to the agriculturally attractive district of Galilee, which became, consequently, the new center of rabbinic learning and synagogue-building.[29] The compilation and redaction of the Jewish oral, legal tradition (Mishnah), which probably occurred during this century, attests a measure of economic and political stability in Galilee. But the fatalities from war, the sale of Jewish prisoners of war into slavery[30] and the Roman ban on proselytism,[31] reduced the Jewish population perhaps to half what it had been in 135.[32] On the other hand gentile immigration into Palestine increased, especially into the new cities founded by Septimius Severus (193–211), Eleutheropolis on the Jerusalem-to-Gaza road and Diospolis (Lydda), and into the southern part of the province.

During the half century between the death of the Roman emperor Severus Alexander (235) and the accession to the throne of Diocletian in 284, when the Roman empire was delivered over to military anarchy, the empire seemed on the verge of disintegration. Then the ideal of the emperor as servant shifted to that of the emperor as master, and his concern with the safety and efficiency of the state was transformed into necessity to maintain himself in office. The military procedures of Roman administration, which had already during the Severan era preempted and replaced the civil, now were applied in rivalry against contenders for the purple; and anarchy became the norm, as no less than eighteen generals were crowned emperor only to be killed shortly thereafter. In all this turmoil the Jewish province of Palestine did not attempt to break free of Roman control, a sign that militant Jewish nationalism had been successfully suppressed.

---

29. E. L. Sukenik, *Ancient Synagogues in Palestine and Greece*, London, 1934. Cf. E. M. Meyers, A. T. Kraabel, J. F. Strange, *Ancient Synagogue Excavations at Khirbet Shema', Upper Galilee, Israel 1970–72, Annual of the American School of Oriental Research*, Vol. XLII, Durham, N. C., 1976.

30. E. M. Smallwood, *The Jews under Roman Rule* (N10), p. 457.

31. Cf. W. G. Braude, *Jewish Proselytizing in the First Five Centuries of the Common Era*, Providence, R. I., 1940.

32. M. Avi-Yonah, *The Holy Land* (N10), p. 220.

SUGGESTIONS FOR FURTHER STUDY:

E. M. Smallwood, *The Jews under Roman Rule* (Leiden, 1976); M. Avi-Yonah, *The Jews of Palestine, A Political History from the Bar Kokhba War to the Arab Conquest* (Oxford: Blackwell, 1976).

X

THE CHRISTIAN CONQUEST OF ROME

Christianity is deeply rooted in the pre-Alexandrian Near East, in Judaism and the Hellenistic and Roman worlds. In its conquest of the Mediterranean world and its claims to ecumenical value and validity, the Christian Church is a political legacy of Alexander. To be sure, the claims of monotheistic religion are necessarily exclusive and inevitably worldwide, but the astonishing missionary zeal of the early church partook in no small measure of the ecumenical drive released into the world by Alexander of Macedon. To say this is not to derive Christian faith from coincidental happenings, contemporary concerns, or local movements of the first century of our era. Rather an awareness of that ecumenical drive sharpens one's focus on the distinctive interpretations Christian thought gave to those forces and events in the midst of which it arose, in the terms of which it was expressed, and against the power of which it fought. The Christian religion and its vehicle the Christian Church shared in Alexander's legacy in remarkable if not predictable fashion.

Christian faith centers in the life and work of Jesus Christ, who lived in Palestine from about 6 B.C. until his death at Jerusalem by crucifixion in about A.D. 30.[1] Born of a Jewish mother, he could trace his genealogy

---

1. Herod the Great, during whose reign Jesus was born, died in 4 B.C.. The census mentioned in Luke 2:1ff. as the official event of Jesus' birth year is confusing. The first Roman census of Judaea and Samaria, not all of Palestine, was taken in A.D. 6, when P. Sulpicius Quirinius was legate of Syria. A census, i.e., "taxation," may have been concluded when C. Sentius Saturninus was legate of Syria 9–6 B.C., as Tertullian suggests. For a review of the problem, cf. E. M. Smallwood, *The Jews under Roman Rule*, Leiden, 1976, pp. 568–71 and G. B. Caird, "Chronology of the New Testament," *The Interpreter's Dictionary of the Bible*, New York, 1962.

through Joseph back to Abraham and Adam and thus to God. (Luke 3:23-38).[2] Beginning his preaching career in A.D. 28 or 29, Jesus celebrated one or perhaps as many as three Passovers before he was crucified on a Friday at the beginning of a Passover feast, perhaps in A.D. 30 or 31.

The story of Jesus' career comes to us not in records that can be identified as having been kept by his contemporaries, but rather in books written by those "who believed in his name," who set down their accounts decades after his crucifixion. Research about Jesus must therefore begin with investigation of the early Christian Church. Our earliest witness to the life of the nascent Christian community is contained in letters of the apostle Paul, who died probably in Rome sometime after A.D. 60. The chronology of his life can be reconstructed on the basis of Josephus' history, the account in Acts in the New Testament, and the few biographical and historical references in his letters. From the available data we can conclude that Paul arrived in Corinth in the early part of A.D. 50 (Acts 18:12).[3] Working back from this date we place his first missionary journey from Antioch in 47–48 and his conversion before that in 33. Working forward from the year 50, we date his arrest in Jerusalem to the summer of 57 and his departure for Rome late in 59. The last we hear of him is in Rome. No ancient author apart from the biblical witnesses mentions Paul, and he remains, therefore, a hero of the Church. The Christian community, to which he wrote between 50 and 60 and in which he worked, produced the authors of the gospel[4] narratives of Jesus.

The gospels were written some time after Paul's death. Mark, the earliest, was probably written after the disciple Peter died and before Jerusalem was destroyed (cf. Mark 13:14), between 65 and 67; Matthew and Luke, both dependent on Mark, seem to know of Jerusalem's fall and may therefore have been written between 80 and 85; the Fourth Gospel,

---

2. It is impossible to harmonize the Joseph genealogies in Matthew (1:1-17) and Luke with each other or with their insistence on Jesus' birth of the Virgin Mary. Evidently Jesus' social position had more to do with his mother's husband than with his divine father. Cf. Cyrus Gordon, "Paternity at Two Levels," JBL 96 (1977) 101.

3. Before the consulship of Gallio (July 51 to June 52) in the early part of A.D. 50 (Acts:18:12).

4. The word Gospel (Anglo-Saxon "god-spell" = good tale, namely a story from or about a god) is a translation of the Latin *evangelium* which itself is a transcription of the Greek, *evangelion*, which in the New Testament refers to the good news of God's purpose.

John, a few lines of which are preserved on a papyrus fragment of the early second century, was most likely written a decade after Matthew and Luke. These accounts are not histories or digests, though they claim to be historical; they are not theological treatises either, though they proclaim doctrine. They are not the result of research so much as they are carefully arranged compilations of traditions, customs and forms necessary to the common life of the Christian community and its message to the world. They are witnesses to "Jesus Christ and the truth about him." As with Alexander and any other person, what Jesus said and did has value both in itself and in what others find in it. Alexander opened to men's eyes a new view of the world; Jesus opened to men's eyes a new view of God. The Church declares that Jesus is God's son and that the work he accomplished has absolute value.

The teaching of Jesus about God cannot be fully summarized though it can be suggested briefly. He taught that God, the Creator and Lord of life, requires of those who would serve him total allegiance, not simply observance of special laws, which could lead a man who thinks he has been obedient to lodge a claim of merit or deserving against God. One cannot, on the basis of one's goodness or achievements, direct God to do anything. Rather, Jesus said, allegiance to God incorporates a sense of obligation, reverence and delight in living; it is that feeling of gratitude and responsibility for the gift of life which leads one to give oneself completely to serving God.

But what does it mean to serve God? Where does one encounter God? In answer to these questions Jesus insisted that God is not remote and inaccessible, but that he comes, meeting men unexpectedly at appointed or unappointed times and places in their lives. His coming is in the everyday events of life, in the lives and demands of other people, in moments of reflection, decision and resolve. God's coming is both an act of grace, because it illuminates what we may become, and a matter of judgment, because it condemns what we are, leaving men without excuse for their mistakes and deserving no reward for what they believe to be their good efforts. This divine-human encounter occurs in a man's dealings with other people, and a major element in Jesus' teaching about God is that a man meets God in his fellow-men and serves God in serving them (Matt. 25:40 " . . . as you did it to one of the least of these my brethren, you did it to me"). Supremely, the church believes, one encounters God in Jesus, who is therefore the Christ (God's messiah, the anointed one); and the salvation Jesus offers is to deliver a man from his past, so that a man's past does not become his fate.

Man's total allegiance to God in the service of mankind is possible, Jesus explained, not by legal observance, but in love. Legal observance itself is distorted without love. Laws are guideposts, marking stages along the road of allegiance; and one traverses the road, not to be rewarded for the number of guideposts passed but for the outcome of the journey. That outcome is love itself, which has been called a turning away from oneself toward God and thus toward one's fellow-men. The supreme example and illustration of that love is, of course, Jesus' crucifixion. These elements in Jesus' doctrine of God undergird the interpretation of his life that developed in the church, and the stages in that development signal steps in the growth of the church.

Gaps in our knowledge of Christian origins are too numerous and significant to permit a coherent historical account. We do not know how or when the churches in Alexandria and Rome arose, how James the brother of Jesus (Gal. 1:19) became head of the church in Jerusalem, what happened to Peter or Paul, what happened to some of Paul's letters (cf. Col. 4:16 "the letter from Laodicea") or why no writings have survived from the church in Jerusalem, which was preeminently important in the mid-first century. We do not know whether Paul had an interest in the Jesus of history (cf. 2 Cor. 5:16), whether he could assume that the recipients of his letters knew the gospel story even as he took for granted their knowledge of the Hebrew scriptures (Rom. 15:4), what their sources of information about Jesus or Jewish history might have been, or when knowledge of the Jesus of history became important to the church. We know only vaguely the fate of the Jerusalem church after the city fell before the Roman armies in 70. The birth of churches in Judaea (Gal. 1:22) and Antioch (Gal. 2:11ff.) is nowhere recorded, and the practices of the early church can be perceived only dimly. The privilege of ordaining apostles, for example, seems to have been reserved for Jerusalem, but was early usurped by Antioch; Ephesus may have been the center of a baptist movement (Acts 19:1ff.; John 1:6ff., 19ff., the Baptist was not the Messiah); and the slow spread of Christianity from the synagogues of the Jewish dispersion to non-Jewish cities like Milan cannot be traced at all. We do know that James, the leader of the church in Jerusalem, was stoned at the instigation of the Jewish high priest in 62,[5] but the reasons for his death are not clearly understood.

---

5. Josephus, *Antiquities* XX.ix.1(197–203).

It is clear, however, that the gradual establishment of Christianity within the Roman world necessitated more and more elaborate and precise organization of the doctrinal and institutional life of the church. Problems of definition and structure, which at first had existed only peripherally, increasingly demanded central attention. That attention required the church in turn to take account of existing philosophical systems and legal structures in society, to give a satisfactory account of itself both to itself and to the world in and for which it worked. But according to what norms could the church properly define its institutional life? And how could it bring its members to accept any credal or institutional norms? Legitimate quarrels over deeply held convictions inescapably arose among Christians and did divide the church, especially in the fifth century. The church did not spring into the world full-blown like Athena from the head of Zeus, and the diverse roots of its heritage inevitably formed and shaped its life in the world.

These roots, which reveal a mosaic of religious belief in the first century, can be readily identified. The church claimed to have received a new revelation of God, but it expressed its message in familiar idioms that derived in the first instance from its understanding of the Jewish scriptures. From those writings Jesus himself learned to regard God not as the organizing principle of the world, who is therefore open to rational discovery and understanding, but as the Creator of all that is, the sovereign and therefore free lord of history. This God can be known only as he reveals himself, and therefore, however important the study of nature may be to human life, for Christianity natural science cannot give answers to man's profound search for justice, meaning and authentic existence. The Christian understanding of God thus derives more from history than from nature.

This biblical approach to God emphasizes man's relationship with the God who encounters him. Speculation about what God is fades into repentance before the commanding voice of God the Creator and Judge who confronts man with the riddles of human existence and exposes human pride (Job 42:1-6). That encounter raises the essential question of purpose, and it directs men to submission and obedience, to the proper relationship of creatures to their Creator. For Christians the Stoic ideal of harmonious equilibrium in the universe is not the goal of human life. The goal is, rather, active assent to the sovereign will of the Creator and Sustainer of life whose purposes are always being revealed. An active involvement in the life of the world was thus an original element of Christian commitment, and withdrawal from the world could be understood only as an opportunity for more effective struggle against the evil forces that threaten to destroy God's good creation.

Also from Jewish scriptures the church adopted the idea of God's chosen, holy people in covenant with him. That covenanted people were to be loyal and obedient to the God who made them a nation, and their loyalty to God demanded release from any structures that could restrict their primary obligation to him. The Christian view of citizenship in a state thus included the state's obligation to provide privacy, the unrestricted opportunity for a person in private life to do whatever was necessary for self-fulfillment as the obedient creature of God. The details of that problem and its satisfactory solution require continuing definition and resolution, but to the church and especially to Augustine (died 430) is due credit for attempting to state and to solve the puzzle of citizenship in two worlds openly and directly.

As a sect of Judaism, early Christianity was centered initially in Jerusalem, where the temple stood and where the crucifixion-resurrection event had occurred. The destruction of that center in the year 70 probably had more to do with the release of Christianity from its Palestinian moorings than any other single event. Thereafter, in their spread throughout the world, Christians adopted the Jewish synagogue as model for their own meeting place and the Jewish scriptures as their holy book containing the record of God's activity among men. Traditions of scriptural interpretation, especially the allegorical method, served as models for the new religion, models which it would in the fourth and fifth centuries subject to critical scrutiny and revision.

The growing church drew support not only from its Jewish antecedents but from its Hellenistic and Roman environment as well. The Hellenic view of the world, contrasting sharply with that of the Near East, made man responsible for understanding and controlling nature and society. Men, according to the Greek view, could discover the secrets of nature and create a society that would make its members good; and the Greeks thus created the disciplines of science and politics. Their interest in these inquiries, however, colored their view of history, which they perceived either as a biological rise and fall of state and people or as superb political pedagogy. History as the record of man's search for meaning seems not to have occurred to them. Greek tragedy, which did explore human responsibility in a revolutionary manner, was never incorporated into history, to which ultimate purpose or goal was not ascribed. The church adopted Greek ideas about nature and society, but it could not accept the cyclical Greek view of history, a view which would not accord with the Jewish conception of God the Creator. The optimistic idea that God is working out his purpose in history remains an article of faith rather than a datum of science.

Nevertheless, the Greek perception of reality, as matter molded into form by reason, made man, a being of reason, responsible to the perfecting powers of reason. He should therefore turn himself into a work of art, a microcosm of God's universe, a wise man, excellent in virtue. This notion of self-perfection turned man inward, away from the world and responsibility for it, to self-improvement and private excellence. The idea has at times strongly influenced Christian thought, if it has seldom dominated it; but the New Testament view that man to be good must be set free from himself by God has always informed the Greek view and shifted its emphasis outward to the life and work of the redeemed community. There excellence and virtue are judged by the purposes of God. The concise statement of a professor of theology sums up the Christian view: "If it works out for the good, God gets the glory; if it turns out for the bad, you take the blame."

The parallels between Christianity and the mystery religions are so numerous that some scholars have dubbed Christianity "the last and greatest of the Greco-Oriental mystery religions."[6] That judgment, however, directs attention to similarities in the paraphernalia of cultic observance rather than to likenesses in central doctrine. The popular religious hunger of the early centuries of our era for redemptive cleansing and power was satisfied by the "refurbished vegetation rites" of the mysteries, without philosophical or theological substance. No evidence of a "mystery theology" has come to light, and it seems indeed probable that the mystery cults borrowed some of their features—baptism for regeneration, the redeemed and knowledgeable community, holy communion, death and resurrection of a divine savior—from Christianity. Their primary power, however, consisted in offering deliverance from fate, security within the world, and participation at the last in the rising of their dying god. Parallels between rites of the Christians and adherents of the mystery religions turn out upon inspection to reveal less about either than about the pervasive religious temper of the age.

A much debated phenomenon in early Christian history is gnosticism,

---

6. S. K. Eddy, *The King is Dead*, Lincoln, Neb., 1961, p. 181; F. C. Grant, *Roman Hellenism and the New Testament*, New York, 1962, pp. 76–79.

the origins of which are not certainly known. For a long time gnosticism was thought to be a Christian heresy of the second century, but its antecedents have been traced to ancient Iranian traditions and to pre-Christian Judaism as well as to Greek thought contemporary but unconnected with Christianity. Gnosticism, which existed in various forms, was a religious or philosophic theory of self-discovery and spiritual liberation. Gnosis was the saving knowledge, transmitted by an emissary from God to the religious devotee, awakening his inner man to its true nature, origin, and destiny in the world of light. Until that knowledge was given, the devotee remained ignorant of the presence of the divine spirit or inner man within himself; but once awakened to its presence he could aid its return to the realm of light and true being by ascetic and cathartic measures. Gnosis was knowledge necessary for physical redemption of a man's heavenly spark of light from its imprisonment in evil matter. Gnosticism, which has parallels in Islamic Sufism and sometimes within Christian thought, presupposes a dualism of light and darkness, being and non-being. The two are locked in a struggle, one consequence of which is that sparks of light have been imprisoned in darkness, and a man's salvation consists in the liberation of his own divine spark, his inner man. Salvation is thus from the world rather than for the world, and the struggle of light against darkness is mythological rather than historical. Gnostic parallels may be observed in the language of the Pauline letters and the Fourth Gospel, but the Christian view of creation as being very good is poles removed from gnostic dualism.

The attempts of the Christian church both to explore the meaning of God's revelation in Christ and to come to terms with its own religious, philosophical and political environment brought it into controversies of far-reaching importance for world history. The early centuries, which saw its confusion with the Jewish synagogue, struggles with pagan polytheism, persecution by the state and spread throughout the world, culminated in the church's being accepted as a legal institution by the emperor Constantine, who ruled 306–337, and its being declared the state religion by the decrees of Theodosius I, who ruled 379–395, forbidding the rites of pagan worship, citing violators of the decrees as offenders against the state and subject to severe penalties, and declaring Nicene Christianity to be the orthodox expression of the faith.

That political culmination came partly as a result of the church's open and prominent discussions about its relationship to the world, not only with its critics but among its own members as well. Christian apologetics (defenses of the faith before the world) were written early in the second century by men like the Syrian convert, Justin Martyr, who died ca. 163. He asserted that the revelation of God in Christ was a completion of the truths proclaimed by Greek philosophers and teachers, and his student, Tatian, drew heavily for his theology on Hellenic thought, even though he condemned the idea that there could be any truth outside the Christian faith. He thus demonstrated that a synthesis of Christian and pagan wisdom was not only possible but inevitable.

The idea that Christian thought and Greek philosophy could be synthesized was propounded explicitly by Clement of Alexandria (ca. 150–c. 215) in a number of treatises, and he was followed by the theologian and "founder of biblical science," Origen of Caesarea (ca. 184–ca. 253). Origen also defined the early Christian view that the secular state had the god-given duty to provide for the material welfare of its subjects and was not an instrument of Satan but of God, even when it violated fundamental laws of God's will. Christians might therefore remain aloof from involvement in state activity and might also criticize the state's rulers, officials and laws; but they could not attempt to destroy the state.[7] This double conviction that Christian truth informs and completes pagan truth, and that the state is God's instrument for good gave urgency to the struggles for truth in the Christian controversies of the fourth and fifth centuries.

Those disputes erupted at the end of the third century when, as Diocletian, who ruled 284–305, was restoring stability to the Roman state in the form of despotism, and later Constantine was able for the first time to bring representatives of the local churches together in a world council, Christians attempted to define their conception of God. Because they insisted on affirming faith in the one God of the Jews and in Jesus of Nazareth as both Christ and God, they had to reconcile the two statements, demonstrating that their faith was both consonant with Jewish monotheism and distinct from pagan polytheism. That theological reconciliation between God the Father and Christ the Son was hammered out in the trinitarian controversies of the fourth century, associated especially with the ecumenical council at Nicea in 325. But the difficulties did not end there, for the church also had to explain the relationship between the divine and

---

7. F. Dvornik, *Early Christian and Byzantine Political Philosophy*, Washington, D.C., 1966, p. 610.

the human in Christ. A satisfactory statement of that relationship was attempted in the Christological controversies of the fifth century, associated primarily with the ecumenical council at Chalcedon in 451. In all, the church met six times in ecumenical conclave to define the essentials of its belief about God. The result of those meetings was to establish as Christian orthodoxy those dogmas accepted by majority vote of the delegates, and to separate from the orthodox church those minorities who could not accept the doctrinal formulations of the majority. The church was thus divided in spite of the best efforts of the emperors, theologians and ecclesiastical politicians who strove for its unity; and the creation of Christian orthodoxy was a new application of the Hellenistic ideal of a single world united culturally and politically.

Christian orthodoxy, as it finally emerged, insisted on four affirmations: that 1. Christ is true God (Council at Nicea in 325); 2. he is true man (Council at Constantinople in 381); 3. he is one person (Councils at Ephesus in 431 and Chalcedon in 441); and 4. the divine and human in Christ remain distinct, with all personal union and harmony (Councils at Chalcedon in 451 and Constantinople in 680). These trinitarian and Christological affirmations should not be understood as systematically coherent with each other, yielding a rational formulation of the nature of God or the person of Christ. They are not explanatory formulas but rather theological boundaries. The Church does not accept or propound a neatly closed system of theology but makes instead affirmations about the mysterious and contradictory facts both of human life and of divine revelation, affirmations which may appear to be logically paradoxical, but with which, nevertheless, the Church is prepared to live and work as it struggles to define and proclaim God's redemptive purposes in the world for human life.

The trinitarian discussion, which dominated Christian thought in the fourth century, concerned the relationship of Christ to God. Are there personal distinctions in God? If there are, is the Son subordinate to the Father? If there are not, was it God who suffered on the cross? But how can God suffer? Is, then, Jesus really God? These problems had already arisen in the Church in the second century, when the notions that if Christ suffered he was not divine[8] or that he only appeared to suffer[9] were rejected as

---

8. Ebionitism. The significance of the name, which means 'poverty,' is not known.
9. Docetism, from the word meaning 'to seem,' as opposed to reality.

robbing the Chist-event of redemptive power. It was the teaching of an elderly Alexandrian priest, Arius, however, that in 318 made the trinitarian problem a burning issue. Arius, following his teachers at Antioch, tried to preserve the unity (monarchia) of God by teaching that Jesus the Son was a created being, God's highest creation to be certain, but not himself God, not of the same substance (homo-ousia) as God, but of a similar substance (homoi-ousia).

That assertion of Arius, which was condemned in Alexandria but found support in Palestine and Asia Minor, brought the Church into controversy, not only about God's unity, but also about human redemption through Christ's suffering. There had been those who said that God had adopted as his anointed (Christ) the man Jesus, in whom God's word had come to dwell in unusual divine power. Those theologians were known as dynamic monarchians or adoptionists because they thought Jesus was exalted by the power of the One God. Others had said that God manifests himself in various forms, one of them being Christ, the Son. Christ, they declared, was a mode of God; and we know these teachers, therefore, as modalistic monarchians, because for them Jesus was one manifestation of the single God. Modalistic monarchians are sometimes known as Sabellians, after their most outstanding spokesman, Sabellius, who came to Rome from Syria ca. 215. The modalists, consistent with their doctrine, taught that God himself hung on the cross, the Father suffered. Monarchian theology thus preserved God's unity, but it did so at the expense of God's redemptive purpose. When Arius thought to solve the difficulties in these conceptions by his doctrine of the created Christ, he made Christ an intermediary between God and man, neither God nor man, and thus denied significance to Christ's incarnation and crucifixion-resurrection, by making them events in which neither God nor mankind were existentially affected.

Meanwhile, Tertullian in the west, who lived most of his life (ca. 160–c. 220) at Carthage, had asserted the one divine substance (substantia) in which the persons (personae) Father, Son and Spirit share, and declared the Godhead to be three "not in quality but in sequence, not in substance but in aspect, not in power but in manifestation."[10] Similar to Tertullian's thought was that of Origen who was born and educated in Alexandria and settled in Palestine at Caesarea in 231. He taught that

10. Quoted by J. C. Davies, *The Early Christian Church*, New York, 1967, p. 186.

Father, Son and Spirit are three species (hypostaseis) of one genus (ousia), the Son being the eternal generation of the Father. These views of Origen and Tertullian, which laid the foundations for what would later be accepted as orthodox doctrine, not only made the Son subordinate to the Father but also raised the problem, how does the Son proceed from the Father?

These were the problems Arius had set out to solve, but his solution, which made of Christ (the Logos, John 1:1) a demigod, caused such commotions in the Church that Constantine took the extraordinary step of convoking a general council of bishops at Nicaea in Bithynia to settle the issue. Arius' first opponent was Athanasius, bishop of Alexandria from 328 until his death in 373. He declared that the Logos was eternal, uncreated and of the same essence with God; and he insisted that in Christ, who encounters us as a man, we confront God as He is.[11] We have no official record of the proceedings of this council, but the statement of faith it endorsed, together with the signatures of the 300 bishops, on various copies of the creed, have survived. The council decided that God the Son was "begotten," not created, "that is to say, of the Father's substance consubstantial with the Father." The reaffirmation of that statement by the Council at Constantinople in 381, with the further qualification that Christ was not only true and perfect God but also true and perfect man, marks the birth of the orthodox, catholic Church.

The importance of those decisions for Christian doctrine should not obscure the political and religious significance of Constantine's initiative in convening the first Council at Nicea. The emperor acted from the conviction that he represented God on earth: he summoned the bishops to consult about an agenda he set beforehand, at a meeting over which he presided but on the resolutions of which he did not vote; he equated the decisions of the bishops, reached under his guidance, with God's will; in the wake of their decisions he banned the works of heretics; and he wrote a letter to the Persian king, Shapur, in which he claimed recognition by all Christians within his own empire and in Persia, too, as God's viceregent on earth. The earlier Alexandrian and Hellenistic claims to universal dominion could hardly have been more clearly expressed.

The Christological controversy in the Church was closely connected

---

11. Cf. Hermann Dörries, *Constantine the Great*, trans. Roland H. Bainton, New York, 1972, p. 146.

with the trinitarian. To solve the problem of the Son's subordination to the Father by removing any question of temporality from the divine relationship and asserting paradoxically that "God is one object in himself and three objects to himself," leaves unsolved the question: If Christ is consubstantial with God, who is Jesus? This problem, like the trinitarian one, also became a matter for state intervention; but the consequences of its solution for the church were more far-reaching. When the Church finally formulated a Christological creed, it found itself divided between orthodox Byzantium and Rome on the one hand and the monophysite Near East on the other (Armenians, Syrians, Copts and Ethiopians). With due allowance for economic and political causes of that division, the rise of "national" feeling in the Near East and the easy Islamic conquest of monophysite territories there cannot be dissociated from the disaffection felt by those Christians with the theological decisions of the Councils. The West was less politically affected because the great councils at Ephesus (431) and Chalcedon (451) in Asia Minor were convoked at the time when the Huns were invading Europe. St. Augustine died during the Vandal siege of his city, Hippo, in North Africa; and Attila met his death probably near Troyes in 453. The Christological dispute could not, therefore, capture in the West the same tremendous energy and passion it consumed in the East. Perhaps this western concentration on its own self-preservation together with its general lack of familiarity with the metaphysical presuppositions of the leading philosophical systems (Platonic, Aristotelian, Stoic and neo-Platonic) and its greater familiarity with law and the satisfaction it demands allowed it to unite behind the paradoxical affirmation of "Christ in two natures, unconfusedly, unchangeably, indivisibly, inseparably," which became the strait gate separating Christological orthodoxy from heresy.

The origins of the Christological dispute, which broke out in the fourth century in spite of strong ecclesiastical opinion that the Nicaean statement "was sufficient to solve all important questions," lie in the earlier efforts of Origen and others in the third century to state adequately the nature of the union of God and man in Jesus Christ, i.e., to reconcile the humanity of Jesus with what later became the Nicene assertion that Christ is "consubstantial with the Father." The question is, "How can the 'one Christ' be both 'true God and true man,' perfect in Godhead, perfect in manhood?"[12] Efforts to answer that question led to the statements of

---

12. Aloys Grillmeier, *Christ in Christian Tradition*, New York, 1965, p. 482.

Apollinarius (bishop of Laodicea in Syria from ca. 374 until his death ca. 390), which were declared by the synods of Alexandria in 362, Rome in 377, Antioch in 379, and Constantinople in 381 to be heretical. Apollinarius insisted on the indivisibility of Christ's person, pointing out that one person cannot be divided into two; if Christ were perfect God and perfect man, he would be two Sons, not one; and he affirmed that in the Incarnation, when the Word became flesh (John 1:14), a composite union of Word and flesh occurred: the one God, manifested in flesh, is not two persons, nor simply God, but a unification, a synthesis of God with human flesh; the man in Christ first became man through the union of the divine spirit and earthly flesh.[13] This 'heavenly man,' as Apollinarius called him, "is neither fully man nor God (alone), but a mixture of God and man,"[14] "a compound unity in human form" in which the divine remains preeminent. "The flesh and the 'determining principle of the flesh' are one prosopon" (person).[15] The trouble with Apollinarius' explanation was that it deprived Christ of his humanity and thus made of his temptation and suffering a charade. What is the glory of sinlessness without a real possibility for sin? Human nature unlimited by human weakness is not human.

The Apollinarian Christology, despite its theological inadequacies, did preserve the oneness of Christ and was therefore widely accepted; and the attempts to remove its shortcomings brought on the debates that resulted in the credal formulation at Chalcedon in 451. Those debates appear in the

---

13. Ibid., p. 222.

14. Ibid., p. 224, citing H. Lietzmann, *Appollinarius von Laodicea und seine Schule*, Tübingen, 1904, p. 234.

15. A. Grillmeier, *Christ in Christian Tradition* (N12), p. 230. On Apollinarius' teaching cf. W. H. C. Frend, *Rise of the Monophysite Movement*, Cambridge, 1972, pp. 113–19. Knowledge of the meanings inherent in the Greek words, *ousia, hypostasis, physis, prosopon* as they were used at various times by the theologians in their understanding of Christ is essential to a proper understanding of their credal statements and arguments. Brief explanatory definitions are given by R. V. Sellers, *The Council of Chalcedon*, London, 1953, pp. 138–39, n. 7, as follows: *ousia* (Latin substantia), an Aristotelian term signifying either a) 'distinctive individuality' or b) 'a common undifferentiated substance,' 'that which is common among a group of particulars'; *hypostasis* (Latin substantia), a metaphysical term for a) 'a particular object or individual' or b) 'that which underlies and therefore possesses reality and genuineness'; *physis*, an empirical term meaning a) 'an individual,' 'the person himself' and b) a generic term equivalent to *hypostasis; prosopon*, a nontechnical, nonmetaphysical term denoting 'appearance,' 'oneness,' 'individuality' of an individual. In Nestorius *ousia* signifies essence, *physis* nature, and *hypostasis* the actual concrete reality.

opposition that arose between the theological school at Alexandria, which emphasized the doctrine of the Word made flesh, and the school at Antioch, which expounded instead the idea of the Word become man.

Basic to these formulations were contemporary philosophical theories about what constitutes a unity. One could think of unity 1. as an "aggregation of component parts" as in a wire cable, 2. as a "union of predominance" in which lesser parts become incidental to the whole, or 3. as a union of "mutual coextension" in which a minor part does not become incidental or negligible but extends through the whole. The Antiochians accepted the view of Christ as being God and man in the first sense, as an aggregation, God dwelling in a Man; the Alexandrians thought of Christ in the second, as a union of predominance, "The Person of the Redeemer is altogether one" out of two (*ek* duo). Both avoided the Apollinarian "mixture," but the danger of the former was to make Christ two persons, God and man, preserving the distinction between divine and human in Christ at the expense of his unity; the danger of the latter was to make Christ one person, God, preserving his unity at the expense of a distinction between divine and human in him. The final formulation, accepted at Chalcedon, one person (hypostasis) in two (*in* duo) natures (physeis), comes close to the third theory of unity, a union of mutual coextension.[16] Western theologians tended to fix their attention, not so much as the Alexandrians did on the meaning of Christ's incarnation nor as the Antiochians did on his resurrection, but rather on his meritorious and atoning death on the cross.

The doctrine of Christ that made him two persons is associated with the teaching of Nestorius, bishop of Constantinople from 428–431. Nestorius, who was considered by one of his contemporary detractors to be a tactless, disgracefully illiterate though fluent preacher of excellent voice, lashed out in his inaugural course of sermons in the capital against the term *theotokos*, "mother of God" as being an inappropriate epithet for Mary, the mother of Jesus. He thought *theotokos* was one-sided and confused the divinity and humanity of Christ; he therefore insisted that Mary was *Christotokos*, mother of Christ. "Not God," he said, "but the temple in which God dwelt was born of Mary." The trouble was that he spoke of the divine and human in Christ as being *conjoined* and thus appeared to espouse

---

16. The argument comes from J. G. Davies, *The Early Christian Church*, New York, 1967, p. 335.

duality in the person of Christ: the Son was not a mixture, as Apollinarius had suggested, but a duality, not only of natures but of persons. What Nestorius actually thought is still a matter of dispute, but in his lifetime his teaching was declared heretical and he was deposed and condemned. It now seems that his banishment at the insistence of Cyril, bishop of Alexandria from 412 until his death in 444, was more politically than theologically motivated. [17]

The leading position in eastern Christendom, bestowed upon the patriarchate of Constantinople by the synod meeting there in 381, had dealt a severe blow to the claims of Alexandria, which to the disadvantage of Constantinople could trace its Christian origins to the apostle, St. Mark, whereas the capital city had to satisfy itself with the fiction that St. Andrew had Christianized it. Whenever, therefore, Alexandrian bishops could denigrate Constantinople before the Church, they did so to demonstrate their own ecclesiastical or theological superiority to the imperial see. An opportunity for such a demonstration had arisen in the *theotokos* sermons of Nestorius, in which Cyril detected a new form of adoptionism, namely that God had chosen the man Jesus as the human dwelling for his Son; and Cyril exploited his opportunity ruthlessly.

The conflict aroused by Nestorius led to his deposition by the council at Ephesus in 431. Thereafter he spent four years in a monastery near Antioch before he was banished to Upper Egypt, where he died sometime after 449. Since his works were condemned to be burned in 435, only fragments of them and his defence of his teaching, *Liber Heraclidis* "the Bazaar of Heracleides," written in 439, have survived. Later, when the emperor Zeno closed the School of the Persians at Edessa in 489, he liquidated the last outpost of Nestorianism in the Roman empire. [18] The School fled to Nisibis, and Nestorianism flourished in Mesopotamia, spreading eastward into India and China and southward into Arabia. Muhammad supposedly owed his knowledge of Christianity to a Nestorian monk, Sergius. In the 13th century the Mongols all but wiped out the Nestorians, whose Syriac-writing survivors today can be found in small communities in northern Mesopotamia and India.

The doctrine of Christ that saw his humanity absorbed into his

---

17. Cf. A. Grillmeier, *Christ in Christian Tradition* (N12), "The Nestorius-Question in Modern Study," pp. 496–505.

18. Cf. J. B. Segal, *Edessa 'The Blessed City,'* Oxford, 1970, p. 95.

divinity, so that his human nature vanished into the divine like a drop of honey when it is mixed into the sea, is associated with the teaching of Eutyches (lived ca. 378–ca. 453), superior of a monastery in Constantinople. He taught that before the union of the divine and the human in Christ there were indeed two natures, but that after the union there was only the divine, the human becoming an accident or property of the divine. This Eutychian doctrine, known an monophysitism, was condemned by a synod at Constantinople in 448, but Eutyches was so confident of the correctness of his view that he persuaded the emperor Theodosius II to covene a Council at Ephesus to settle the matter. The Council was duly convoked in 449, presided over not by Flavian, patriarch of Constantinople, but by Dioscurus, bishop of Alexandria; its representatives were so carefully chosen (the Antiochenes were excluded) and its procedures so prescribed that its conclusions in favor of Eutyches were a foregone certainty. The delegation from Rome was not permitted to speak, and Flavian was so mauled by the attendants of the partisan bishops that he died of his wounds. Leo, the bishop of Rome, whose delegation to the meeting departed secretly so as not to be forced to subscribe to the council's decrees, appropriately dubbed the meeting 'Robber's Synod,' a name that has endured. When the emperor Theodosius II, who had supported Eutyches, died in the summer of 450, his sister Pulcheria and her husband Marcian espoused the orthodox position and convened a Council at Chalcedon in October 451 to undo the mischief of Ephesus. This Synod condemned Eutyches and formulated the doctrine of Christ, "known *in* two natures (which exist) without confusion, without change, without division, and without separation,"[19] which remains the creed of the orthodox church.

The Council of Chalcedon established orthodoxy at the expense of Christian unity. Its confession of Christ in two natures seemed to reaffirm Nestorianism and to oppose the teachings of Alexandrian bishops in favor of those from Constantinople. The monophysite opponents of the creed rejected the distinction between 'nature' and 'person' and clung to the notion that one person logically implies one nature, even to the paradoxical assertion that God was crucified. In general, the "heretical" views of Christ turn out upon inspection to be rationalizations of the mystery of his person and nature, rationalizations which the Church finally could not accept

19. R. V. Sellers, *The Council of Chalcedon* (N15), p. 211.

because they compromised what it perceived to be the original message of the Bible. The monophysites, like the Nestorians, have maintained themselves in the East as separate sects under their own bishops and patriarchs to the present day. They supported the Arabs and Turks in weakening and at last defeating Byzantine rule in the East, and they are found today in Armenia, Syria, Mesopotamia, Egypt and Ethiopia.

The great Christian Councils established the limits of Christian orthodoxy, but those limits were based on concepts which the bishops made no attempt to define philosophically or analyze carefully.[20] Their formulations did preserve both divine transcendence of the world and God's immanence in human history, leaving the mystery of God intact.[21] The bishops reached their decisions more or less democratically, by consensus, on the basis of biblical and ecclesiastical traditions which they interpreted in light of the Hellenic and Hellenistic conceptions of their time. One cannot claim, therefore, that orthodoxy is a private matter or the matter of a faction within the Christian body. It was achieved in an imperial society, by political manipulation to be sure, and at the cost of Christian unity. But it was achieved by the Church as a whole. It is scarcely either a historical necessity or a heritable possession, even though it emerged in the 4th and 5th centuries as an imperial effort at uniformity of thought. The Church tried to bring together Near Eastern and Western views of man and God, and that task proved to be impossible of satisfactory, rational fulfillment.

SUGGESTIONS FOR FURTHER STUDY:

From the vast literature on the Christian church, the following books will provide orientation for the main problems of this discussion. A succinct and uncluttered history of Christianity from its origins to recent times is given in the classic volume of Edwyn Bevan, *Christianity* (London, 1932). For the early period, Hans Conzelmann's *History of Primitive Christianity*, translated from the German by John E. Steely (Nashville, 1973), containing one appendix devoted to the history and legends of leading personalities in the early church and another reproducing important non-biblical documents, is a lucid, informative and reliable account. J. G. Davies, *The Early Christian Church: A History of its first five centuries* (New York, 1967), contains in addition to its clear and comprehensive text a judiciously selected reading list. The Hellenistic background is brilliantly sketched by Rudolf Bultmann, *Primitive Christianity in its Contemporary Setting*, translated from the German by R. H. Fuller (London,

---

20. A. Grillmeier, *Christ in Christian Tradition* (N12), pp. 482–83.
21. A. Grillmeier, *Christ in Christian Tradition* (N12), p. 491.

1956), and by F. C. Grant, *Roman Hellenism and the New Testament* (New York, 1962). The classic statement of T. R. Glover *The Conflict of Religions in the Early Roman Empire* (London, 1909), is supplemented by the extraordinary summations of John Ferguson, *The Religions of the Roman Empire* (Ithaca, 1970), including his informative bibliography. W. H. C. Frend, *Martyrdom and Persecution in the Early Church* (Oxford, 1965), is unsurpassed, and the same author's *Rise of the Monophysite Movement* (Cambridge, 1972), is a good guide to the literature. Superb guides to understanding the Christological problem are Aloys Grillmeier, *Christ in Christian Tradition*, translated from the German by J. S. Bowden (New York, 1965); J. N. D. Kelly, *Early Christian Creeds*, 2nd. ed. (London, 1960), *Early Christian Doctrine*, 2nd. ed. (London, 1960); and R. V. Sellers, *The Council of Chalcedon: a historical and doctrinal survey* (London, 1961). On Gnosticism see Elaine H. Pagels, *The Gnostic Gospels*, New York, 1979; Bentley Layton, ed., *The Rediscovery of Gnosticism*, London, 1980.

On Constantine, read the concise and authoritative account of A. H. M. Jones, *Constantine and the Conversion of Europe* (New York, 1949); and the theological account of Hermann Dörries, *Constantine the Great*, translated from the German by Roland H. Bainton (New York, 1972), with excellent bibliography. Ferdinand Lot, *The End of the Ancient World* (New York, 1961), is a model of clarity and scholarship. N. H. Baynes, *Constantine the Great and the Christian Church* (1929), has upheld the sincerity of Constantine's conversion to Christianity.

A stimulating overview of the period is given by Francis Dvornik, *Early Christian and Byzantine Political Theory*, 2 vols. (Dumbarton Oaks, Washington, D.C., 1966). A convenient and useful collection of documents in English translation has been made by J. Stevenson, *Creeds, Councils and Controversies: Documents illustrative of the history of the Church* A.D. *337–461*, 2nd ed. (London, 1973).

XI

THE BYZANTINE EXPERIMENT

What the church failed to accomplish theologically, the Christian Byzantine state tried to achieve politically. A survey of that early history from Constantine, who ruled from 324–337, to Heraclius, who ruled from 610–641, is necessarily incomplete and sketchy; but it will highlight the final effort of the Mediterranean world before the rise of medieval Europe to achieve the political and cultural unity that had been so often envisioned as a result of Alexander's Macedonian conquests. What the Greeks had dreamed and the Romans tentatively structured, the church tried to create with its grand vision of God's saving purpose and the Byzantine rulers tried to organize under the rubric of God's imperial and universal rule. The Byzantine strategy failed of its own weight in contest with a renascent Near East, but it left a political imprint for the later Ottoman statecraft and for more recent dreams of bringing the world under manageable control.[1]

The later Roman civilization which is the subject of this chapter takes its name from the Greek City, Byzantion (Latin Byzantium), which the Greeks founded about 600 B.C. on the European side of the Bosporus, commanding the entrance to the Black Sea. After the emperor Severus razed its walls in 196, the city remained neglected until Constantine selected it in 323 for his capital and rebuilt it, changing its name in 330 to Constantinople, now Istanbul. Historians have adopted its ancient name to designate the new church state of which it was the soul, mind and impregnable geographic center. Constantine's city became Christian, because of his

---

1. See the remarks of P. N. Ure, *Justinian and his Age*, Harmondsworth, 1951, pp. 166–67.

allegiance to the Christian God whom he believed to have given him his crown with the command to unify his people in peace and concord, and as a consequence of the decree of Theodosius I, that Christianity was to be the only acceptable religious faith of the state.[2] Both the new capital, which at the Council of Constantinople in 381 was declared to be "New Rome," and the new religion distinguish the later Roman (Byzantine) empire from its Latin predecessor.

The new capital was not intended to be a new creation. Its emperors did not propose to do away with Rome as a capital,[3] but they did recognize that their inescapable political and military commitments made their presence in the eastern part of the empire essential to the state's welfare. Constantine and his successors ruled in the traditions of old Rome, but Constantine ruled also as a Christian who saw perhaps that a Christian empire would one day invigorate, direct and finally supplant the aging and weakened pagan, Roman state,[4] supplying it with unassailable divine authority and sanction, exercised in the emperor's power as God's viceregent on earth. Constantine's successors accepted his vision and adopted it as their own. Their successful repulse of the barbarians westward seemed to them a proof of divine favor, which they determined to preserve by defining and maintaining proper declarations about God's nature and work among men (orthodoxy). The eastern episcopacy thus became the indispensable servant of the state, which itself adopted the absolute authority and trappings of earlier eastern empires. The emperor Julian's brief effort to reverse the process which had been set in motion by Constantine only sharpened the Christian vision in the mind of Theodosius I (the Great), who set about to realize it in his lifetime.

Theodosius brought the Arian controversy virtually to an end, establishing Nicene orthodoxy in the empire, but he did not unify the church;

---

2. *Vide supra*, p. 192. The edicts of 391 and 392 forbade access to pagan temples, that of 393 prohibited holding the Olympic games; earlier in his reign, Theodosius had looked with favor on the Christian destruction of the Serapeum, temple of the god Serapis, in Egypt. On Theodosius' attitude toward paganism see A. H. M. Jones, *The Later Roman Empire*, 2 vols., Norman, Okla., 1964, vol. 1, pp. 168–69; Paul Lemerle, *History of Byzantium*, Paris, 1961, p. 33.

3. F. Lot, *The End of the Ancient World and the Beginnings of the Middle Ages*, London, 1931, rpt. new York, 1961, pp. 36–37.

4. Norman Baynes, *Byzantium*, p. xvii–xviii.

his armies deflected the Gothic attacks westward, but at the expense of accepting overwhelming numbers of Arian Germans into their number. Theodosius' rule devolved upon his death on his two sons: the 18-year-old Arcadius, who was assigned to rule the East, i.e., Macedonia, Thrace, Asia and Egypt; and the 10-year-old Honorius, who should govern Italy, Gaul and Africa from his residence at Ravenna. By then, however, the imperial, Christian vision had lost some of its rosy hue: the Huns were harassing the borders of the state, military power rested with the Goths whom Theodosius had settled in the Balkan peninsula, and the populace no longer shared the political optimism of Theodosius or Constantine. A sign that all was not well came when the young Arcadius found himself forced to demonstrate to his impetuous appointee as patriarch of Constantinople, John Chrysostom ("golden mouthed"), the sovereignty of the state over the church. In his claim to authority over the state, and especially in his denunciation of the pleasure-loving empress Eudoxia, the patriarch was following the precedent of Ambrose, bishop of Milan from 340–397, who had excommunicated Theodosius for his massacre of the citizens of Thessalonica.[5] Chrysostom enjoyed widespread popular support, but his uncompromising spirit gradually eroded his secure position. At last the emperor deposed him and banished him to the eastern frontiers of the empire, where he died in 407. At Arcadius' death the following year, his seven-year-old son, Theodosius II, became emperor.

Regent for the first six years of Theodosius' reign was the general, Anthemius, who had become praetorian prefect of the East. Guardian for the boy-king, however, seems to have been the Sasanian monarch, Yazdagird I, who ruled from 399–421.[6] He apparently understood and respected the powerful force Christians could exert in Armenia and Syria on behalf of a ruler who would maintain their civil rights, and Arcadius no doubt had turned to him as being a more trustworthy and reliable guardian of Theodosius' royal rights than any of the Byzantine royal family or court officials would be. But the boy grew up in Constantinople under the

---

5. On St. John Chrysostom see J. C. Baur, *Der heilige Johannes Chrysostomus und seine Zeit*, 2 vols., Munich, 1929–30, English translation by Sr. M. Gonzaga, Westminster, Md., 1959, London, 1960; *Oeuvres complètes de saint Jean Chrysostome*, trans. M. Jeannin, Bar-le-Duc, 1863–67.

6. A. A. Vasiliev, *History of the Byzantine Empire*, 2 vols., Madison, Wis., 1958, vol. 1, p. 96.

208 / VISIONS OF ONE WORLD

watchful eye of his pious sister Pulcheria, who even chose his wife for him, Eudocia, the Christian daughter of an Athenian philosopher. Doubtless under Pulcheria's direction Theodosius became a devout defender of Christian orthodoxy, going so far as to exclude pagans from imperial service.[7] One of his major tasks was to defend his orthodoxy against the heretical views of his appointed patriarch Nestorius, who was finally banished to Egypt, where he died. The eastern Christians, recipients of Yazdagird's good will, seem to have abused their good fortune and brought down around their ears their benefactor's wrath, consequences of which were Yazdagird's persecution of Christians in his empire and his war on Roman Armenia.

The Romans, however, were having disastrous trouble elsewhere that prevented their march into Armenia. The shock to the empire when Rome was sacked by Alaric, king of the Visigothic federation, in 410 forced Theodosius and his advisers to find more effective ways of halting barbarian incursions across the Danube into Thrace. Seeking to reduce their dependence on military occupation, they and their successors gradually learned, as Justinian would later demonstrate, to turn money into "a technology of survival."[8] Beginning, in 421, to establish peace with the Huns, the Romans closed their borders to rebellious Hunnic subjects and agreed to pay the Hunnic king a modest tribute of gold for keeping them at home. Thirteen years later, still to maintain the peace, the Romans doubled the tribute, and in addition returned or ransomed rebels and escaped Roman prisoners, and improved trading privileges along the frontier for the barbarians. Nevertheless, in 441, Attila crossed the Danube into Singidunum (Belgrade) and Sirmium (Srem), and two years later he destroyed Naissus (Nish) and Sardica (Sofia), soundly defeating the Roman armies sent out to halt his advance. Theodosius was at last able to divert Attila from the capital by an immediate cash payment of 6000 pounds of gold and a promised triple increase in the annual tribute to 2100 pounds of gold; and Attila, having apparently satisfied himself that he could hope for little more in the Balkans, moved with his armies into Gaul. When he died there in 453 the Hunnic threat to Rome disintegrated. Theodosius, however, had earlier determined to protect Constantinople against barbarian threats with a new

---

7. A. H. M. Jones, *The Later Roman Empire* (N2), vol. 1., p. 208.

8. Peter Brown, *World of Late Antiquity*, A.D. *170–750*, New York and London, 1971, p. 155.

city wall. He therefore, three times during his reign, strengthened and extended the city walls, making the capital virtually impregnable and at the same time barring enemy access from Europe into Asia Minor.

Probably the emperor's greatest achievement was his order that there be collected all the decrees issued by all the emperors beginning with those of Constantine in 312, a collection which we know as the Codex Theodosianus. Nine years in preparation, the codex became at its publication in 438 the exhaustive and authoritative legal reference for the empire and later a primary source for Justinian's legal reform. Since it brought together all decrees of the Christian emperors, it is a major source for determining the influence the new religion exerted on Roman legal thought and practice.

Equally revealing of the cultural aspirations of Theodosius' court was his reorganization in 425 of what may be called the university of Constantinople, giving to it alone the privilege of higher education in the city and making it thus rival and in the sixth century surpass the philosophical academy at Athens.[9] Instruction by 31 professors, who were to be appointed by the senate, was to be in Latin and Greek, the number of Greek masters exceeding that of their Latin colleagues by two. Special provision was made for one chair in philosophy and two in law, reflecting no doubt the now practical goals of education in contrast to the view, expressed by the Antiochene rhetor, Libanius in the latter half of the 4th century, that Latin and law were "twin enemies of Greek higher education."[10]

When Theodosius II died in 450, his aged sister Pulcheria married a retired military commander, Marcian, whom, at her insistence, the senate and army had elected emperor. He became the first emperor to be crowned by the patriarch of Constantinople. An orthodox Christian, under the influence of his strong-willed wife, Marcian sought recognition by Leo, the bishop of Rome, whose orthodox views regarding the natures and person of Christ had been rejected by the Robber Council at Ephesus in 449. Leo's desire that his doctrinal statement be accepted by the church, and Marcian's desire to be accepted as orthodox emperor by Leo, led Marcian to summon the fourth ecumenical coucil of the church to Chalcedon in 451. There the monophysite doctrine of Christ, which had been upheld by the Robber

9. The decree is contained in *Codex Theodosianus*, xiv.9.3; vi.21.1, ed. Th. Mommsen, Berlin, 1905. Cf. the English translation by C. Pharr, M. B. Pharr and T. S. Davidson, Princeton, 1951.

10. A. H. M. Jones, *The Later Roman Empire* (N2), vol. 2, p. 989.

Council two years earlier, was totally rejected, and Leo's position was fully adopted. This decision alienated the monophysite provinces of Syria and Egypt from Constantinople, and reinforced their tendency to consider withdrawing from the empire. In Egypt the church ceased to use Greek, replacing it with Coptic. The Council, against Leo's will, also conferred on the patriarch of Constantinople a rank second to that of the bishop of Rome and gave the former the right to ordain bishops in Asia Minor and Thrace. Thus, when Marcian died in 457, Pulcheria having predeceased him by four years, serious cracks were appearing in the theoretically unified Roman empire, despite the church's efforts to achieve orthodoxy and the imperial efforts to compel unity.

The reigns of Leo (457–474), Zeno his Isaurian[11] son-in-law (474–491) and Anastasius (491–518) are not well documented but are noteworthy for bringing to an end the German (Ostrogothic) threat to the eastern part of the empire and, during the reigns of Zeno and Anastasius, reviving the monophysite strength of the church. Both Zeno and Anastasius saw that reconciliation with the dissident monophysite provinces was essential to the health of the state, and both acted accordingly. Zeno in 481 issued an imperial Decree of Union (Henotikon), in which he confirmed the credal statements of Nicaea (325) and Constantinople (381), anathematized Nestorius, Eutyches and their followers, and avoided any statement about one or two natures in Christ, condemning any who taught divergent doctrine "at Chalcedon or elsewhere."[12] The patriarchs of Alexandria and Constantinople accepted the Henotikon, but the bishop of Rome found it unacceptable not least because it asserted the emperor's right to legislate theological doctrine for the church. The pope therefore anathematized the patriarch of Constantinople for agreeing to it, and the patriarch in turn refused to pray for the pope. In general the vague, new formula failed to satisfy either the monophysites or the orthodox, and Anastasius (to whom Zeno's widow, Ariadne, gave her hand in marriage), felt compelled to take stronger measures for union.

Anastasius had such pronounced monophysite leanings that the patriarch of Constantinople refused to crown him emperor before he had signed a written profession of orthodoxy. But the emperor was also a man of

---

11. Isauria, the mountainous and wooded part of western Cilicia.

12. Cf. J. B. Bury, *History of the Later Roman Empire from the Death of Theodosius I to the Death of Justinian* (London, 1923), reprint, 2 vols., New York, 1958, vol. 1, p. 403.

compromise and concord, to whom Zeno's Henotikon seemed a reasonable solution to the religious controversy. When, therefore, his patriarch at the capital persisted in agitating against him, Anastasius had him condemned as a Nestorian and deposed (496). As his successor the emperor appointed Macedonius, an adherent of the Chalcedonian formula, who was popular in Constantinople. But increasing restiveness among the monophysites, together with Macedonius' intrigues against the emperor, led Anastasius in 511 again to have his patriarch deposed. This time the emperor selected a monophysite, who soon caused a riot in the Hippodrome, the favorite place for public assemblies in the capital, after his introduction of the mono-physite version of the Trisagion ("Holy, Holy, Holy") into the liturgy at the patriarchal church. The two assembled and opposing factions of Blues, who tended to be orthodox and aristocratic, and Greens, who were commoners and inclined toward monophysitism,[13] were stilled only after the emperor appeared at his accustomed seat in the arena without his imperial regalia and offered to abdicate his office. Thereafter, however, the religious lines of battle were firmly drawn and nothing could be done to resolve the issues. Neither the compromise measure of Zeno nor the partisan solution of Anastasius had brought the desired harmony to the church.

By the time Anastasius died in July of 518, leaving as a legacy of his prudent administration gold reserves amounting to 320,000 pounds in the state treasury, Constantinople had become finally established as the political and cultural center of the Roman empire. After nearly two centuries of being fortified and beautified by imperial decree, successfully warding off Gothic and Hunnic invasions, and exploring and debating the philosophical, political and theological conceptions and consequences of church doctrine, the young capital had established political and cultural traditions which gave it a sense of its power in the world and the directions in which it would seek to govern. Anastasius left to his successors an administratively and economically stable state, prepared to assume control of the world. The man in whom this new self-consciousness first became operative was one Flavius Petrus Sabbatius, of Thracian descent, who after he was adopted by his mother's brother, the new emperor Justin, became Justinianus.[14]

---

13. On the circus factions see A. A. Vasiliev, *History of the Byzantine Empire* (N6), vol. 1, pp. 155–56, especially the notes on p. 156.

14. On Justinian's origin cf. A. A. Vasiliev, *History of the Byzantine Empire* (N6), vol. 1, p. 129, where Justinian is called an Illyrian or perhaps Albanian.

Justin had been a chief of the Excubitors, the palace guard, and had succeeded the childless Anastasius on the throne in the wake of a palace intrigue. Having no children himself, the 65-year-old emperor had long promoted the careers of his nephews, among whom Justinian appears to have been his favorite. Thus, under the aegis of his royal uncle, the favored nephew now advanced rapidly from chief of the palace guard (518) to consul (520) to Caesar (525) until he was finally crowned Augustus and co-regent in April of 527, four months before Justin died; thereafter Justinian became sole emperor.

Justin, a convinced upholder of Chalcedonian orthodoxy, had endeavored throughout his nine-year reign to heal the religious rift between Constantinople and Rome, and his religious policy had entailed persecution of the monophysites. Justinian also seems to have been partisan to the Chalcedonian creed, but it seems likely that the monophysite sympathies of his wife Theodora made him lenient with the monophysite heretics in an enlightened effort to preserve their loyalty to the empire. His belief that his rule should not diminish the Roman empire of the Caesars was certainly the strongest of his religious convictions, and Theodora no doubt persuaded him that the eastern parts of the state were vital to its health. Justinian, nevertheless, perceived the empire's primary enemy to be the Germanic peoples of the west, rather than the Slavs to the north, the Persians to the east or the religious factions within his state. He believed the Arians outside the empire had to be subdued to restore Rome to its former extent, and he bought off the Persians, while he expected the monophysites within the state to remain politically loyal. That faulty conception of his empire, derived from what was generally perceived to be the current failure to continue a glorious past, and supported by a self-serving Christian optimism about the kingdom of God on earth, was the rock upon which the Byzantine ship of state nearly foundered. Justinian, caught by impossible dreams of empire, nearly bankrupted the state with his tireless industry and best efforts. In him Alexander's vision of one world seemed more capable of realization than perhaps at any time in history, and that dream is both the glory and the tragedy of his reign.

Justinian's military campaigns against the Vandals in North Africa, the Visigoths in Spain, and the Ostrogoths in Italy were brilliantly successful but economically exhausting to the state. Justinian could maintain authority over these reconquered territories only with the continued use of forces that he could not afford. Furthermore, he had to cede to the Franks in Gaul virtual independence, and to buy truce after truce with the Persian king Chosroes. These peace treaties with Persia, besides costing Byzantium huge sums, established the boundaries and regulated trade with Persia, but they could not legislate or enforce religious tolerance among Christians or between Christians and Zoroastrians. Christian proselytizing posed a constant threat of "Byzantine cultural imperialism" to the Persian king, just as Persian persecution proved a menace to Christian existence in Persian territory. In the Balkans the imperial forces slowed but could not halt the dogged incursions of the Slavs, who penetrated westward to the Adriatic Sea, the Hellespont and the northern shores of the Aegean. For these campaigns Justinian first exhausted the gold reserves of Anastasius, then levied, with the brilliant advice of his shrewd and ruthless minister of finance, John of Cappadocia, unbearable taxes on his people, and at last resorted to underpaying his troops and thereby reducing the numbers and morale of his soldiers.

In addition to his dream of reconquest, Justinian's conception of his task as Roman emperor included responsibility to make and interpret law, a duty he undertook soon after his arrival in Constantinople.[15] To correct the legal chaos that had arisen in the long history of Roman imperial and juridical jurisprudence, Justinian in 528, the year after his coronation, appointed a ten-man commission, among whom was Tribonian, a native of Pamphylia and a pagan, to compile a codex of imperial decrees. The lawyers[16] completed their work in ten months, compiling the imperial edicts from the reign of Hadrian to that of Justinian. In 530 Justinian appointed another commission, again headed by Tribonian, to revise and compile the legal writings; they published their work (the *Digest*, or *Pandects*) in 533. That same year a handbook for students of law (the *Institutes*) was also published. The following year a new edition of the *Codex* appeared, which supplanted the edition of 529, with the result that the first edition has not survived. All these works, written in Latin, were supplemented after 534 with new decrees, called *Novels* (new laws), written in Greek; and the entire work became known in the twelfth century as the *Corpus juris civilis* ("Body of Civil Law"). This legal work is one of the great monuments of Byzantine history, but the man who inspired it, Tribonian,

---

15. Cf. A. A. Vasiliev, *Justin the First*, Cambridge, Mass., 1950, pp. 389–413.

16. Three recognized schools of law, at Constantinople, Rome and Beirut graduated the best legal minds of the day. The school in Beirut was moved to Sidon in 551, after an earthquake had leveled Beirut.

was hated in Constantinople apparently because of his avarice. His particular detractors seem to have been the aristocrats, who doubtless saw their privileges disappearing as he tampered with the law. [17]

A grim signal that all was not well in the state was given early in Justinian's reign (532) by a six-day rebellion in Constantinople that has become known as the Nika revolt, from the battle cry of the rioters ("Conquer!"). The orthodox Blues and monophysite Greens found themselves united in revolt against the new king, with his religious and economic policies, and in determination to supplant him with one of Anastasius' nephews. They burnt half the city and nearly forced Justinian and his advisers to flight. Only Theodora's unwavering courage, immortalized in her reminder to her husband, "the purple is a glorious shroud," drove Justinian to crush the revolt. His generals, Belisarius and Mundus, blocking the exits from the Hippodrome, where the mobs had assembled to proclaim as king Anastasius' nephew, Hypatius, turned their troops against the rioters and slaughtered more than 30,000 of them. Thereafter Justinian had the nephews of Anastasius executed. That grisly episode strengthened Justinian's grip on the reins of state and no doubt confirmed his imperial desires, propelling him resolutely on his brilliant but misdirected career.

The Nika revolt had left Constantinople in ruins, and given the emperor occasion for creating a splendid new city. Making full use of what he no doubt considered to be a divinely sent opportunity, Justinian adorned the city with public baths, buildings for the care of the sick and indigent, assembly halls and colonnades, an improved water system, and above all, numerous monasteries and churches including the magnificent Hagia Sophia (Holy Wisdom). (The cathedral was turned into a mosque in 1453 and a museum in 1935.) Byzantine pride in that building was expressed in the words attributed to Justinian at its dedication, "Solomon, I have outdone you."

But Justinian did not limit his works of construction to the capital. He dotted the frontiers of his empire with numerous fortresses, increased communications with new and improved bridges and roads, and was responsible for building such monuments in far off places as the great complex of St. Catherine of Mt. Sinai, the church of San Vitale in Ravenna

---

17. A. H. M. Jones, *The Later Roman Empire* (N2), vol. 1, pp. 157ff., who discusses Justinian's struggle with the owners of vast estates.

and its nearby basilica of San Apollinare in Classe (the Ravenna port), and a basilica at Dory in the mountains of the Crimea. Justinian's ambitious building program, together with his great legal reform and energetic wars of reconquest, all of which were carried out in less than forty years, reveals a grand vision of empire, the astonishing realization of which, partial though it was, must have excited the grudging admiration of even the Persian king.

Scarcely any aspect of imperial necessity or grandeur escaped the vigilant concern of the emperor who dispensed with sleep.[18] To eradicate paganism he closed the Academy in Athens by depriving it of funds; he persecuted Jews and Nestorians as being enemies of the true faith and tried to reconcile the monophysites to his rule while at the same time preserving his own good relations with the pope in Rome. He promised honesty and efficiency in government to encourage willing and prompt payment of higher taxes, regulated the essential importation of grain from Egypt to Constantinople, sought new trade routes with the east through the Red Sea to bypass the Persian stranglehold on Byzantine imports,[19] and succeeded somehow in introducing the silkworm and thus silk production into the Byzantine empire. He was certainly a man with a sense of divinely given mission, which made him hopelessly but honestly autocratic. His fault lay in tirelessly and obstinately attempting too much, not too little; and his became the last great attempt to rescue the world of antiquity from its inevitable transformation into the new world of Persians, Arabs and European peoples. In his resolution and Christian vision he evokes our profound admiration and generous pity.

One noteworthy aspect of Justinian's rule, related to his competition with the Persians for control of trade through Syria and Mesopotamia, was his connection with the Arab tribes inhabiting "the soft underbelly of the Fertile Crescent."[20] To Justinian these Beduin seemed capable both of tipping the balance of power between himself and his Persian adversaries and of providing an alternative route to trading centers further east. He undoubtedly knew the story of Palmyra which, guided by its royal pair, Odenathus and Zenobia, had theatened Rome's trade with the east until the

---

18. Procopius, *Anecdota* xiii.28; xv.11.

19. In the sixth century, according to one report, "all the nations carry on their trade in Roman money." Quoted by A. A. Vasiliev, *History of the Byzantine Empire* (N6), vol. 1, p. 166.

20. Peter Brown, *World of Late Antiquity* (N8), p. 170.

emperor Aurelian destroyed it in A.D. 272. In his own lifetime he had been in contact with the "ephemeral desert empire"[21] of Kinda in northern Arabia, which was at its height in the early sixth century as one of the first known Arab efforts at intertribal cooperation. More important, though, in Justinian's eyes was the Arab principality of Hira on the southern borders of Iraq, dominated by the dynasty of Lakhm. The Lakhmid princes, who were not Christian, dominated a region populated largely by Nestorian Christians whose loyalties after their condemnation at Chalcedon were to Sasanid Persians. This buffer dependency of Persia was flourishing under its greatest ruler Al-Mundhir III (Almoundaros in Greek) during Justinian's reign, and Justinian therefore sought an Arab dependency of his own to restore the military balance. In 529 he appointed Harith ibn Jabala (Arethas in Greek), leader of the Ghassanids (Banu Ghassan) who occupied the region between Damascus and the Yarmuk river, to the rank of patrician with the title phylarch, thus creating for Rome an Arab client state. The Ghassanids were monophysite Christians who fought regularly for Byzantium against the Persians and their Arab allies, the Lakhmids. In 554 Harith defeated and killed Al-Mundhir, and within fifty years thereafter the Lakhmid state came to its end. The Ghassanids early in the seventh century were swept up in the Muslim advance which cost them their political identity too.

Further south and west in the Yemen and in the African, monophysite state of Abyssinia (Axum) Justinian attempted to create Christian bulwarks against Arab paganism and the Persian trading monopoly with the east. The Himyarite rulers of the Sabaeans in the Yemen were Jewish converts who inaugurated a series of persecutions against the Christians, especially those of Najran, culminating in a massacre in 523. In response to that Justin and Justinian encouraged the Abyssinian Negus (king) to invade Arabia in 525. The latter's successful attack destroyed the Jewish Himyarite rule and established an Abyssinian dependency which controlled the Yemen for the rest of Justinian's lifetime. It must thus have seemed to Justinian that his hope for by-passing the Persian trade route was being realized in the Red Sea, but the merchants of Axum could not compete in India with those of Persia.[22]

---

21. B. Lewis, *The Arabs in History*, rev. ed., London, 1958, p. 30.

22. During Justinian's reign there appeared a literary and geographical work known as *The Christian Topography of Cosmas Indicopleustes*, "sailor to India," which is our primary source for knowledge about commerce between India and the west in the sixth century. Consult E. O. Winstedt, *The Christian Topography of Cosmas Indicopleustes*, Cambridge, 1909; A. A. Vasiliev, *History of the Byzantine Empire* (N6), vol. 1, pp. 163–67.

The fifty years after Justinian have been called "one of the most cheerless periods in Byzantine history, when anarchy, poverty, and plagues raged throughout the empire."[23] They came when "the sleepless one" slept at last, and there were none to keep his tireless watch over the relentless forces of change and decay or to recall in angry justification of the present disorders the problems and mistakes of his long rule; the splendor of Constantinople remained to overshadow the hard times that had brought it into being. But the problems against which Justinian had struggled also remained. He had died childless and without naming a successor, and that failure exacerbated the insistent demands for solutions to the dangerous and demoralizing threats to imperial peace. The dangers were well-known: migration and warfare among the western and northern barbarians (Avars, Slavs, Franks and Lombards) with the Byzantine armies; the renascent Sasanid state of the Persians in conflict with Rome over territorial boundaries and their Christian subjects, the Armenians; revolts of the Berbers (Moors) in North Africa and Goths in Spain; unrest among the dissident monophysites coupled with the emperors' vigilant efforts to remain on good terms with the orthodox bishop of Rome; the increasingly high costs of government and defense combined with persistent disaffection within the imperial armies with their pay and other imperial policies. The contemporary records are meager, and our knowledge of the period deficient. What survives are the impressions recorded by later chroniclers of the ninth century, in whose time the empire was no longer that of Justinian "the Great."

One imperial attempt to control the western foci of the sprawling state was the creation late in the sixth century, during the reign of Maurice (522–602), of the exarchates of Ravenna and Carthage, in which civil administration and judicial procedure were placed in the hand of military rulers, the exarchs, who exercised unlimited powers. Brought into being by the continued depredations of the Lombards in Italy and Berbers in Africa, these new officials had the authority to compel order, but at the price to the state of independence from the emperor. They ranked among the highest officials in the realm and could nourish imperial pretensions. The emperor Heraclius (610–641) was son of the exarch of Carthage.

The relative success of the exarchates in preserving order in the empire led Heraclius in the seventh century to extend military rule in provinces organized and known as Themes, i.e., districts defended by detachments of

---

23. A. A. Vasiliev, *History of the Byzantine Empire* (N6), vol. 1, p. 169.

troops recruited locally and rewarded for their services with small grants of land. Each Theme was governed by a *strategos*, general, whose office corresponded to that of the earlier exarchs. The new administrative and defense system, which was fully organized by Heraclius for Armenia only, proved to be extraordinarily successful in knitting together the diverse peoples of the empire in the Balkan peninsula and the Near East.

Heraclius may be credited with inaugurating a new era in Byzantine history, though he was more the defender of Byzantium against forces beyond his control than the originator of the forces of change. He ascended the throne in the wake of the savage rule of Phocas (602–610) to face the threats of Persians on the east, Avars and Slavs on the north, and at home rebellion among the troops and a lamentable lack of funds. In 611 the Persians occupied Antioch, in 613 Damascus, and the next year they invested Jerusalem, killing great numbers of Christians and pillaging the city. Five years later Alexandria fell before them, and other Persian forces advanced to Constantinople. During these same years the Avars also advanced against Constantinople, and the Slavs invaded the Balkans. Against marauding expeditions such as these the Themes eventually constituted a strong defense. Heraclius was badly hampered, however, by the near bankruptcy of his treasury, and in desperation he even contemplated moving the capital to Carthage. That drastic proposal brought the previously wavering Church staunchly to the support of Constantinople. The Patriarch placed its wealth at the empire's service, and Heraclius between 622 and 628 was at last able to launch successful, counter-offensive "crusades" against the Persians. Those victories were the death blow to the Sasanid state, and Heraclius now assumed the title, basileus (king, emperor), perhaps to emphasize his victory over the Persian King of kings. Unknown to Heraclius, however, the Arabs of Mecca were enjoying an economic and religious awakening, which would shortly propel them into concerted military action against the Byzantine armies.

The cultural and political dreams of Later Rome to rule a united, Christian Mediterranean world had been too grand. The enthusiasm of Constantine and his biographer Eusebius about God's rule through his appointed viceregent on earth had reached its fullest religious pitch in the achievements of the Theodosian dynasty which established orthodox Christianity as the state religion. Justinian accepted and incorporated the political consequences of that fervor into his program of reconquest. But the religious, economic and political costs of his rule were greater than the state could bear, and at his death the Church was divided, the treasury empty, the empire ringed by hostile and restive claimants to the harvests of classical civilization, and Byzantine society itself restless and divided in purpose, allegiance and belief. Byzantium did become the champion both of Christianity against paganism, Judaism and Islam, and of civilization against barbarism. It preserved traditions of Christian and Classical antiquity and transmitted them to the new powers in Europe and the Near East. Its deeply religious and conservative spirit made it a rock againt which the changing tides of history would dash for centuries before it finally gave way. But that basic conservatism was not the spirit of Alexander of Macedon; it was rather the bastion protecting the backwaters of tradition from the invigorating new life and spirit of change. The thrust of conquest now passed from the West to the Near East, where a rising new civilization would inherit and cherish Alexander's vision but finally divide for centuries his inchoately united world. "The ancient world had died in the imagination of the inhabitants of the eastern Mediterranean."[24]

SUGGESTIONS FOR FURTHER STUDY:

The best survey of early Byzantine history for the general reader is by John W. Barker, *Justinian and the Later Roman Empire* (Madison, Wis., 1966). Both in organization and style he provides an informative and interesting panorama of Later Roman development, centering on Justinian's reign. The book is provided with helpful lists, dates and bibliographical guide for the novice. More detailed are the classic two volumes of J. B. Bury, *A History of the Later Roman Empire from the Death of Theodosius I to the Death of Justinian* (Dover paperback, New York, 1958; reprint of the original edition, London, 1923). A stimulating discussion of the third to eighth centuries in the West is the superb volume by F. Lot, *The End of the Ancient World and the Beginnings of the Middle Ages* (New York, 1961, a paperback reprint of the English translation from the French, London, 1931), containing enlightening introduction and bibliographical comments by G. Downey. The first volume of the *History of the Byzantine Empire, 324–1453* by A. A. Vasiliev (Madison, Wis., 1958, a paperback reprint of the edition of 1952), covering the years 324–1081, is less easy to read than Barker, Bury or Lot but filled with valuable information, annotation and interpretation. Particularly useful is the first chapter on "The Study of Byzantine History." The two volumes of A. H. M. Jones, *The Later Roman Empire* (Norman, Okla., 1964), are indispensable for social and economic history. An exceptional survey, noteworthy for its concise, elegant style and trenchant insight is *The World of Late Antiquity AD 170–750*, by Peter Brown (New York and London, 1971). A superb account of Justinian was written by P. N. Ure, *Justinian and His Age*, (Harmondsworth, 1951).

---

24. Peter Brown, *World of Late Antiquity* (N8), p. 187.

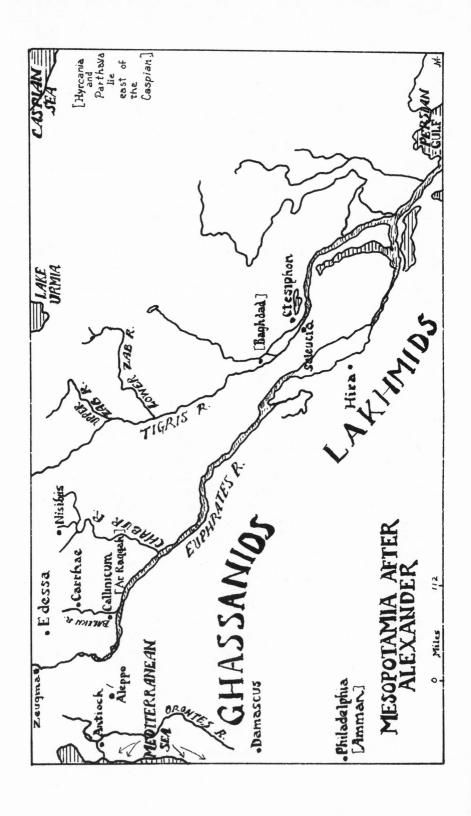

CASPIAN SEA

[Hyrcania and Parthava lie east of the Caspian]

PERSIAN GULF

LAKE URMIA

UPPER ZAB R.

LOWER ZAB R.

TIGRIS R.

[Baghdad]

Ctesiphon

Seleucia

Hira

LAKHMIDS

•Nisibis

Edessa

•Carrhae

Callinicum [Ar Raqqah]

BALIKH R.

CHABUR R.

EUPHRATES R.

Zeugma•

Antioch•

Aleppo

MEDITERRANEAN SEA

ORONTES R.

•Damascus

GHASSANIDS

•Philadelphia [Amman]

MESOPOTAMIA AFTER ALEXANDER

0 Miles 112

XII

SASANIAN NATIONALISM

The great Byzantine dream of ecumenical, political and religious unity, which evaporated at last before the thrust of Arab resistance and expansion, had a contemporary parallel in the Sasanian dream of restoring the great Achaemenid empire of Darius, which had come to its inglorious end before the advance of Alexander. That Sasanian dream, like the Byzantine, was rooted in a brilliant past that now seemed capable of reconstruction, fortified as it was by the new elements of a universal religion. But those opposing Byzantine and Sasanian dreams inspired the continued, enervating clashes of Roman and Persian armies that left Syria, Mesopotamia and Palestine easy conquests for the vigorous Arab forces. That those visions arose in the same centuries, vanished and were then dreamed anew by the victorious Arabs, is evidence for the persistence of Alexander's vision in the still unified thought world of the eastern Mediterranean. The Arab conquests, however, would divide Iran from Europe, allowing East and West again to develop their independent traditions in relative isolation, and withdrawing the Alexandrian dream from any hope of fulfillment for centuries.

Sasanian history began when Ardashir (the Greek form is Artaxerxes) of Fars, perhaps from Istakhr near Persepolis, overthrew Artabanus V, the last of the Arsacid kings in A.D. 226 and claimed for himself sole rule of the Parthian vassal kingdoms, taking the royal title *shahanshah*, King of kings. He called his father Papak a king, and it is generally assumed that his grandfather, also a lord, was Sasan. But the relationship of Sasan to either Papak or Ardashir is not known. The suggestion that 'Sasanian' was a patronymic designation, deriving from a "remote progenitor whom the

221

royal family of the new empire believed to have been their founder" is perhaps as close to historical probability as one can come.[1]

The Persians, of whom Ardashir was prince, seem to have constituted a vassal state of the Parthians,[2] but since the story of Ardashir's rise to power is more legend than sober fact, the nature of Fars' subjection to the Parthian king remains unknown. An essential element of the tradition, however, is Ardashir's descent from Sasan and Sasan's descent from the Achaemenids, a tradition which the Persian epic poet Firdousi, continued in his national epic, *Shah-nameh* (Book of Kings), making Sasan a son of Artaxerxes I Longimanus, who ruled Persia from 465–424 B.C. That tradition was basic to "the systematisation of the legendary history of Iran . . . carried out under the Sasanians when the real history had been forgotten."[3] The Sasanian kings considered themselves to be the lineal descendants of the Achaemenids and the inheritors of their great empire, though they had no clear knowledge of that empire's history, a knowledge won only in the last century by archaeological and historical research. That ancient heritage, made more illustrious by association with Alexander who destroyed it, seemed to the Sasanians fortuitously destined for bountiful harvest when in the chaotic events of the third Christian century the great Rome must have seemed on the brink of collapse.

Ardashir inherited the Parthian vassal organization and compelled the feudatories to submit to his authority, no doubt replacing the recalcitrant with the compliant or with favorites from his own court. Thereby he gave renewed unity to the disintegrating Parthian territory, pulling its fragments together from the customary administrative center, Ctesiphon-Seleucia, which he preserved as the working capital. The centralized administrative organization he forged served the Sasanian empire throughout its four-hundred-year history. Ardashir is also credited with reestablishing the religion of Zoroaster as the national cult, creating the religious office of chief mobad (i.e., pope), though this may have been attributed to him in later times when an appeal to traditional values was thought to give current

---

1. R. Rawlinson, *The Seventh Great Oriental Monarchy*, 2 vols., New York, 1876, vol. 1, p. 33, who also suggested that 'Sasanian' was first used by Armenian writers from whom it was adopted by the Byzantine historians.

2. Strabo XV.15.3.24 (C736).

3. R. N. Frye, *Heritage of Persia*, New York, 1963, p. 35.

practice sanction and authority.[4] Undeniably, however, the Sasanian state was Zoroastrian, and the new-found faith, the organization of which may have followed that of the Christian church, gave the state a single religious center which the Parthian had lacked. Further, the religion of Zoroaster sharply distinguished Persians from Christian Romans and contributed to the phenomenon which became evident in the sixth century, that a man was defined by his religious rather than his political commitment.[5]

We are informed by his inscriptions, especially the trilingual inscriptions in Greek, Parthian and Middle Persian at Naqshi-Rustam near Persepolis,[6] about the 31-year reign of Shapur (the name means "king's son"), which after a short co-regency followed that of his father Ardashir in 241. In these writings Shapur proclaims himself king of kings, not only of Iran but also of non-Iran, and glories in his three victorious campaigns against Rome, the last of which resulted in his capturing the emperor Valerian in 260 and imprisoning him for the rest of his life. Shapur's campaigns seem to have restored the eastern boundaries of the Achaemenid empire and, with his capture of Antioch on the Orontes, to have pushed his western frontier to the Mediterranean. His use of Greek in his inscriptions, his interest in Greek and Indian thought revealed in translations of their works he commissioned,[7] and his employment of Roman legionaries, captured in his campaigns against Valerian, to build bridges, dams and other public works in Iran—all these attest the magnitude of western influence in the Near East in the mid-third century. The extent to which that interest can be attributed to Ardashir and Shapur alone cannot at present be known.

The attention paid by Ardashir to the establishment of national Iranian religious observances was increased by his son Shapur. During the latter's reign, Kartir, a priest who by the end of the century would become a noble and the religious chief of the state, and who may deserve to be called the "real founder of Zoroastrian orthodoxy under the early Sasanian kings,"[8] began his rise to power. He appears in his inscriptions both as *mobad* and

---

4. R. N. Frye, *Heritage of Persia* (N3), p. 209.

5. P. Brown, *World of Late Antiquity, A.D. 170–750*, New York and London, 1971, p. 186.

6. Cf. the translation by A. Marico in *Syria* 35 (1958), pp. 295–360.

7. R. Ghirshman, *Iran*, Harmondsworth, 1954, p. 294.

8. R. N. Frye, *Heritage of Persia* (N3), p. 209.

herbad, priestly designations that have been interpreted as applying to the priests of northern Iran with their cultic center at Shiz-Ganzak[9] and those of southern Iran centered at Istakhr.[10] Kartir's use of both designations leads to the assumption that he succeeded in forging an acceptable religious union between the Parthian cults of the north and that of Fars in the south, thus establishing a national, Sasanian church.

The appearance of a culturally organized political and religious authority during Shapur's reign, however, has not been confirmed by the discovery of state archives and may therefore be misleading. Indeed the frequent internal upheavals in Sasanian history suggest for all periods a less than stable political structure. It seems established, nevertheless, that priests, soldiers and various officials of the bureaucratic secretariat were effective checks in Sasanian society to the powers of the land-owning nobility from whose various ranks the political leaders were drawn. Among the highest officers in the state in the later empire, next to the king himself, were his chief administrator, the vizier, his religious chief, the *mobad* of *mobads*, the chief of tax collections, and the highest generals of the army. The existence of these offices reflects an intended administrative centralization, however effective or long-standing it may have been. The extent to which the centralized Sasanian political structure of the fourth and following centuries was modelled on that of Diocletian is an intriguing problem that deserves further investigation.[11] It may be that the structure of Iranian nationalism owes more to Roman influence than has been suspected, even after full allowance is made for ancestral Iranian cultural and religious traditions.

Shapur belongs to a new era in religious thought. The third century which saw Christianity in struggle against gnostic doctrines and heading for a definition of orthodox belief, structure and canon, witnessed in addition the regeneration and elaboration of Zoroastrian thought, the brief popularity of Manichaean syncretism and successful attempts by the Zoroastrians to bring together their own sacred writings (the 21-book Avesta, our earliest manuscripts of which date only to the thirteenth century A.D.). The compilation of the Jewish Talmud can also be dated to

---

9. On this site see above, ch. VIII, n.54.

10. Cf. S. Wikander, *Feuerpriester in Kleinasien und Iran*, Lund, 1946, pp. 37–42.

11. On taxation cf. A. H. M. Jones, *The Later Roman Empire*, 2 vols., Norman, Okla., 1964, vol. 1, pp. 61–68 with annotation.

these years. In them the "failure of nerve" that characterized the previous period was transformed into certainties about invisible powers that, in cooperation or combat with a supreme being, order the universe and human destiny, requiring of man less of obedience than of illumination, not so much of ethical striving as of proper knowledge and mystical union with the divine. When faith in human processes of ordering the world failed, men looked inward and found gods of the spirit who revealed the true nature of being, serenely unconcerned with the visible, prevailing powers of the world. New orthodoxies, born of imperialism and the new religious currents from further east, overcame the "failure of nerve" of previous centuries. Man's "unworthiness" changes from an occasion for despair to an occasion for salvation, when a supreme being's ordering providence and purpose could finally work its will. Emboldened by this novel awareness of ultimate truth, men became crusaders for their God, and in their battles against evil turned their energies once more to building their states, to bring them into conformity with God's will.

An index to the prevailing spirit is given by the religion of the Manichees, the disciples of the Iranian teacher Mani (or Manes) who lived in Babylon during Shapur's reign. Strongly influenced by Christianity and claiming to be "the comforter" promised by Christ to his disciples (John 14:26), Mani became a missionary of what he perceived to be the truth: namely, that the universe is the arena in which a cosmic struggle is being waged between the kingdom of goodness and light on the one hand and that of darkness and evil on the other. Mani taught that man's spirit, created by God, is good; but all matter including man's body was created by the devil and is therefore evil. The great battle will end with the triumph of light, when matter will be destroyed. Mani's optimism about the final victory of goodness, and his appeal to each man to liberate his own spirit from the matter that enslaves it, made his eclectic religion initially widely popular, as his extant letters reveal. After his death adherents of his faith could be found in Asia Minor, India and as far east as China as late as the twelfth century. Mani's pessimism about creation, however, led the religions of the world to brand his teaching a heresy and to persecute his followers. No enduring religion has ever been so heavenly-minded as to have no earthly good, and Manichaeism inevitably gave way before monotheistic Judaism and Christianity, dualistic Zoroastrianism and finally Islam, all of which reckon with God's good creation. In the struggle for religious certainty Manichaean optimism and humanism triumphed over Manichaean pessimism, and men believed again that their efforts could and would restore the world to its originally created order. Mani was executed probably at the urging of the Zoroastrian priests, during the brief reign of Varahran (later called Bahram) I (273–276).

The four decades following Shapur's death saw eight kings succeed one another to the Sasanian throne, accompanied by continuing Roman military expeditions to increase their share in, if not to dominate, the lucrative trade with the east that passed through Mesopotamia to the Mediterranean.[12] The paucity of information for these decades is traceable to continuing political upheavals in Rome and perhaps in Iran as well. Not until Diocletian stabilized the government in Rome after 285 are we again able to trace in somewhat greater detail the course of political events in Iran. By that time Varahran II was king, and he saw the Romans recover Mesopotamia, while Armenia, which had been a Persian province for more than twenty-five years, fell under Roman control in the person of Tiridates, an Arsacid prince. The Romans continued, under the able direction of Diocletian, to press their advantage, and they compelled Narseh in 297 to sign an unfavorable treaty by which he ceded to Rome all of Mesopotamia west of the Tigris as well as five provinces in Armenia and Kurdistan to its east.[13] Narseh's son, Hormizd II, did not contest the Roman acquisitions but spent his brief reign improving public buildings and the administration of justice, especially for those poor oppressed by the rich.

With the long reign of Shapur II, who in 309 as an infant was declared to be Hormizd's successor, we reach another illuminated era in Persian history. His Roman contemporaries on the Byzantine throne were Galerius and the entire Constantinian house, including Jovian, as well as Valens who died in 378. Since these emperors were actively engaged in the Near East, supported by a centrally organized government in Byzantium, source material for Persian history through Roman eyes is more plentiful, especially in the great history of Ammianus Marcellinus of Antioch who took part in the emperor Julian's Persian campaign in 363, the letters of

---

12. Cf. Herodian, *History of the Empire*, Loeb, iv. 10.4, who reports the Roman offer of an alliance by marriage with the Parthian king, Artabanus V; one advantage of which would be that " . . . the locally grown spices of the Parthians and their wonderful clothes, and on the other side, the metals produced by the Romans and their admirable manufactured goods would no longer be difficult to get and in short supply, smuggled in by merchants."

13. For a discussion of the treaty cf. G. Rawlinson, *Seventh Great Oriental Monarchy* (N1), vol. 1, pp. 129–35.

Libanius and the writings of Julian himself. By the time Constantine became sole ruler of Rome in 324, Shapur was a young man of sixteen years, humiliated by years of Roman control over Persian territory and the depredations of marauding Arab bands, and prepared to take active control of the affairs of his kingdom. Because Constantine had confessed himself a Christian, all Christians under Sasanian control looked to him for succor and therefore became identified in Shapur's eyes as a "fifth column" in his Zoroastrian state. The resulting, unfavorable Christian position in Iranian lands became particularly precarious after Constantine died in 337 and Shapur energetically renewed his efforts to retake Sasanian territories from Rome. Christians who spoke openly against the war, like Aphraat bishop of Syria, were subjected to systematic persecution, especially during the years immediately following Constantine's death. Syriac literature abounds in Christian martyr stories, many of which come from this period, that describe vividly the sufferings of the Christian church. Since most of the stories were written for edification of the faithful, their value for under-standing contemporary history is marginal. Nevertheless they do reveal the mutual hostility of Zoroastrians and Christians in the Near East and the political rather than religious motivations of Shapur, who, even though the Zoroastrians hated Jews as much as they did Christians, did not molest the Jews, since they were not a political threat to him.

Shapur fought to restore to Iranian control the territories lost by his predecessors to Rome. In a letter addressed to Constantius responding to Roman feelers for peace, Shapur reminded the emperor that Persia had a historical claim to "the entire tract within the river Strumon and the borders of Macedon" which could now be pressed did not Shapur delight in moderation. But because that was his rule of conduct he would therefore be content if the Romans should restore "Mesopotamia and Armenia which were fraudulently extorted from his grandfather." That land, which right-fully belonged to him, had been a continual cause of dispute and bloodshed, and Rome would live in peace and security henceforth if Constantius would relinquish what did not belong to him anyway.[14] Constantius' reply that Rome could not honorably surrender any territory, and his reminder to Shapur that Rome had always secured advantage by war, even though she was occasionally defeated in a battle, sums up the Byzantine stance in the

---

14. Ammianus Marcellinus *Res Gestae* xvii.5.

world. The Alexandrian dream of a single world empire was still alive in
Byzantium, though by the end of the sixth century that vision had faded to
the extent that a Byzantine historian could put in the mouth of a Persian
envoy for peace with Rome the words: "The whole human race knows that
the Roman and Persian kingdoms resemble two great luminaries, and that,
like a man's two eyes, they ought mutually to adorn and illustrate each
other, and not in the extremity of their wrath to seek rather each other's
destruction."[15]

Shapur succeeded generally in restoring the old boundary of the
Euphrates River between his kingdom and Rome, but the Romans were able
to insist on the freedom of their cities from taxation. Armenia remained
nominally a Roman province, though in fact it was divided between
Zoroastrians faithful to Shapur, Christians loyal to Rome, and the
nationalist Armenian nobility seeking Armenian independence. After a
long reign, marked by constant wars with Rome in the west and the Kushan
nomads on the east, Shapur died in 379, having more clearly defined a new
era in Persian history. Within one hundred fifty years the Sasanian kings,
especially Ardashir, Shapur I and Shapur II, had created a powerful state
which they forced Rome to treat as an equal. Zoroastrianism had become the
established religion of the state, and authority had become strongly centralized in the hands of rulers who boasted the political heritage of the
Achaemenids. The precarious economy, however, the developing rift
between the nobility and the Zoroastrian priesthood, and the pressures for
political decentralization combined with the social unrest among the poor
were serious problems awaiting solution.

These problems became evident soon after Shapur's death, when his
successors did not engage either in warfare or in great building enterprises at
home. The virtual absence of records from the two decades following
Shapur's reign suggests a period of national inactivity; but the events of the
next century, which reveal the Sasanian royal family in vigorous dispute
with the nobility for control of the empire, together with the contradictory
epithets assigned to two of Shapur's successors and the suspicious deaths of
others from "accidental" blows on them by falling objects, suggest the
beginnings of an internal power struggle that would only later become

---

15. Petrus Patricius, quoted by G. Rawlinson, *Seventh Great Oriental Monarchy* (N1),
vol. 1, p. 124.

known to the world.[16] The reasons for that dissension must remain largely conjectural, but it seems clear that religious differences and desires for economic prerogatives pulled royalty and nobility increasingly apart.

Yazdagird I, for example, who ruled from 399 to 420, was celebrated by western authors for his generosity and irenic disposition, but by those of the Near East he was condemned as despotic, harsh and wicked. The reason for the contrary representations appears to have been Yazdagird's indulgence and active support of the Christians early in his reign. He is said at one time even to have considered being baptised and, at the dying Arcadius' request, to have become guardian for the latter's young son, Theodosius II. Later, however, he espoused the Zoroastrian cause. The change from Yazdagird's early favorable Christian inclination to antipathy and active persecution of Christians is not explained satisfactorily either as the reaction of one "who, after nearly embracing truth, relapses into error,"[17] or simply as his just response to Christians' abuses of their privileges. It seems more probable that the king sought the political support of the large numbers of Christians in his realm against the increasing autonomy and power of the Zoroastrian nobility. His expectations of Christian allegiance to his rule, however, were disappointed when Christians refused to become identified with Iranian nationalism and instead used their privileged status in religious missionary activity rather than for the political purposes Yazdagird must have intended. In anger, therefore, he turned against them. Yazdagird died "from the kick of a horse," i.e., more than likely a palace coup that sought either to bolster or to restore the deteriorating status at court of the noble aristocracy.[18]

The struggle for the throne that erupted between Yazdagird's sons after their father's death seems to have been motivated to a great extent by the rivalry between Christians and Zoroastrians for the royal power. The claims of Varahran, who had grown up among the Christianized Arabs of Hira and whom his father had chosen to succeed him, were contested by Shapur who

16. Cf. Masoudi, trans. C. Barbier de Maynard and Pavet de Courteille, *Prairies d'Or*, 9 vols., Paris, 1861–71, vol. 2, p. 189.

17. G. Rawlinson, *Seventh Great Oriental Monarchy* (N1), vol. 1, p. 275; J. Labourt, *Le Christianisme dans l'empire perse sous la dynastie sassanide*, 2nd ed., Paris, 1904, pp. 105–06; R. Ghirshman, *Iran* (N7), p. 298.

18. The story appears in Tabari, *Chronique*, trans. H. Zotenberg, 4 vols., Paris, 1867–71, vol. 2, p. 104. Cf. T. Nöldeke's translation of Tabari, Leiden, 1879, p. 77, n. 1.

had been governor in Armenia. The Zoroastrians, however, who desired neither son as king, managed to place their own candidate, a certain Khusro, on the throne; but Varahran succeeded with the aid of his Arab patron, Mundhir, in making good his claim to the kingdom and was crowned Varahran V, the Bahram-Gur of Arab chronicles.[19] Any illusions Christians may have had, however, about Varahran's support were short-lived. He appointed a zealous Zoroastrian as vizier, continued his father's persecution of the Christians and had himself depicted on his coins wearing a mural crown adorned with crescent and circle, probably representing moon and sun. It appears therefore that Varahran made certain concessions to the Zoroastrian nobility in exchange for their allegiance to his rule.

Those harmonious relations, however, did not endure. It seems that the nobility had an economic stranglehold on the king. The state's primary income was from taxes on the crown lands and their products. But the major part of Persian land belonged not to the king but to the nobles, and it could be taxed only indirectly. Varahran apparently had won the support of the landowners on the strength of his pledges not to increase their tax levies or alter the tax structure in any way. But those pledges left him only victories in war as a source for increased state income; the bulk of the plunder doubtless went to the troops, while the crown gained any new lands as well as the yearly tribute from the defeated. Warfare thus became an economic necessity for the centralized Sasanian government, and the king was inevitably pitted against the nobility to preserve his own power.[20]

During Varahran's reign, the Sasanians had to repel new invaders from central Asia known as Hephthalites or "White Huns." Some sources designate the same invaders as Chionites, conjecturing their origin to have been in the north. These newcomers were probably a Turkic people, but their linguistic identity is not certainly known. The identities and history of the peoples of central Asia, known variously as Scythians, Huns, Mongols and Turks, were discerned only dimly by the Greeks, Romans and Arabs; and scholars have been unable to dispel the resultant confusion.[21] The invaders crossed the Oxus river into Iran sometime during Varahran's 18- or 19-year

---

19. "Hunter of wild asses"? Cf. Genesis 16:11-12, "Ishmael . . . a man like the wild ass," New English Bible.

20. Cf. R. Altheim, *Ein Asiatischer Staat*, Wiesbaden, 1954.

21. Cf. R. N. Frye, *Heritage of Persia* (N3), pp. 216–18; F. Altheim, *Geschichte der Hunnen*, 4 vols., Berlin, 1959–62.

reign only to be thoroughly routed and pursued by the victorious Sasanian troops across the Oxus deep into their own territory. The plunder that fell into Varahran's possession was enormous, including a crown richly set ("plusiers milliers de perles") with pearls.[22] The soundly defeated Hephthalites did not trouble Varahran again, and the loot taken from them no doubt went far in helping the Sasanian king meet his expenses of state.

Varahran, remembered in Persian literature as an ideal ruler, a sportsman, musician and ladies' man, was undoubtedly an able monarch who presided over an era of relative domestic and foreign peace. He succeeded, for example, in 422 in having Rome renew her fifty-year commitment to contribute funds for the defense of the Caucasus and in making the Christian church of Iran independent of Byzantium, thus removing some of the suspicions that had plagued his father. The idealized memory of his reign no doubt rests on reasonably historical foundations. His fullest praise was sung in the twelfth century by the Persian poet Nizami in a work called *Haft Paykar*.[23]

Varahran's son and successor, Yazdagird II, was not as fortunate as his father had been, either in his relations with the Christians or his wars against the Hephthalites. Both groups represented threats to the state that the Zoroastrian king determined to crush, in Armenia by enforced conversion of the Christians there to Zoroastrianism, and in the east by overwhelming military expeditions against the invaders. His extreme policies, however, bore little fruit because he did not appreciate the full strength of either foe. The Armenians would not convert, and Armenia therefore remained vulnerable on the Sasanian west to Roman influence. The Hephthalite nomads to the east could not be stopped or their advance reversed, and they remained to trouble the Sasanian state for the rest of its life. They became so strong, in fact, that they made and unmade Sasanian kings during the next four decades, apparently considering themselves to be conquerors of Persia during the reign of Peroz (459–483). Perhaps that claim persuaded Byzantium, thinking rather to bear the ills she had than fly to others she knew not of,[24] to underwrite some of the costs of Peroz's campaigns against the Hephthalite nomads. Peroz also admitted the heretical Nestorians into his realm, perhaps in an effort to create a distinctive and

---

22. Tabari, trans. H. Zotenberg (N18), vol. 2, p. 120.

23. Ed. H. Ritter and J. Rypka, Prague, 1934.

24. *Hamlet*, III.1.81-82.

separate Christian Church in his state. These Christian heretics, exiled from Rome, established their headquarters at Ctesiphon and a school at Nisibis, located some 60 miles southwest of the Tigris on the plains of the Habur river, from whence they Christianized extensive districts of Arabia. When, however, the Armenians became monophysite Christians, any royal Sasanian hopes for a united, nationalist, Persian church were greatly diminished. Peroz's reign ended apparently during one of the worst famines in Sasanian history, the consequences of which would trouble Iran for several decades.

Kavadh I, Peroz's son, had spent his youth under the protection of the Hephthalites, perhaps as a hostage. He succeeded to the Persian throne, supported by an Hephthalite armed force, on the death of king Balash in 488, probably in exchange for his promise to continue paying Sasanian tribute to his former guardians. The kingdom he inherited, however, was experiencing serious internal turmoil caused by a long-standing cleavage between the aristocracy and common people. The abyss that separated them derived from the unequal division of land in Iran and the ruling myth of blood purity.

Land had traditionally been held in large tracts by the nobility, who interpreted their ownership as their deserved reward for faithful obedience to God, while many villages were comprised of virtual slaves. In an agricultural economy this left the majority of the population landless, poor and undeserving in God's sight. The Seleucid kings had attempted to remedy the situation and at the same time introduce a strong support for their rule by founding free cities for Greeks, whose industrial and mercantile acumen and skill increased the tax income for the state. That practice of royal city-founding was continued by both Parthians and Sasanians, and was no doubt a mainstay in the Sasanian struggle for power with the Parthian and Persian nobility. Among the principal Persian trading centers were Ctesiphon-Seleucia and Babylon, but the list of Sasanian royal foundations is long.[25] The oppressive social stratification which placed the majority of the Iranian population in a subject caste of slaves was made worse by the entrenched custom of polygamy which sharply restricted the number of women available for marriage.[26] The severe famine of Peroz's reign, together

---

25. O. Klima, *Mazdak. Geschichte einer sozialen Bewegung im Sassanidischen Persien*, Prague, 1957, p. 76.

26. Ibid., pp. 104–05.

with the major Persian defeat at the hands of the Hephthalites in 484, brought the latent social upheaval into open assaults by the people against the nobility, assaults which Kavadh, no doubt finding in the rebellion support for his rule, did little or nothing to restrain.[27] The nobility therefore, in the eighth year of his rule, seized him, put him in prison,[28] and placed his brother Jamasp on the throne in his stead. Kavadh managed, however, to escape to the Hephthalites who once more set him upon the Sasanian throne after a three-year interregnum of Jamasp.

The popular revolt that broke out during the first part of Kavadh's rule, perhaps in the year 494–95, is connected with the teaching of Mazdak, which Kavadh accepted opportunely and rejected when it no longer furthered his own purposes. Mazdak, whose father appears to have been a Manichee, may have grown up, as the Arab historian Tabari reports, in Babylonia in a village called Madariya on the Tigris river,[29] a region strongly pervaded by Semitic as well as Iranian religious conceptions.[30] He appears diligently to have studied religious doctrines and finally to have decided that the teachings of a Manichaean secretary, Zaradusht, were the truth about life.[31] Zaradusht differed with Mani in declaring that the good and purposeful God had already fought and vanquished blind and purposeless Evil and should therefore be worshiped as victor, but also that man's redemption was a matter of chance rather than choice. Those doctrines of God's present rather than future victory over Evil and man's accidental salvation lie at the root, in ways that we do not yet understand, of Mazdak's belief in the equality of all men and their equal claim to that which constitutes human happiness. As men have equal claims to water, fire and pasture, he declared, so should they have equal claim to women and the material goods of happiness.[32] Mazdak's interest was less a communism of

---

27. Ibid., pp. 138–39.

28. Near modern Dizful according to O. Klima, ibid., p. 141.

29. T. Nöldeke, *Geschichte der Perser und Araber zur Zeit des Sassaniden aus der Arabischen Chronik des Tabari übersetzt*, Leiden, 1879, pp. 153–55.

30. O. Klima, *Mazdak* (N25), pp. 159ff., who suggests that Mazdak might even have been a Jew who converted to Magianism.

31. O. Klima, *Mazdak* (N25), p. 234: "Mazdak was at best a popular preacher, who could have belonged originally to a Manichaean sect. He adopted all kinds of ideas, which he picked up from his evironmnet or his travels, and incorporated them unsystematically into basic Manichaean teachings."

32. O. Klima, *Mazdak* (N25), p. 241.

goods and wives than a man's right to take from those with superabundance the woman and goods that were required for his own God-ordained happiness.

In a sermon reported by Firdousi, the poet lets Mazdak declare:

> Five things lead one astray from righteousness—
> The wise one can add nothing thereto—
> They are these: Envy, Wrath, Vengeance and Need,
> And the fifth, that is greater than they, is Greed.
> If you can be victor over these five Devas,
> The way of the Lord of the World will be shown you.
> Because of these five we have wives and goods,
> And thus true religion in the world is made feeble.
> It is needful that wives and property be shared,
> If true religion is to suffer no harm;
> For in these two reside Envy, Greed and Need
> Which secretly unite with Wrath and Vengeance.
> The Deva always turns away the Wise one's head;
> Both must be declared common possession.[33]

And again:

> Men should be equal with respect to property,
> And abundance should be forbidden the more mighty;
> Wives, houses and property must be shared,
> The poor man must become the equal of the mighty.[34]

The supposed social revolution during Kavadh's reign, which was Mazdakitism, made of no account the Persian aristocratic claims to purity of blood, since, according to Tabari, when the uprising ended no man knew his son, and no son knew his father. If that did occur, the aristocratic, Sasanian pride of "higher ancestry" had become groundless. It seems likely, however, that Kavadh supported Mazdak not to destroy the nobility but to restrain and subdue it, and once that aim was accomplished he dispensed with the troublesome movement. He did that toward the end of his reign

---

33. Tehran Ed. IV p. 364, 11.3–9; quoted by O. Klíma, *Mazdak* (N25), p. 194.
34. Tehran Ed. IV p. 363, 11.5–8; quoted by O. Klíma, *Mazdak* (N25), p. 196.

when, in order to secure the succession to the throne of his son, Chosrau, whom the Mazdakites feared because he was unsympathetic to their teachings, he had Mazdak and some of his chief advisers executed. Thereafter in Persia and also in the Byzantine empire a persecution of the revolutionaries and their Manichaean co-religionists ensued, which deprived them of all strength and popular appeal.[35]

When Kavadh died in 531 in his eighty-second year, Chosrau I Anushirwan ("of immortal soul") ascended the Persian throne. His 47-year reign, contemporaneous with those of Justinian and Justin II in Constantinople, is remembered as one of the most outstanding in Persian history[36] and represents the cultural and administrative apex of the Sasanian era. Its brilliance rests on Chosrau's victories in war against the Byzantine, Armenian, Abyssinian, Hephthalite and Turkish armies, his domestic governmental reforms, and his broad cultural interests. Undefeated in wars abroad, largely because he reorganized the command and paid the troops himself rather than leaving their remuneration to the nobles, Chosrau modified at home the tax laws (we know of both a land and a head tax) to encourage increased production and provide the means for estimating and predicting the national income; and he restored to their original owners properties seized during the Mazdakite revolt. He subjected to royal contol the Zoroastrian priesthood, which was indebted to him for exterminating the Mazdakites, entered upon projects of public building, and created a functional, efficient bureaucracy headed by the king to replace the traditional, patrimonial one controlled by a few great families, which had troubled his forbears. After Justinian closed the philosophical school at Athens in 529, Chosrau welcomed the fugitive professors, sometime after his accession in September 531, to the Persian court[37] to discuss the works of Plato and Aristotle, which he had commissioned to be translated into Pahlavi along with numerous Indian tracts. At Gundeshapur, near Susa, he established a medical school which later became a university.

---

35. Cf. Tabari, by T. Nöldeke (N29), pp. 154–55. Evidence for the contemporary persecution of the Manichaeans in the Byzantine empire is cited by O. Klima, *Mazdak* (N25), p. 275.

36. R. N. Frye, *Heritage of Persia* (N3), pp. 215, 218; Rawlinson, *Seventh Great Oriental Monarchy* (N1), vol. 2, p. 100; Bausani, *The Persians*, trans. from the original Italian (1962) by J. B. Donne, London, 1971, p. 61.

37. Agathias, *History* II 30.

It is noteworthy that Chosrau succeeded in strengthening the central authority and administration of the Persian state in those same years when Justinian was vainly seeking to reunite and strengthen the traditionally Roman empire. Chosrau's success was due in part to his suppression of the Mazdakite uprising and the consequent Zoroastrian submission to his rule, and it freed him to acquaint himself with Greek philosophy. Nothing reveals better the pervasive influence of Greek thought than its reception at Ctesiphon by Chosrau at the moment when Justinian was closing the philosophical schools and trying to solve the theological divisions in the Christian church. Chosrau's interest in Greek thought was no doubt genuine,[38] but his knowledge was superficial[39] and the Greek philosophers were soon disillusioned with their life at the Persian court and returned home, encouraged by the treaty of "Endless Peace" of 532 which stipulated that Justinian was not to molest them or force them to convert to Christianity.

Chosrau ruled a centralized state, religiously unified, socially bureaucratized and under strict economic regulation. His internal reforms, more significant and lasting than any changes he was able to effect in the frontiers of his empire, reduced the traditional power of the aristocracy in favor of a new bureaucracy comprising court officials, an internal revenue service and military leaders. The traditional and patrimonial Iranian society had become altered under Kavadh and Chosrau so that social rank was now an earned as well as an inherited privilege. So successful were the reforms that when Chosrau died in 578, the Sasanian empire seemed stronger than ever; but the success was not to endure. When, within sixty years the Persian state crumbled before the Muslim advance at Qadisiyah near Hirah in 637, it was the traditional Persian way of life, not the reforms of Chosrau, that was cherished and that survived Persian political defeat.

Chosrau's son and successor, Hormizd IV, seems to have been unworthy of his father. He began his reign with a diplomatic gaffe by not sending notice of his coronation to Constantinople,[40] and with a political miscalculation by refusing the terms of peace with Rome that had been worked out by his father and the emperor, Tiberius. During his reign he oppressed the nobility under the pretext of concern for the poor, and the Zoroastrian

---

38. Cf. John of Ephesus, trans. from the Syriac by R. Payne Smith, Oxford, 1860, vol. 6, p. 20.

39. Agathias, *History* II 28.

40. T. Nöldeke, *Aufsätze zur Persischen Geschichte*, Leipzig, 1887, p. 121.

priesthood in his refusal to ostracize Christians. He doggedly fought against Rome and was forced to repulse a Turkic invasion from the north, though he never took the field against his enemies. His able general, Varahran Chobin, distinguished himself in wars against the Turks, but when the Romans defeated him in Armenia in 589, the envious Hormizd used the occasion to disgrace the general by relieving him of his command and insulting him as a coward. Chobin in rage led a mutiny against the king, in the course of which Hormizd was blinded, dethroned and killed, and his son Chosrau II Aparvez, was crowned in his stead in 590.

Chosrau, however, had been crowned without the consent of Chobin, whose command of the troops and victories in war had strengthened his will to be king. When his own forces deserted to Chobin, Chosrau sought refuge with the Romans, many of whom may have seen in his flight an opportunity for an easy renewal of Alexander's ancient conquest. The emperor Maurice, however, seems to have realized that Rome's best interests lay not in conquest but in political stability in the East as an antidote to anarchy and the possible designs against Rome of unknown leaders and powers. He therefore welcomed Chosrau and, in exchange for the Persian surrender of claims to most of Armenia, provided him with an army and funds to regain his throne. Thus armed, Chosrau advanced into Mesopotamia, rallying to his support the Persian armies and finally forcing a defeated Varahran Chobin to flee across the Oxus river to asylum with the Turks of central Asia, who soon thereafter killed him.

Having retrieved his throne, Chosrau Aparvez ("the victorious") apparently feared for his life, for he requested and received from Maurice a personal bodyguard, said to number one thousand. In addition, perhaps partly as a gesture of political and religious friendship with Rome, he married a monophysite Christian, Shirin, whose great influence over her husband before she died brought down upon them the wrath of the Zoroastrian priests.[41] Chorau's zeal for her faith[42] did not long outlive her, and toward the end of his 37-year reign he resorted to persecuting his former Christian brothers. As long as Maurice lived, nevertheless, peace reigned

---

41. T. Nöldeke, ibid. (N40), p. 125 note; Nöldeke thought it probable that Maurice gave his daughter, Maria, in marriage to Chosrau sometime after the third year of Chosrau's rule. *Geschichte der Perser und Araber zur Zeit der Sasaniden*, Leiden, 1879, p. 283, n. 2.

42. T. Nöldeke, *Geschichte der Perser und Araber* (N29), believed Chosrau was far from being Christian, p. 287, n.2.

between Sasanians and Romans, and Chosrau ruled with admirable vigor and wisdom.

The death of Maurice in 602 at the hand of Phocas marked a turning point in Chosrau's career. Chosrau made Phocas' usurpation of the Byzantine throne a cause for war, and with the initial support of Narses, Maurice's commander in the East, embarked on a series of successful military campaigns against Rome, which the murder of Phocas and coronation of Heraclius in 610 did not halt. The Sasanian forces ravaged Syria, and, supported by a large army of Jews, invested Jerusalem, where they killed thousands of Christians, carried thousands more into captivity, and had the "True Cross" carried to Ctesiphon.[43] The victorious armies then advanced into Egypt as far as Ethiopia, while other Sasanian forces marched through Asia Minor as far as Chalcedon, which capitulated in 617. The armies of Chosrau were now encamped across the Bosporus within sight of Constantinople, and a reconstituted empire of the Achaemenids appeared imminent. Constantinople, however, proved to be impregnable; and after Heraclius, by threatening to flee to Carthage, forced the Byzantine church in 622 to support his military campaigns against the armies of Chosrau, the Romans achieved victory after victory against their adversaries.

The military setbacks suffered by Chosrau's armies, coupled with the successful uprisings of the Beduin Arabs of Hira against their Sasanian overlords[44] and the hatred of his rule nourished both by the nationalist Zoroastrians and the Christians who bewailed the desolation of Jerusalem, embittered Chosrau and made him tyrannical. But his cowardice in combat cost him the respect of his troops, and when in addition he executed and imprisoned the military commanders who had been unable to withstand the Roman armies and sought to substitute his younger for his first son as his royal successor, he was seized in a palace coup, imprisoned briefly and executed in 628. Remembered for his love of Shirin, his life of ease, and his dazzling court and vigorous administration, he left at his death a land impoverished by war and burdened with taxes.

The exhausted Sasanian state never recovered from Chosrau's rule. His son and successor, Kavadh II, reigned only six months, during which time he concluded a peace treaty with Heraclius, by which he surrendered all

43. The evidence is cited by G. Rawlinson, *Seventh Great Oriental Monarchy* (N1), vol. 2, pp. 165–66.
44. Cf. T. Nöldeke, *Aufsätze zur Persischen Geschichte*, (N 40), p. 125f.

conquered territories and prisoners as well as the "True Cross" to Rome. At home he seems to have remitted taxes, released political prisoners and tried to ease the severity of his father's reign; but when he slaughtered his brothers and half-brothers in a misguided effort to secure his throne he so outraged his court that his own death shortly thereafter, perhaps as a victim of the plague, was not greatly mourned. Kavadh's killing of the royal males and his own early death introduced anarchy in Iran until in 632 a new prince, Yazdagird III, a grandson of Chosrau II, was made king. He was to be the last of the Sasanian kings. In the month of his coronation Muhammad, "ruler in Arabia" died, ushering in the age of Muslim conquest, and the final years of Sasanian empire were drawing to a close.

Leadership passed after Muhammad's death to his father-in-law Abu-Bakr, who in 633 sent an expedition against Hira, the success of which reduced the fertile lands on the right bank of the lower Euphrates to Muslim domination. Three years later, Yazdagird, in an effort to regain the lost territory, sent an army under Rustam across the Euphrates against the Muslim command post at al-Qadisiyah. The armies fought inconclusively for three days, but on the fourth day an adverse sandstorm severely crippled the Sasanian forces, Rustam was killed and the Persian armies were routed. The next year the Muslims renewed their advance and entered Ctesiphon in 638 one day after Yazdagird had fled with his court to the Zagros mountains. That same year a bloody battle at Julula in the mountains opened to the Muslims the mountain passes and led finally in 641 to their resounding victory over the Persians in Nihavand, not far from Hamadan on the road between Besitun and Burujird. That disaster extinguished Sasanian power. Yazdagird lived another decade, constantly in flight until he was murdered, as legend has it, for his costly garments; but the Sasanians fought no further battles.

The Sasanian state, which had arisen on the ruins of the Parthian, succumbed to the same evils that had destroyed Parthia: it could not achieve enduring stability in the face of barbarian invasions and threats of invasion from the east, Roman aggression from the west, internal dissension over religion, and the absence of clear political purpose. The external threats entailed a huge drain on Sasanian manpower and economic resources; Zoroastrianism, which had once united the Sasanians and permitted them to overthrow Parthian rule, could no longer unite them sufficiently to permit them to overthrow Christianity or withstand Islam; the struggle between the partisans of centralized authority and the exponents of political decentralization kept the administration in constant turmoil; and that internal confusion diverted trade between the Mediterranean and Indian oceans from its route through Iran to a safer route by way of the Red Sea, further weakening the Persian state. The Sasanian efforts to recreate the Achaemenid state of Darius, which had fallen before Alexander, crumbled before the Muslim religious and military advance.

The driving power in Mediterranean affairs was now to be no longer Greek or Roman but Near Eastern. The Semitic revival in the person of the Arabs meant a resurgence of the ancient Mesopotamian drive to empire, based as it was on the sovereignty of a single god, and expressed in the rule of his chosen sovereign over a people conceived as his servants.[45] That ancient conception of the state, grafted as it now was onto the successful methods of Alexander, has determined the course of Near Eastern history, turning what might have become an eastern political legacy of Alexander into a romance. According to the ancient Near Eastern tradition, the world belongs to God, whom men must serve in obedience rather than freedom. In Islam, Greek cultural and political humanism are subjected to God's will, and truth is a matter of will rather than discovery and surprise.

SUGGESTIONS FOR FURTHER STUDY:

The basic work in English is still G. Rawlinson, *The Seventh Great Oriental Monarchy*, 2 vols. (New York, 1876); but the best work, containing comprehensive bibliography, is A. Christensen, *L'Iran sous les Sasanides*, 2nd ed. (Copenhagen, 1944). T. Nöldeke's translation of Tabari, *Geschichte der Perser und Araber* (Leiden, 1879), on which his work, *Aufsätze zur Persischen Geschichte* (Leipzig, 1887), is based, is invaluable. The article, "Persia," by Eduard Meyer, in the *Encyclopaedia Britannica*, 14th ed. (1929), gives an excellent survey. Good introductions to Manichaeism have been written by H.-Ch. Puech, *Le Manicheisme. Son Fondateur. Sa doctrine* (Paris, 1949), Geo. Widengren, *Mani und der Manchäismus* (Stuttgart, 1961), and O. Klima, *Manis Zeit und Leben* (Prague, 1962). For Mazdak see O. Klima, *Mazdak. Geschichte einer sozialen Bewegung im Sassanidischen Persien* (Prague, 1957). A history of eastern Christianity was written by S. Labourt, *Le Christianisme dans l'Empire Perse sous la dynastie sassanide*, 2nd ed. (Paris, 1904). The brief surveys of Sasanian history by R. Ghirshman (1954) and A. Bausani (English translation, 1971), and the notes of R. Frye (1963) are helpful for general orientation.

Volumes 3(1) and 3(2) of the *Cambridge History of Iran*, ed. Ehsan Yarshater (1983), are devoted to the Seleucid, Parthian, and Sasanian periods. They appeared when this disuccusion was in page proof.

---

45. The later dispute in Islam over the theocratic basis and form of the state depended on the conviction that Muslims are the people of God, serving him as his state on earth.

POSTSCRIPT

The Alexandrian millennium left firmly implanted in the Mediterranean world conceptions of empire that would develop in familiar and recognizable patterns both in the east and the west during the succeeding centuries. In the Near East and Spain the Muslim conquest was a continuation of ancient Mesopotamian and Persian patterns of rule fortified and informed by a new, monotheistic religious faith that adopted the scholastic methods of Greek reason for its own development but ignored the Greek political experience. In the west the Christian church adopted the Roman conception of empire and became as politically ingenious as the Muslim scholars were theologically and philosophically subtle.

The western notion of empire matured in Roman times. The Latin word, *imperium*, from which our English word, *empire*, is derived, originally meant the legal power to enforce law. The Roman people granted that power to enforce their authority to the highest magistrates of their city, and thus for a man to have *imperium* meant for him to be invested with the highest public responsibility. By the time of Augustus, however, the meaning of *imperium* had begun to shift from the power a man had to enforce law to the territory over which he enforced it, i.e., to the territorial or administrative whole that was subject to law. But *imperium* began in addition to denote something superhuman, emanating from the divinity of Rome itself, until the *imperium* of the Roman people at last became simply the Roman *imperium*, suggesting a divine personality men were bound to respect and obey. The imperial people in the end surrendered their imperial power to the emperor, the representative of the *imperium*, who benevolently bestowed the benefits of Roman peace and eventually Roman citizenship on conquered peoples. When in 212 all people became Roman citizens the transfer of *imperium* from the Roman people to Rome itself was complete.

The Christian church thought of *imperium* in this exalted way, declaring the Roman empire to be God's world and the emperor God's chosen representative. The bishops in the early fifth century addressed the emperor Honorius with the title, "Imperium vestrum," and thus accorded to *imperium* the status of an eternal, divinely established institution. The Christian conception of empire grew as the actual empire which had given that conception birth crumbled before the incursions of Germanic, Slavic and Arab peoples. It was nourished as the Roman emperors created an imperial doctrine of religious orthodoxy in a vain attempt to hold the empire together from within. [1]

Revolts against the imperial will to orthodoxy can be observed in the heresies, one of which has persisted to the present time. It arose in the popular teaching of a British monk, Pelagius, who lived from about 360 to 420. Being particularly upset by the Augustinian doctrine of Original Sin, which maintains that a man is completely unable to do good and that God alone can redeem men from their innate and inescapably evil natures, Pelagius taught that men are free to do good or evil, that there is no original or inherited sin, and that men do not therefore need redemption. God, he said, had granted to mankind freedom of will, the laws of the Bible, and the example of Christ; and men are therefore responsible themselves for the good or evil of their own lives. Against the imperial proponents of divine sovereignty, Pelagius rose to defend human freedom, declaring that God's will can indeed be thwarted.

Theologically, however, Pelagius was unable to explain what it must then mean to be God. If God's will can be thwarted, how can God be God? and if God's will cannot be thwarted, in what sense is man free? Augustine declared that God's will is not contingent on human action, but that declaration is for many an unsatisfactory statement of man's freedom. There is no satisfactory answer to the problem of why a man created by God can or should rebel against God.

It was inevitable that the teachings of Pelagius should be declared

---

1. The extent to which the original ideas surrounding *imperium* have shifted can be seen in our modern conception of empires, implying plurality, and of imperialism, implying only one. This discussion of empire is drawn from the illuminating book, *Empire*, by Richard Koebner, Cambridge, 1961, pp. 1–32.

heretical, as they were by a council of bishops at Carthage in 418. Furthermore, given the western aggressive estimate of man, it was no doubt inescapable that someone in the western church should have radically asserted man's freedom, even at the sacrifice of God's sovereignty. Pelagius, unfortunately, did not define the theological problem thoroughly, and his teaching has therefore continued to be condemned. Nevertheless, his condemnation reveals the conflicting concerns of Near Eastern and European theology. The church insists against Manichaeism that the created world is good, and against Pelagius that mankind is sinful, lost without redemption wrought on his behalf in Christ. But the Greek experience exalts human freedom, while the the Near East emphasizes human dependence on God. Given its mission in the world to bring men to the knowledge of their redemption in Christ, the church vigorously espoused orthodox confession of faith and the imperial, ecumenical view of the world that had been set loose by the career of Alexander.

The sovereign rule of Christian orthodoxy, however, prevailed only in the west. In the Near East Islam conquered the Christian territories of Syria, Egypt and North Africa, no doubt in part because its strict monotheism appealed to the monophysite Christians there. Islam might indeed have conquered the entire Mediterranean world but for its unbreakable bond with Arabia, just as the Christian conquest finally quickened after the Romans unwittingly separated the Church from its Palestinian moorings when they destroyed Jerusalem. The Church did survive in the Near East, of course, but the eastern patriarchates lost all importance in the west, and the eastern Christians were cut off from fruitful dialogue with their western peers. The rule of religious orthodoxy in the Near East was assumed by the Muslim leaders, who thereby perpetuated in Islam some of the religious conflict known previously in the Church.[2]

Islam did take the southern Mediterranean, driving the power of Christianity to retrenchment in the north and west. France became the victorious defender of orthodox Christianity and thereby buttressed Rome's leading ecclesiastical position. The eastern Church, faced by a formidable

---

2. From the available, extensive bibliography on Islam, the following works are helpful: H. A. R. Gibb, *Mohammadanism*, 2nd ed., 1953 (reprinted, 1963); B. Lewis, *The Arabs in History*, revised ed., London, 1958; F. E. Peters, *Allah's Commonwealth*, New York, 1973; Marshall G. S. Hodgson, *The Venture of Islam*, 3 vols., Chicago, 1974; R. M. Savory, *Introduction to Islamic Civilization*, Cambridge, 1976.

opponent in Islam and effectively separated from the Church in the west, succumbed to the puritanism of Islam and revolted against images in the church in the Iconoclastic controversy of the eighth century, which resulted in the loss of much Byzantine art.

The failed Alexandrian attempt of the fourth century B.C. to incorporate the Near East into a Mediterranean world opened to the world, in a new way, an ecumenical vision. The Macedonian, Roman, and Byzantine rulers struggled in vain to transform a political and cultural vision into reality, until the Sasanian state in the third Christian century exposed the western goal for the dream it was. The Sasanian military and economic threat to the west ended in 628 with the military triumph of the Byzantine Heraclius, which was in turn rendered insignificant by the Muslim advance. The Muslim conquest, which eventuated in the largest territorial empire the world has known, brought the Near East once more to a political and cultural supremacy that would not be destroyed until the defeats of the Arabs at Poitiers in 732 and the Ottomans at Vienna in 1683 fixed the future frontiers of the Islamic world at Gibraltar and the Danube. The Christian conquest of Europe gave the western world an exalted vision of human potential for good, as long as men submit to their commonly accepted vision of God. Evaporation of the religious vision also blurred the vision of human potential for good.

Thus new conceptions of empire, originating with the Semitic Akkadians (2300 B.C.), enlarged and modified by Alexander, further developed at Rome, embraced by the Christian Church, and adopted by the Arabs and by one after another of the European and more recent eastern nations, persist in changing but recognizable forms as an indirect legacy of Alexander 'the great.'

House of Ptolemy

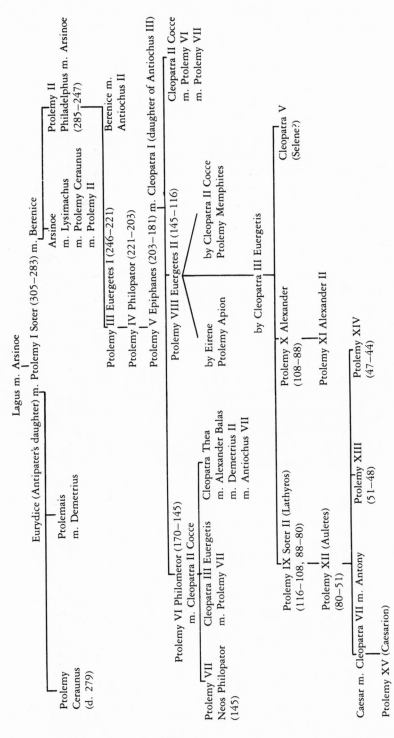

Lagus m. Arsinoe

Eurydice (Antipater's daughter) m. Ptolemy I Soter (305–283) m. Berenice

Ptolemais
m. Demetrius

Arsinoe
m. Lysimachus
m. Ptolemy Ceraunus
m. Ptolemy II

Ptolemy II
Philadelphus m. Arsinoe
(285–247)

Berenice m.
Antiochus II

Ptolemy III Euergetes I (246–221)

Ptolemy IV Philopator (221–203)

Ptolemy V Epiphanes (203–181) m. Cleopatra I (daughter of Antiochus III)

Cleopatra II Cocce
m. Ptolemy VI
m. Ptolemy VII

Ptolemy VIII Euergetes II (145–116)

by Cleopatra II Cocce
Ptolemy Memphites

by Eirene
Ptolemy Apion

by Cleopatra III Euergetis

Cleopatra V
(Selene?)

Ptolemy X Alexander
(108–88)

Ptolemy XI Alexander II

Ptolemy XIV
(47–44)

Ptolemy VI Philometor (170–145)
m. Cleopatra II Cocce

Cleopatra III Euergetis
m. Ptolemy VII

Cleopatra Thea
m. Alexander Balas
m. Demetrius II
m. Antiochus VII

Ptolemy IX Soter II (Lathyros)
(116–108, 88–80)

Ptolemy XII (Auletes)
(80–51)

Ptolemy XIII
(51–48)

Ptolemy VII
Neos Philopator
(145)

Ptolemy
Ceraunus
(d. 279)

Caesar m. Cleopatra VII m. Antony

Ptolemy XV (Caesarion)

245

Antigonids and Seleucids

Antigonus I (d. 301)

Phila (daughter of Antipater) m. Demetrius (d. 293) m. Ptolemais (daughter of Ptolemy I)

Stratonike
m. Seleucus I
m. Antiochus I

Antigonus II Gonatas (276–239)

Demetrius II (239–229)

Philip V (221–179)

Demetrius (The Fair)

Antigonus III Doson (229–221)

Apame I (daughter of Spitamenes) m. Seleucus I Nicator (312–281) m. Stratonike (daughter of Demetrius)

Antiochus I Soter (280–261)

Achaeus

Phila II m. Antigonus Gonatas

Laodice I (daughter of Achaeus?) m. Antiochus II Theos (261–247) m. Berenice (daughter of Ptolemy II)

Seleucus II Callinicus (247–226)

Antiochus Hierax

a son

Stratonike m. Ariarathes III of Cappadocia

Laodice m. Mithridates II of Pontus

Seleucus III (226–223)

Antiochus III (223–187) m. Laodice III daughter of Mithridates II of Pontus

Antiochus

Seleucus IV (186–175)

Demetrius I (162–150)

Demetrius II (145–139) (129–125)

Antiochus IV Epiphanes (175–163)

Antiochus V (163–162)

Antiochus VII Sidetes (139–129)

Cleopatra m. Ptolemy V

Hasmoneans and Their Seleucid Contemporaries

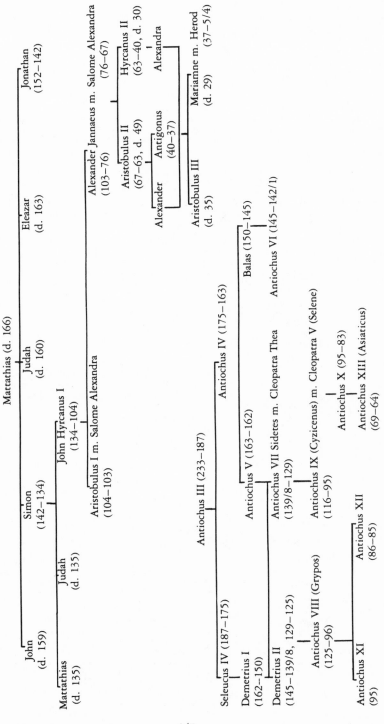

Byzantine Emperors

(For full lists consult J. W. Barker, *Justinian and the Later Roman Empire*, Madison, 1966, pp. 276–285.)

Constantine I (The Great)	324–337
Constantine II	337–340
Constans I	337–350
Constantius II	337–353 (alone, 353–361)
Julian	361–363
Jovian	363–364
Valens	364–378
Theodosius I	379–395
Arcadius	395–408
Theodosius II	408–450
Marcian	450–457
Leo I	457–474
Zeno	474–491
Anastasius I	491–518
Justin I	518–527
Justinian I (The Great)	527–565
Justin II	565–578
Tiberius	578–582
Maurice	582–602
Phocas	602–610
Heraclius	610–641

The House of Sasan
(according to Herzfeld)

Sasan

Papak

1) Ardashir I (223–241)

2) Shapur I (241–272)

3) Hormizd I (272–3)

4) Bahram I (273–6)

5) Bahram II (276–93)

6) Bahram III (293)

7) Narseh (293–302)

8) Hormizd II (302–9)

9) Adarnaseh (309)

10) Shapur II (309–79)

11) Ardashir II (379–83)

12) Shapur III (383–88)

13) Bahram IV (388–99)

14) Yezdegerd I (399–420)

16) Bahram V (420–438)

17) Yezdegerd II (438–57)

18) Hormizd III (457–9)

19) Peroz (457, 459–483)

20) Balash (483–88)

21) Kavadh I (488–96, 499–531)

22) Jamasp (496–499)

23) Chosroes I (531–578)

24) Hormizd IV (578–590)

25) Chosroes II (590–628)

28) Kavadh II (627)

29) Ardashir III (628)

Shahrigan

30) Yezdegerd III (632–33, 651)

INDEX

Cynoscephalae, 95f.
Cyprus, 52
Cyrenaica, 52, 117, 144; Roman province, 130
Cyrene, 117 n.52
Cyrus the Younger, 16

Danube River, 21
Daphne, 109, 112
daric, Persian, 31
Darius I, 14
Darius III Codomannus, 35
Darius' laws, 15
Decapolis, 132, 171
Delos, 66, 101
Demetrius of Phalerum, 51, 52
Demetrius Poliorcetes, 52, 55; death of, 55
Demetrius II, 89
Demetrius of Pharos, 90f.
Demetrius (son of Seleucus IV), 114
Demetrius II Nicator, 120, 121
democracy, Greek, 17
Demosthenes, 23, 25, 32, 43, 50, 51
diadochi, 49
Diocletian, 193, 224, 226
Diodorus of Sicily, 26
Diodotus Tryphon, 120f.
divine right to rule, 69
Droysen, 27
dynastic rule, 86

East-West relationships: eras of, 5
(the) ecumenical idea, 69
Edessa, 200
Edomites, 131
efficiency, 79f.
Elephant corps, 57
Empire: conception of, 243f.
Epaminandos, 29
Epicurus, 71
Epiphaneias, 110
Epirus, 21
Eucratides, 112
Eudocia, 208
"Euergetes," 33
Eumenes, 51, 98ff.
Eumenes I, 65
Euripides, 21, 157
European feudalism, seeds of, 22
Eusebius, 218

Eutyches, 201
exarchate, 217
Excubitors, 212
Ezekiel, 5

Fars, 14, 15
Firdousi, 222, 234
Flamininus, Titus Quinctius, 95
Four quarters of the world, 11
France, 245
freedom, 2–3; for Greeks, 44, 66; of the sea, 66

Gabae, 112
Gabinius, 138, 171
Gaius Popillius Laenas, 101f.
Galatians, 56, 162
Galilee, 174; as Rabbinic center, 182
Gaugamela, 39
Gedrosian desert, 25, 42
Ghassanids, 216
Gnosticism, 192
Gordian knot, 40
Gospels, 186f.
government: forms of, 9
Granicus River, 38, 39
(the) Greek ideal, 80f.
Greens and Blues: circus faction, 211, 214
Gundeshapur, 236

Hadrian, 167
Hagia Sophia, 214
Hammurapi, 10
Hannibal, 91; flight to Antiochus, 96
Harith ibn Jabala, 216
Hasidim vs. Hellenizers, 108f., 111
Hasmonean state, 103, 111 n.19
Hebrew slaves, 5
Hecatompylos, 147
Hellenistic, 21, 47
Hellenistic states: characterisitcs of, 82–86
Henotikon, 210
Hephthalites, 230
Heraclides, 114, 118, 121
Heraclius, 4, 205, 217f., 238
Herod, 158, 161, 173; the Great, 173f.
Herodotus, 5, 21
hetairoi, 23, 29, 37
Hierapolis-Bambyce, 156
Himyarites, 216